The East Kent Railway

Volume One:
The History of the
Independent Railway

by
M. Lawson Finch & S.R. Garrett

THE OAKWOOD PRESS

© Oakwood Press & M.L. Finch & S.R. Garrett 2003

British Library Cataloguing in Publication Data
A Record for this book is available from the British Library
ISBN 0 85361 608 6

Typeset by Oakwood Graphics.
Repro by Ford Graphics, Ringwood, Hants.
Printed by Cambrian Printers, Aberystwyth, Ceredigion.

Was it the visiting sailor who hung the lucky horseshoe from *Hecate's* lamp iron? The pattern of point lever suggests that this photograph was taken at Tilmanstone.

Front cover: East Kent Railway No. 2 in fine condition in Shepherdswell yard *c.*1938.
Colour-Rail

Published by The Oakwood Press (Usk), P.O. Box 13, Usk, Mon., NP15 1YS.
E-mail: oakwood-press@dial.pipex.com
Website: www.oakwood-press.dial.pipex.com

Contents

An Index, Bibliography and table of Acknowledgements will appear in Volume 2 which completes the history of the East Kent Railway, describes its route and details the history of its locomotives, carriages, wagons and working practices.

0-6-0 No. 3 passes Hernden siding. Eastry South Halt is to the left of the level crossing that the train is about to cross.   *Colonel Stephens Railway Museum*

Foreword

In 1949 Maurice Lawson Finch published a history of the Kent & East Sussex Railway. Each copy contained a sheet of paper advertising the forthcoming publication of a companion history of the East Kent Railway. However, Maurice soon realised that the East Kent was to prove a far more difficult railway to chronicle than the Kent & East Sussex. For the first 20 years of its existence the East Kent had attempted to create a network of railways to serve the newly discovered Kent coalfield with severely limited resources and often in the teeth of opposition from the very collieries the East Kent hoped to serve. Mountains of paper - hearings, investigations, letters, maps and surveys - were generated by the East Kent's endeavours to achieve its aims and it was through what remained of these mountains that Maurice persevered to put together a coherent account of the East Kent's history.

In the 1980s I was having exactly the same problems as Maurice in writing my own history of the East Kent when a chance introduction brought us together. By adopting a strict chronological approach we found that it really was possible to tell the East Kent story without entirely losing the main plot. A lot of material has had to be left out for the sake of coherence and there will undoubtedly be a rash of information to answer our unanswered questions the minute this book goes for publication. Has it not always been so?

Regrettably Maurice died in 2000 without seeing this history published but his enthusiasm for the East Kent can be seen in this extract from his original introduction:

> It must be said that, for the light railway enthusiast and to the many who find pleasure in the unusual or eccentric, the railway was a delight. For many it was a last link with the disappearing relics of a bygone age; an age of benevolent gentry in high wing collars and drooping moustaches, each and every one of whom was endowed with the capacity, obvious from the straining buttons of their waistcoats, for enjoying numerous celebratory luncheons. It was an age when ordinary people were much nearer to nature than they are today and if it was a beautiful day everyone knew it and the guard would most likely comment upon it. It was also an age when individual contribution seemed to count for something, if the carpenter-painter put the wrong markings on a carriage door it remained good subject for conversation for a lifetime. For many the passing of the 'East Kent Light' has closed forever the door to a retreat where, for a shilling or so, one could shed many burdens and return fortified against the tedium of modern existence. Without such sanctuaries many of us are lost indeed.

Stephen Garrett
May 2003

Chapter One

In the Beginning

While it is usual to set the scene before embarking on the story of a railway, the reader may be rather dismayed at the amount of scene setting that the story of the East Kent Light Railways Company requires. Most railways were, however, conceived as enterprises in their own right or as the self-contained offspring of greater enterprises. The East Kent Light Railways Company, on the other hand, began as but one enterprise in a complex federation of enterprises whose ultimate goal was to transform East Kent into a thriving industrial centre to rival Glamorgan or Lancashire. Its genesis is to be found in the thwarted hopes of a Channel Tunnel, in the prolonged birthpains of the Kent coalfield and in the monopoly over rail transport in East Kent held by the South Eastern & Chatham Railway (SECR) whose strained finances made it reluctant to engage in rural branchline construction. To add colour there were plenty of lords, some of them a-leaping, a golfcourse with maritime ambitions, obstruction by venerable religious and educational foundations, an almost front line role in the two World Wars, much jockeying between captains of industry, a great deal of good will and not a little ill.

The birth of the Kent Coalfield

Although the Weald of Kent and Sussex had been noted for its iron industry in the past this had been a small-scale operation and depended on charcoal for its fuel. The exhaustion of easily exploited surface deposits of iron ore and increasing competition for the dwindling supplies of timber from ship-building and house-building had effectively extinguished the industry long before new methods using coal enabled large scale iron production to prosper elsewhere. This left Kent with no characteristic industry to distinguish it from many other parts of the country and to be known instead for the prosperity of its agriculture.

During the 19th century two major new industries came to be associated with Kent, although largely ignored in most conventional accounts of the Industrial Revolution. These were the cement and paper industries and both created a heavy demand for coal. Even without these industries there was a growing need for coal in Kent. The development of the steamship created a demand for bunkering coal at Kent's civil and naval ports. The gas industry and the use of coal for domestic heating, the brickworks to supply the growing towns, even the laundry industry, all added to the demands for coal. Kent, together with London and the rest of Southern England, provided an enormous and growing market for coal which, in the absence of a local source of supply, enriched the coalowners of Wales, the Midlands and the North, to say nothing of the main line railways which carried it.

The credit for first suggesting the existence of a concealed coalfield beneath Southern England is usually accorded to R.A. Godwin-Austen who addressed

Two views taken in 1957 showing the original Channel Tunnel workings of the 1880s.

the Geological Society in 1855 on the subject. The essence of his argument was that the Somerset coalfield was not a local phenomenon but a surfacing or re-emergence of the coalfields of the Ruhr and Northern France. Whilst acceptable as a theoretical proposition there was no shortage of acceptable theoretical propositions in the 19th century and, in the absence of hard factual evidence, Godwin-Austen's address had no immediate impact either in 1855 or when submitted to the Royal Institution in 1858.

As is frequently the case when theories are subsequently proved correct there are other apparently legitimate claimants to Godwin-Austen's mantle. As early as 1826 two geologists, Buckland and Conybeare, had pointed out the similarity between the coalfields of Somerset and Northern France and in 1846 Sir Henry de la Beche elaborated on this to suggest that 'a mass of coal measures may be buried beneath the Oolites and Cretaceous rocks on the East'. In 1848 a Mr Dunn published a paper entitled 'Winning and Working Coal' in which he made the point that, although coal is not usually associated with chalk, just such a combination could be found at Grand Hornue Colliery near Mons in Belgium. As it was the same chalk that continued to the Channel Coast and most probably was the same chalk that formed the cliffs of Dover, there was an equal possibility that the coal would extend to Kent too.

It was not until 1871 that the Royal Commission on Coal Supplies gave the first official support for the theoretical existence of a coalfield in Southern England. In 1872 the British Association took the first practical steps towards resolving the question by instigating the formation of a Sub-Wealden Committee to bore for coal at Netherfield in Sussex. The Committee included Godwin-Austen as well as many of the foremost scientific and industrial luminaries of the time such as Darwin, Bessemer, Hawkshaw, Siemens, Laing and Vignoles. Amongst the concerns that subscribed to the expenses of the undertaking were the London Brighton & South Coast Railway and the South Eastern Railway.

With the benefit of hindsight it is clear that a boring in Sussex was doomed to failure, but the difficulty with discovering a concealed coalfield is precisely that it is concealed. Boring continued until 1875 by which date a depth of 1905 feet had been reached and some £7,000 spent. Although no trace of coal was found the boring did discover a rich vein of gypsum which is still being exploited at Mountfield. The Committee subsequently suggested that Dover might have been a more likely site to have found coal but there appears to have been no move to follow this suggestion.

That a successful boring was eventually made at Dover came about for reasons that owed almost everything to a chance opportunity rather than to design. In 1881 the South Eastern Railway embarked upon a scheme that has often been credited as being the brainchild of its Chairman. Sir Edward Watkin was not only Chairman of the South Eastern Railway, but also of what was then the Manchester, Sheffield & Lincolnshire Railway and of the Metropolitan Railway in London. The conventional version is that by linking the former to the latter and the latter to the South Eastern and by building a tunnel beneath the English Channel he hoped to see trains running from Manchester to Paris. In fact, on the available evidence, Sir Edward seems to have been converted rather later to the possibilities offered by a Channel Tunnel than the popular version would have it.

A number of schemes for a Channel Tunnel had been vigorously promoted since the mid-1850s and Parliamentary approval for exploratory works had been granted in 1875. In 1876 the French and British Governments had reached agreement on what was known as the Tunnel Charter to settle the various novel problems of international law posed by the enterprise. At this point the scheme began to languish for lack of financial backing and might have gone no further had not William Low, a long-standing supporter of the Tunnel, solicited the active support of Sir Edward Watkin. Whatever the strength of his earlier interest in the Tunnel may have been, Watkin now took up the cause with vigour. Not only did he persuade the South Eastern Railway to authorise expenditure of £20,000 from its limited funds, but he was also able to obtain the necessary Parliamentary authority for the railway to undertake exploratory work under the South Eastern Railway Act 1881.

Excavation of a first heading was promptly begun at Shakespeare Cliff to the west of Dover under the supervision of Francis Brady. By April 1882 a 7 ft diameter shaft had advanced 2,026 feet when word came from the Board of Trade that work should come to a halt. The War Office had grown increasingly alarmed at the strategic threat to Britain's defences posed by the Tunnel and had gathered sufficient support to persuade the Prime Minister, William Gladstone, to their point of view. Legally, the Board of Trade's advice did not amount to an actual prohibition and work continued until July 1882. Certain minor works were kept in hand until July 1883 but all work on the Tunnel then ceased and in 1884 all authority for the undertaking was withdrawn. Meanwhile the workings had been sold by the South Eastern Railway in 1882 to the Submarine Continental Railway Company, also under Sir Edward's control, which in turn bought out a rival, The Channel Tunnel Company, and adopted its name.

One of the members of the Sub-Wealden Committee which had organised the unsuccessful Netherfield boring was Professor William Boyd-Dawkins. He had continued to take an active interest in the possibility of a coalfield in Southern England and in 1886 approached Sir Edward to propose that the workings and equipment at Shakespeare Cliff might be used for a new boring to test the possible presence of coal beneath the chalk. Sir Edward took up the idea and Brady was instructed to proceed with the new task. Progress with the boring was not particularly rapid but on 15th February, 1890 a 30 in. seam of coal was encountered at a depth of 1,180 feet. The existence of coal beneath Southern England was no longer solely a theoretical proposition. Now that the first hurdle was passed a number of new questions had to be answered. Was the coal exploitable in commercial quantities? How far did the coal extend? Who was going to get the coal up?

Developments at Dover and related enterprises 1891-1910

Sir Edward Watkin reported the results of the Dover boring to the Annual Meeting of the South Eastern Railway in July 1891. To date the boring had cost £10,000. He had been advised that the estimated cost of sinking a permanent shaft at Dover to prove the extent of the coal measures was £30,000. He could not recommend that the company invest more than £1,000 in such an enterprise. It was, in any event, not within the railway company's powers to enter the coalmining business.

Somehow boring continued at Shakespeare Cliff and over the next three years six further seams of coal exceeding a width of 24 inches were encountered. There had been fears that the first coal proved might have been an isolated pocket but the finding of further seams and comparison with the Pas-de-Calais coalfield reassured optimists that a coalfield of commercial potential had been discovered. Pessimists, particularly established coal owners, were more wary and were happy to leave the proving and exploitation of the coalfield, for the time being at least, to the optimists. Optimism was to prove to be an enduring characteristic of the Kent coalfield and the many enterprises that went with it, not least the East Kent Light Railways Company.

The retirement of Sir Edward Watkin in 1894 put paid to any active involvement in the Kent coalfield by the South Eastern Railway. Development of the coalfield was instead taken up by a group of businessmen who, in 1896, promoted the Kent Coalfields Syndicate Limited. Prominent amongst these were Henry Potter of Dunstable, described as a Stockbroker, Harcourt Marley of East Molesey, described as a Surveyor, William Cousins of London, described at first as a Chemist and later as a Land Agent, and Arthur Burr of Lingfield, Surrey.

Arthur Burr had been a lead merchant and had also had some responsibility for coalmines in North Wales. In 1896 he was living in Lingfield where he had not only played a part in the establishment of the racecourse there but had also, on learning of the possibility of coal measures beneath Southern England, bored for coal on his own lands. Losing all his money, it is not clear on which particular venture, he had been forced to resign from Surrey County Council but had stood again and been re-elected. His employees, upon learning of his financial ruin, had donated their last week's pay to enable him to continue with whatever enterprise it was that had lost him his fortune. All of this is by his own account and may not stand up to too close a scrutiny but gives some measure of the man without whom, it seems likely, there would have been no Kent coalfield. He must have been a man of extraordinarily persuasive powers and was credited, by friend and enemy alike, with an enormous capacity for hard work. It must also be said that above all he was an inveterate optimist.

The Kent Coalfields Syndicate began by buying out the interests of the Channel Tunnel Company and the South Eastern Railway in the Shakespeare Cliff site. A subsidiary firm, The Colliery & General Contract Company, was set up to carry out the actual sinking of a colliery on the site. Two further subsidiary companies were also founded: a Mid-Kent Coal Syndicate was set up in 1897 to bore for coal on the estate of Lord De l'Isle and Dudley at Penshurst and a Kent Coal Exploration Company was founded to explore generally for coal in Kent. Of all these early companies, the Mid-Kent Coal Syndicate, was the only one on which Arthur Burr formally held a Director's seat.

Besides purchasing the Shakespeare Cliff site the Kent Coalfields Syndicate, with a capital of £200,000, also purchased 575 acres in the locality from Henry

Potter and George von Dadelszen, described as a London metal broker, for £130,000 in fully paid shares, thereby immediately divesting itself of a substantial proportion of its potential working capital. At Shakespeare Cliff the Colliery & General Contract Company, undertook to sink and equip two 1,800 ft shafts in 18 months for £55,000 to be paid 60 per cent in Syndicate shares and 40 per cent in cash. Payments would be made monthly at the rate of 85 per cent of actual expenditure. Since the Contract company had only raised £3,047 in actual cash and the Syndicate had only raised £17,612 this was not a sound footing upon which to base such a major enterprise. Sinking was, nevertheless, begun in 1896. Even considering the limited resources available it is surprising that no provision was made by the Contract company for pumping equipment. An inrush of water into the No. 1 pit in 1896 seems to have been ignored and the company was still unprepared when a flood in No. 2 pit in March 1897 killed eight workmen and stopped the sinking at 303 feet.

Meanwhile Stock Exchange dealing had seen Syndicate shares selling for four to five times their face value. At a later date Burr, Potter and Marley were accused of achieving this by bogus sales of shares. A libel action by Burr in 1901 led to a retraction of this allegation in his case. It is a matter of record that by June 1897 there had been a 250 per cent turnover in the ownership of Syndicate shares. In October 1897 the first of a series of reconstructions took place when the Kent Collieries Corporation was set up to acquire the assets of the Syndicate for £1,275,000. The intention was to offer this as £775,000 in cash and £500,000 in fully paid Corporation shares, but many Syndicate shareholders chose to take shares in lieu of cash. The faith of these shareholders was to be severely tested over the coming years.

An early setback was a decision to abandon the sinking of No. 1 pit and to start a No. 3 pit on the site of the original borehole. This proved to be a poor choice as water coming up the borehole was to be a constant problem with this shaft. Flooding was to be a persistent problem throughout the Kent coalfield with several major water-bearing strata lying adjacent to most of the coal measures. Insufficient attention had been paid to the cores taken from the original boring which would have warned of this hazard. Equally unknown at this time, and a matter that a single boring could not have revealed, was the degree of variation in the coal measures and adjacent strata that was also to prove characteristic of the coalfield.

Further borings, under the auspices of the Kent Coal Exploration Company, were being undertaken at this time to try to establish the limits and extent of the coalfield. Acting on the advice of Boyd-Dawkins that the probable line of the field was to the North-West, borings were put down at Ottinge, Hothfield, Pluckley and even at Old Soar close to Tonbridge. No coal was found in any of these borings. Only at Ropersole, about mid-way between Dover and Canterbury, was any coal found but of the 12 seams encountered in a 2,129 ft boring the best was only 15 inches thick. A boring put down by the Kent Collieries Corporation at Brabourne was abandoned at 2,010 feet without meeting coal.

If coal was elusive elsewhere the Dover Colliery was having no difficulty in finding water. By November 1898 it was estimated that 54,170 gallons were entering the workings every hour. A happier discovery was the uncovering in 1899 of a 12 ft seam of iron ore, but this on its own was not enough to cure the increasingly shaky finances of the various coal companies. Accordingly a second reconstruction took place in 1899 with a Consolidated Kent Collieries Corporation being set up to acquire the assets of the existing companies. Unfortunately these assets were accompanied by considerable liabilities and, despite an influx of French shareholders, the new Corporation was not significantly better placed than its predecessors to finance the progress of the mine.

Shareholder confidence in the Directors and in others like Burr, Potter and Marley who still remained the chief protagonists of the Kent coalfield was beginning to weaken. The employment of French engineers in 1900 led to a dramatic improvement in progress with the sinkings but this was brought to a halt in May 1901 when No. 2 pit was only 90 feet from the coal measures. A length of steel rope falling down this shaft managed to smash the pumping pipes and the pit was immediately flooded. It took four months to drain the pit and with the water went the remaining financial resources of the Corporation. A Receiver appointed by the mine's creditors threatened to sell off the whole concern and was only prevented from doing so by an appeal to the shareholders for £7,000.

Rather than taking their Directors' advice to set up yet another new company the shareholders agreed in 1902 to raise funds by issuing preference shares and debentures. At the same time they dismissed all but one of the Directors. This was Jean Leroy of Calais who had been introduced to the Corporation by Arthur Burr and who had represented the interests of the French shareholders on the Board. As for Burr, he had not only lost his own fortune with the collapse in the value of the Kent Collieries Corporation but was also widely blamed for all the misfortunes which that concern and its predecessors had suffered. Burr was later to reply that his fault had been to leave the management of the enterprise in the hands of Directors who were not prepared to take risks. With the new Board pledged to have nothing to do with Burr or his associates, his connection with the Dover Colliery was at an end but his real role in the Kent coalfield was yet to come.

As far as the story of the East Kent Light Railways Company is concerned the history of the Dover Colliery fades into the background at this point, but since it later resumes some importance it is as well not to abandon it entirely. The issue of preference shares was not particularly successful but, when augmented by the proceeds of a debenture issue, did raise sufficient capital to resume sinking the colliery using the Kind-Chaudron process. This process is not unlike the use of a boring shield of the type frequently used to create railway tunnels and involves drilling vertically with a large boring tool, removing the spoil created and lining the cylindrical shaft thus created with watertight iron tubbing. Water would, of course, enter at the foot of the bore but once the shaft was into dry ground the water could be pumped out and normal sinking resumed in what would then be a dry shaft. The process had been widely used on the Continent but was unusual in Britain. It enabled good progress to be resumed in 1903 and by September 1904 No. 2 pit was announced as being within feet of the coal measures.

A less auspicious announcement in the same month was that of the resignation of Jean Leroy whom the other Directors had accused of continued complicity with Burr. Whilst there was considerable justification for this allegation, the actual bone of contention appears to have been Leroy's opposition to the Corporation taking a loan of £20,000 on the security of unissued debentures. Leroy argued that this would not only further reduce the credit of the Corporation but would also prove insufficient to complete the sinking.

Coal was actually reached in February 1905 and 12 tons were raised for examination. Although the coal was pronounced suitable for household and steam purposes the seam was found to be only 20 inches thick. Commercial exploitation of the coal would also require sinking of the second shaft to be completed. This would take time and money. Since the Corporation had little of the latter it was necessary for yet another reconstruction to take place. Thus was created the Kent Collieries Ltd in August 1905.

Aware that the market for shares in the new company might be limited, the Directors arranged for the issue of 550,000 of the 1,200,000 new shares to be underwritten by the Share Guarantee Trust owned by Richard Tilden Smith. He had successfully mined for coal in Australia before returning to England and equally successfully set up in business as an expert in company reconstruction. The share issue was sufficiently successful to avoid the need to call on Tilden Smith to take up the shares he had underwritten. When the *Daily Mail* began to recommend the company's shares in 1907 the future of the colliery seemed assured. Unfortunately it was at this point that the pumping equipment failed and the mine was once again flooded. By September 1908 Kent Collieries Ltd was in need of further capital. An attempt to issue preference shares failed and the debenture holders called in a receiver. By December 1909 the company owed £131,181. The subsequent rescue of the Dover Colliery and its relevance to the East Kent Light Railways Company will be dealt with later.

Meanwhile developments had been taking place elsewhere in the coalfield which held out far greater hope than the long-running saga of the Dover Colliery might have suggested. While the Dover enterprise lurched from crisis to crisis Arthur Burr had been busy founding an even more ambitious scheme to establish the Kent coalfield as a reality.

The founding of the Concessions empire

Since the 1899 reconstruction there had been little attempt by those connected with the Dover Colliery to continue exploratory works elsewhere in Kent. They probably considered that their hands were full enough with Dover's problems and had no spare funds to develop new pits. Further discoveries might have assisted their ability to raise funds but further unsuccessful borings would have been counter-productive.

Arthur Burr had parted company with Dover but he certainly had no inclination to part company with the Kent coalfield. His first independent step was to found the Dover Coalfield Extension Ltd in 1901. With a capital of

£25,000 it was intended to acquire mineral options in likely areas and to prove the existence of coal there. If coal were to be proved in commercial quantities Burr would set up new companies to exploit it.

Although the company was able to build up an impressive portfolio of mineral options and leases these were mostly located in the Dover-Canterbury-Folkestone 'Triangle' and were doomed to be of little mineral value. They did, however, include Lord Guilford's Swingfield Estate which, whilst of little mineral value in itself, seems to have laid the foundations for future co-operation with the Earl. They also included a substantial area between Tilmanstone and Eythorne to the north of Dover, a direction previously ignored in the search for the coalfield.

Uncovering a previously untried area appears to have been too much of a gamble for the Dover Coalfield Extension Ltd who, after purchasing the options, only had sufficient funds left for one boring. The site chosen was at Ellinge, mid-way between Folkestone and the earlier boring at Ropersole where there had at least been some thin seams of coal. Although the Ellinge Boring also proved the presence of thin seams of coal it was abandoned at 1,805 feet when the company's funds were exhausted. Had the boring been carried on it is thought that it would have met much more promising seams . However, Ellinge would have been too close to the edge of the coalfield to have made a reliable site for a colliery as the coal measures thin abruptly at such points. Without further funds the company went into liquidation in 1903.

In April 1904 the Kent Coal Concessions Company was founded to acquire and exploit the assets of the Dover Coalfield Extension Ltd. The first Directors of the Kent Coal Concessions were Jean Leroy, now also parting company with Dover, and Frederick Wells but it was later admitted by Arthur Burr that he had been the real instigator of the Kent Coal Concessions. He chose not to show his hand at this point and it was left to Leroy to steer the company into public view.

The first task for Kent Coal Concessions was to obtain the Dover Coalfield Extension options and leases by issuing 20,000 Concessions £1 shares at 12s. 6d. each to the shareholders of that company. Further mineral concessions would be obtained and added to these and the resulting area would be divided into six districts. In each district subsidiary companies would sink a pit at an estimated cost of £150,000. The estimated production of each pit would be at least 1,500 tons daily for the next 50 years. The Concessions' geological adviser, Professor Boyd-Dawkins, had selected a 'particularly promising site' for the first pit upon which work would soon commence. He had also given his opinion that the troublesome water-bearing strata encountered at Dover were likely to thin out or disappear entirely inland. The estimated cost of £150,000 for each pit was to prove optimistic but, since the pits were to be sunk by subsidiary companies, the risk would not fall directly on the Concessions company.

To safeguard the issue of shares another company, Central Trust Ltd, would underwrite the issue of 15,000 shares on the home market and Maurice Pelletier of Calais would underwrite 5,000 shares for sale in France. Pelletier later assigned the underwriting of these shares to Leroy. The Central Trust also entered an agreement with Concessions to procure mineral options over a large

Early days at Guilford colliery. All the materials seen here would have been brought in by road. The lack of a railway severely slowed work here and at Tilmanstone.

Group taken at Fredville boring in 1906. *Left to right:* A. Burr, M. Burr, G.H. Hollingworth, F.C.A. Godden, W. Boyd-Dawkins, C.H. Smithers, foreman borer.   *A.E. Ritchie, The Kent Coalfield*

estate at Denton, near Ropersole, and over a large area of land at Waldershare on the unexplored side of the Dover to Canterbury main railway line. This was another estate belonging to Lord Guilford and, like the lands at Eythorne, was to prove to be a better prospect than any of the areas to the West.

In October 1904 Leroy and Wells were joined as Directors by Henry Johnston of Co. Armagh. A fourth Director, Sir Henry Dering, Bart, joined the Board in January 1905. In the same month the first of the promised subsidiary companies was formed. This was the Sondage Syndicate and its creation marked the open return of Arthur Burr. Instead of having a Board of Directors the Syndicate was to be managed by Burr as Manager for Life with the additional right to nominate his son, Dr Malcolm Burr, to the position in his place. Burr was to be paid 20 per cent of the Syndicate's net profits but could choose to use part of this sum to pay any members of a consultative committee of shareholders that he selected to assist him in his duties. In practice this role seems to have been confined to Harcourt Marley, an associate from the Dover period, and Arthur E. Ritchie, a mining engineer who later wrote the first extensive history of the Kent coalfield.

There were further unusual aspects to the Syndicate. It was to have the exclusive right to carry out borings for Kent Coal Concessions on sites nominated by Concessions. If a boring was successful then it would be paid a 100 per cent cash bonus on its capital outlay, together with 10 per cent of the nominal capital of any company formed to work a pit on the site of the boring or 10 per cent of the net profits raised by sale of the site. On the other hand, if the boring was unsuccessful then Concessions was under no liability to make any payment to the Syndicate at all.

No sooner had the Syndicate been created than it commenced work on its first boring at Waldershare. A second boring, this time at Fredville on land belonging to Henry Western Plumptre, was begun in August 1905. Coal was struck twice at Waldershare in September 1906 in the form of the 20 in. Welcome seam and the 40 in. Alexandra seam. In October the 54 in. King Edward seam was also reached.

The creation of the Sondage Syndicate was directly related to changes that were then taking place in the management of Kent Coal Concessions. Frederick Wells had resigned in January 1906, his place being taken by Algernon Hervey from Norfolk, and in May Jean Leroy had 'ceased to act' as a Director. Leroy, it will be remembered, had taken over the underwriting of 5,000 shares to be sold in France. Unfortunately, after he had received his underwriting commission it was discovered that his cheque for the proceeds of the share issue was worthless. This had severely depleted the Concessions' resources and had effectively left it no means to exploit the coal options it had obtained. In 1912 Burr described the situation thus, 'Hence the creation of the Sondage Syndicate on the principle of "No coal, no pay", and tempting as was the speculation, I found it more difficult to raise that £5,000 than to raise £500,000 today. But, although my friends were few in number, they were enthusiastic and staunch, and with their help we struggled on until in the Autumn of 1906 we struck our first workable coal at Waldershare'. In the event there was such speculation in Concessions and Sondage shares in the wake of the first coal discoveries that

Guilford Colliery.

Tilmanstone Colliery at an early stage of development. This original postcard was postmarked
1907.   *M. Lawson Finch Collection*

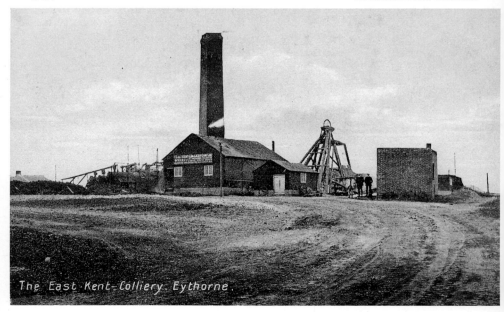

Burr was able to re-sell his shares at four to five times their purchase price. Burr later felt it necessary to defend himself against accusations of self-interest in this matter, 'I was enabled thus to relieve myself of my heavy commitments, loans, &c., upon the blocks of shares that I had been compelled to load myself with, and which, consequently, became a most profitable investment, whether I liked it or not, and enabled me to finance the company and its sister undertakings over many an awkward stile during the next few years'.

Leroy was succeeded on the Board of Concessions by Henry Close of Dublin. During the year and despite Burr's references to the difficulty of raising capital, Concessions increased their share capital, first to £75,000 in June and then to £100,000 in December.

1906 also witnessed the creation of a second subsidiary company. This was the Fonçage Syndicate and its structure was similar to that of the Sondage Syndicate with Burr as Manager for Life on the same terms. Its remit was somewhat wider than that of the Sondage Syndicate and it was essentially created to pick up wherever or whatever the Sondage Syndicate had left off. Its initial task was to make a start on a colliery at Waldershare. This was to be sunk at some distance from the Sondage boring and, to distinguish the two enterprises, permission was obtained from Lord Guilford to give his name to the new colliery. Initially a 7 ft diameter shaft was begun but when this had reached 300 ft in October the Syndicate increased its share capital and commenced two 18 ft diameter shafts instead.

The Fonçage Syndicate's second undertaking was carried out jointly with the Sondage Syndicate. This was to create a colliery at Tilmanstone where Concessions had acquired the mineral options amongst the assets of Dover Coalfield Extension. Presumably the site was considered sufficiently close to Waldershare as to be able to rely on the findings of the boring there and thus dispense with the need for any trial boring at Tilmanstone itself. Sondage was to sink the shafts while Fonçage was to provide and erect the surface equipment including second-hand winding engines. As at Guilford initially a 7 ft shaft was sunk but this was subsequently enlarged to 14 ft.

In September 1906 the Fonçage Syndicate also began work on a colliery at Snowdown where the Fredville boring, on the opposite side of the Dover to Canterbury main line, had just reached its first seam of coal, albeit only 18 in. thick. Two shafts were commenced but when one of these reached 275 ft in 1907 it began to take water and all work was halted while efforts were concentrated on Tilmanstone.

Besides continuing with the borings commenced in 1906 and undertaking the joint works at Tilmanstone with the Fonçage Syndicate, the Sondage Syndicate also commenced a new boring at Goodnestone on land owned by Henry Fitzwalter Plumptre, brother to the landowner at Fredville and Snowdown.

By the end of 1906 it is clear that Arthur Burr's plans for Concessions to develop the Kent coalfield were proceeding as intended. A large area of mineral options had been obtained, borings were finally uncovering the real location of the coalfield and three of the six intended collieries had been set in motion. It was at this point that Arthur Burr assumed the position of Managing Director of the Concessions.

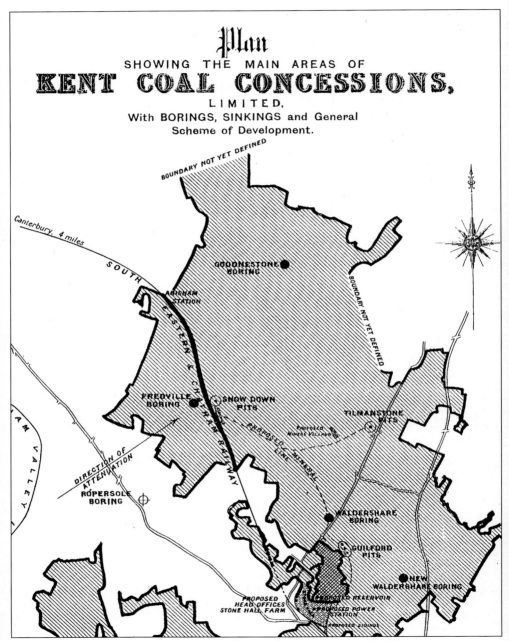

Kent Coal Concessions map showing the proposed mineral railway.

1907 saw a dramatic change of pace in the implementation of Burr's plans for the Kent coalfield and saw the creation of four new companies. It was also a year in which it became evident that developing the coalfield away from Dover did not guarantee immunity from some of the same problems and in which some new problems appeared. Additionally, it was to be the year in which the first firm proposals for a railway to serve the coalfield were mooted.

It was a condition of most mineral options or leases that the holder could not only exploit the minerals beneath the land but could also lay tramways on the surface of that land. Since the Concessions' mineral options and leases were in many cases adjacent it was feasible for a rail network to be constructed which could link up much of the coalfield. A Prospectus for preference shares issued in 1907 was accompanied by a map showing the extent of the lands over which the Concessions held powers; it also indicated a 'proposed mineral line' running between the Snowdown Colliery Sidings and Stonehall Sidings on the Dover to Canterbury main line via Waldershare boring and Guilford pit with a branch to Tilmanstone pit.

Although this scheme was not implemented, possibly because of problems crossing public roads which no amount of mineral options could authorise, it is interesting that even at this stage the Concessions contemplated a single railway system to serve the coalfield instead of individual lines to the nearest railhead. The absence of rail facilities was already proving to be a distinct handicap in the development of the pits and was one of the problems that the Dover Colliery, situated alongside the South Eastern main line, had not had to face.

The Guilford pit was particularly affected by its dependence on road transport. Its situation on the narrow Singledge Lane, which had never had to cope with much more than occasional confrontations between flocks of sheep and hay carts, was particularly unsuited even in dry weather for the frequent coming and going of traction engines hauling the many loads of bricks, coal, machinery, timber and other materials that the sinking of a colliery required. In wet weather the approaches to the colliery rapidly became impassable.

Even without transport problems the Guilford sinking was running into problems. The Fonçage Syndicate was running out of money. Its original capital of £5,000 had been increased to £20,000 but less than £15,000 of this had been taken up by the end of 1906. A Prospectus was therefore prepared for the creation of a new Guilford (Waldershare) Colliery Company with a capital of £300,000. Amongst the Directors would be the Earl of Essex who would be Chairman, Isaac Storey of Messrs Storey Bros, Lancaster, and James Mathew of Hawthorn, Leslie & Co., the locomotive manufacturers. Mathew was already one of the larger shareholders in Concessions and in both of the Syndicates and seems to have had an appreciation that the development of the Kent coalfield would be a long-term proposition rather than an immediate source of wealth.

Unfortunately it was not possible to raise the capital required for the company and the project was abandoned. Instead a Guilford Syndicate was created in August with a smaller capital of £40,000. For £18,000 it acquired all the Fonçage Syndicate's interests at Guilford. These comprised mineral rights over 1,500 acres, all the equipment, buildings and plant on site, and the incomplete sinkings. The Guilford Syndicate was not intended to complete a full working colliery but to complete one shaft into the coal measures and then to put the pit on the market for £500,000. Management of the Guilford Syndicate was wholly vested in the Fonçage Syndicate which was, of course, effectively under the sole management of Arthur Burr. The original 7 ft shaft was enlarged to 12 ft diameter to be used as a reservoir for the pit's water requirements. No. 2 shaft was left at its already completed depth of 30 ft and work was resumed on sinking No. 1 shaft.

Similar financial and transport problems had also slowed progress at Tilmanstone. Again it was decided to create a new company, the East Kent Colliery Company, to put the development of the pit on a firmer footing. The share capital was to be £250,000 of which £240,000 was to be issued as 5s. ordinary shares and £10,000 as 1s. vendor's shares. These latter were divided between Concessions, 125,000 shares, Fonçage Syndicate, 50,000 shares, and Sondage Syndicate, 25,000 shares. There was no immediate public issue of the remaining shares but 670,000 were to be held by Central Trust Ltd and sold off as needed to finance progress at the pit. The Directors were to be Arthur Burr and Harcourt Marley. They were later joined by Henry Gompertz, a stockbroker from Bedford, who already held shares in Concessions and the Syndicates. The first practical consequence of the creation of the new company was the commencement of a second shaft in November. The ceremonial cutting of the first sod was performed by Burr's three-year-old grand-daughter, Gabrielle, and the shaft was subsequently named the 'Gabrielle'.

Another aspect of the development of the coalfield that had slowed with the over-commitment of Concessions' resources was the acquisition and exploration of further mineral areas. It could be argued that this was the time to concentrate on what had already been taken in hand but there seems to have been a conviction that, to remain credible with the share-buying public, the Concessions Group had to be seen to be actively expanding. It was also intended to keep development in the hands of the Concessions Group and out of the hands of any potential interlopers who could reap the rewards of all the work that Concessions had put into identifying the extent of the coalfield without contributing to the expenses. There do not seem to have been any serious rivals interested in the area at this stage but if and when they were to arrive, as they did, the price of mineral options would be likely to rise.

There were other sound, though less noble, reasons for creating new companies to take on any developments beyond the means of the existing companies. The Dover Colliery had shown the debilitating effects of creating a new company simply to take on the liabilities of an existing company. Expanding the share capital of either of the two Syndicates would put any money raised at the risk of existing claims against those concerns. Although their credit was still good at this time there was the chance that it might not remain so. Concessions itself would need further funds to service its existing obligations. The decision was therefore taken to create the South Eastern Coalfield Extension Ltd with a share capital of £25,000 to be managed by Arthur Burr as Director General for Life at 20 per cent of net profits. Its main function would be to acquire further mineral options and to explore them by putting down borings. Delays with the share issue prevented the new company from playing any significant role in 1907.

Financial considerations were very much the reason for the creation of the last of the new Concessions Group companies to be formed in 1907. This was the East Kent Contract and Financial Company which was registered in December with a share capital of £50,000. Inevitably its management was vested solely in Arthur Burr as Director General but for the first time Burr took a large personal shareholding of £4,000. Apart from his forced assumption of shares to make good Leroy's depredations, Burr had previously held only small parcels of shares in the various companies and even these had sometimes been held jointly with Marley and others. His son and daughter-in-law, Malcolm and Fanny Burr, frequently appeared in the lists of shareholders and it seems that Arthur may have preferred to invest on their behalf rather than in his own name. Malcolm had, after all, given up his chosen career in languages in order to study mining so that he might assist his father. Not only that but he had financed his studies himself by taking private students in Russian.

A shareholding of £4,000 by anyone was a considerable rarity amongst the companies of the Concessions Group. As with the Dover Colliery, the main market for Concessions Group shares seems to have been amongst the middle classes. Institutional interest or participation by existing coalowners was extremely limited and the lists of shareholders for the East Kent Contract & Financial are typical of those of all the Concessions companies. Many shareholders held fewer than 25 shares and examples can be found of investors holding only one or two shares. A typical trawl through shareholders holding less than 25 shares in the company reveals nine widows, 17 spinsters, an admiral, a butler, a tramway inspector, a commercial traveller, seven clerks in holy orders, many clerks of the ordinary sort, a missionary, a butcher and a cigar merchant. Many of the French shareholdings, for despite Leroy's activities there had been a steady flow of share applications from France, were of a similar nature.

Although East Kent Contract & Financial Company was empowered by its registration to undertake an enormous variety of tasks it was primarily to become a vehicle for moving funds between the various Concessions companies. Arthur Ritchie described its operations in the following terms: 'Thus it would happen that the managing director of Concessions (Mr Burr) would interview the director-general of Contract (Mr Burr) with a view to a loan. Contract, not having any money at the moment would approach the director-general of, say, South Eastern Coalfield Extension (Mr Burr), borrow the required sum from that company and make the loan to Concessions'. Inevitably such a procedure was fraught with risk for all concerned, not least for Arthur Burr who would wear himself out attempting to keep all the companies afloat. In the short term the existence of East Kent Contract & Financial served to conceal the intrinsic capital weakness of the Concessions companies. In the longer term it was to create enormous problems for the individual companies and to have a fundamental effect on the career of the East Kent Light Railways Company.

With so many new companies entering the scene it should not be assumed that the existing companies were entirely idle in 1907. The Concessions company raised its capital to £150,000 by the issue of £50,000 preference shares to meet its liabilities to the Syndicates for their work on its behalf. Although the

Fonçage Syndicate was handing its constructional activities over to others it still retained a management role in respect of the Guilford Syndicate. After 1907 it effectively withdrew from active participation in the work of developing the coalfield but remained alive to nurse its various holdings in the other companies. The Sondage Syndicate, on the other hand, started a new boring at Barfreston, mid-way between Snowdown and Tilmanstone, having successfully completed its borings at Fredville and at Waldershare where it had struck the 62 in. thick Rockefeller seam. Ritchie refers to the Goodnestone boring being completed in 1907 but elsewhere it is said to have been as late as 1910. This matter cannot be settled as easily as it might seem because the Concessions Group had taken to referring to its borings by code letters to protect their findings from potential competitors whilst at the same time being able to extol the extent and richness of the coalfield. Unfortunately there appears to be no surviving key to these codes.

The Concessions Group contented itself with the creation of only one new company in 1908. This was the Snowdown Colliery Company which was promoted by East Kent Contract & Financial to take over responsibility for the development of that colliery from the Fonçage Syndicate. Management of the company was placed in the hands of Arthur Burr on behalf of the East Kent Contract & Financial and of Henry Johnston and Henry Close on behalf of the Concessions company but, since the latter two lived in Co.Armagh and Dublin respectively, it is unlikely that they played a major role in the running of the company.

A photograph of Goodnestone boring issued by Kent Coal Concessions. This was one of the many Concessions borings carried out to establish the location and value of coal seams in the area under their control.

Although a share capital of £251,250 was registered there seems to have been little haste in issuing significant numbers of shares and the general approach to developing the colliery appears to been leisurely. A new shaft was started to replace the one that had been flooded in 1907 and work was resumed on the other shaft. Progress on both shafts was slow as the main efforts of the Concessions Group were now centred on Tilmanstone.

At Tilmanstone rapid progress was being made, particularly with No. 1 shaft. Unfortunately it had been decided to continue sinking this shaft without a brick lining. This may possibly have been due to the demand for bricks outstripping the supplies available or the difficulty of transporting bricks to the site. Whatever the cause, there were 300 feet unbricked when the shaft reached 913 ft and the sides began to collapse. It was necessary to refill this bottom section with rubble which had then to be gradually re-excavated as the brickwork lining was extended. This task occupied the remainder of the year.

At Guilford there was steady progress and the shaft had reached a depth of 752 ft by October. Work then had to be suspended in the face of claims for compensation from the County Council for damage done to the roads. The cost of these claims came to £2,776 9s. 2d. and was borne by the Concessions company. The 250 workmen employed at Guilford were laid off though some may have been re-employed on the road repairs which the Concessions Group undertook as part of their settlement with the County Council.

By 1908 South Eastern Coalfield Extension had raised sufficient funds to acquire new mineral options and to commence exploratory borings upon them at Walmestone, Woodnesborough, and Mattice Hill. These new borings were to the north of any of the areas previously tried and would show whether the coalfield extended in this direction. It is interesting in this respect to note that Malcolm Burr replaced Professor Boyd-Dawkins as the Concessions 'geological adviser' at this time. There was some expense involved in compensating Boyd-Dawkins but since the borings were all successful this was money well spent.

Just as 1909 had been a bad year at the Dover Colliery it also began badly for the Concessions Group. Scarcely had sinking resumed in the No. 1 shaft at Tilmanstone than a further calamity occurred. Instead of using pumps it had been possible up until now to remove water from the shaft by raising it in a hoppit. On 14th January the hoppit was over-wound and fell to the bottom of the shaft. Three workmen were killed and the ventilation pipes were smashed. It was decided to suspend work on No. 1 shaft and to press on with No. 2 shaft until it reached the same level. A connecting road could then be driven between the two shafts. Work therefore proceeded apace in No. 2 Shaft but in April this shaft suddenly began to take water at a faster rate than it could be wound out. It was nine months before sinking could be resumed in No. 2 shaft. In the meantime work was resumed on No. 1 shaft and, since it was evident that Tilmanstone would now take longer to complete than had been hoped, it was decided to resume sinking at Guilford.

Possibly scenting the imminent collapse of the Concessions Group, a Medway Coal Exploration Syndicate was founded at about this time with the backing of Lord Harris of the Consolidated Goldfields of South Africa and Welwyn Achille de Rothschild. As the Concessions Group failed to oblige this concern by foundering it was forced to seek coal measures outside the Concessions area. It chose to go rather too far outside the area and its borings at Bobbing, near Sittingbourne, and at Chilham were unsuccessful. The Syndicate went into liquidation in 1912. Its brief existence is relevant in that it was the first serious appearance of wealthy backing for the development of coal in Kent. It should be noted that its geological adviser was Professor Boyd-Dawkins.

South Eastern Coalfield Extension's success with its mineral options encouraged the formation in November of yet another concessions company which was named, with a remarkable lack of imagination or sense of the absurd, Extended Extension Ltd. There was the usual arrangement for Burr to serve as Manager for Life at 20 per cent of net profits. The company was created too late to do much in 1909 but seems to have set about the acquisition of further mineral options fairly promptly, as by April 1910 it had spent over £10,000 of the £23,739 it had so far raised. It had loaned a substantial portion of the remainder to East Kent Contract & Financial.

Elsewhere within the Concessions Group 1909 was a year of consolidation. The Concessions company increased its share capital again to £200,000 with a total of 171,516 shares issued by the end of the year. The South Eastern Coalfield Extension also increased its share capital but is of more interest for a letter written by its solicitor to the Ecclesiastical Commissioners: 'Our clients also desire to have facilities for laying a railway over the surface of the Coldred portion to connect the adjoining pits already sunk at the Guilford Colliery with our clients freehold at Stonehall, which abuts on your land at Coldred; they would guarantee to at once start work on this railway, and thus be able to give employment, practically at once, to some 200 hands'. Apart from the fact that the Concessions Group seem still to have been thinking in terms of a mineral tramway the letter is interesting for a number of reasons. A line direct from Guilford to Stonehall, which this would have been if it had to pass over the lands of the Ecclesiastical Commissioners, would have involved a precipitous gradient to descend into the valley at Stonehall. When the East Kent Light Railways Company later planned a line between these two points it followed a very circuitous loop in order to descend along the side of the valley and even this required an exceptionally steep gradient. A descent straight down the side of the valley would probably have required some sort of inclined plane.

The letter is also of interest in that the Ecclesiastical Commissioners effectively declined to entertain any agreement on any subject with anyone acting on behalf of Arthur Burr. There seems to have been a major estrangement between Burr and the Commissioners at some time which not only prevented the Concessions Group from acquiring mineral rights over their lands but was also to cause considerable difficulties for the East Kent Light Railways Company. It is not clear whether it was thought that an approach by the South Eastern Coalfield Extension would be more agreeable to the Commissioners than an approach by the Concessions company or the Guilford Syndicate. Certainly the South Eastern Coalfield Extension had no direct interest in the Guilford or Stonehall areas.

The whole question of the Stonehall area is something of a mystery. Amongst all the rights, leases, and options possessed by the Concessions Group the land at Stonehall appears to have been the only major freehold area to have been owned and yet Concessions were very slow to make any effective use of the site. There had briefly been plans in 1907 to build a power station here but it was not until 1910 that Concessions made any serious proposal for the site. Possibly it was thought that, since this was freehold property, it could safely be left until time and funds permitted development. Options and leases, on the other hand, not only eventually ran out but also required the payment of deadrents on a rising scale. If an area subject to deadrents could be worked profitably then the deadrents turned into royalties and could be paid quite happily from those profits. If an area proved unsuitable for development the options over it could be surrendered and the liability to deadrents would cease. Unfortunately for the Concessions Group, its acquisition of options over such a large area and the time taken to earn any sort of profit from any of them had meant that deadrents were proving to be an unexpectedly heavy liability. This was the sixth year of the Concession Group's existence and the only profits made so far had been those arising whenever one of the companies sold something to one of the other companies or charged interest on a loan. As shares rather than cash constituted the usual currency within the Group, even these 'profits' were of somewhat hypothetical value.

1910 proved to be a year of renewed activity for the Concessions Group. At Tilmanstone this activity was of an unwelcome sort. Initially progress on both shafts made good progress. By May No. 1 shaft had reached 1,140 ft and it was

Interior of the electrical power house at Tilmanstone Colliery, reproduced from publicity material issued by Kent Coal Concessions in 1910.

decided to halt work on the shaft to enable No. 2, then at 1,087 ft, to draw level. While work proceeded on No. 2 shaft a test borehole was drilled from the base of No. 1. This borehole started drawing water at 10 ft but was plugged without too much difficulty. No. 2 shaft reached 1,140 ft in July and it was decided to drill a test borehole here as well. At 18 ft from the base of No. 2 shaft the borehole began drawing water at an estimated rate of 2,000 gallons each minute. It was not possible to plug the borehole and when pumping was attempted the water was found to contain so much sand that the pumps became clogged. It was therefore decided to start a third shaft, this time named 'Rowena' after a further grand-daughter, to order electric pumps and to take advantage of the necessary delay by re-equipping No. 1 shaft with new winding gear.

At Snowdown work progressed steadily on both No. 2 and No. 3 shafts throughout 1910 but at Guilford sinking was halted in May to enable new winding equipment to be installed. In the meantime sinking was resumed on No. 2 shaft. This change of policy resulted from the impending creation of a new company to take over the Guilford site and to complete the pit there as well as beginning a new pit at Stonehall. There would also be potteries at Stonehall to take advantage of the rich deposits of fireclay that accompanied the coal measures in this area. The Guilford (Waldershare) Coal and Fireclay Company, as it would have been known, was to have had a capital of £460,000. However, apart from the laying in of sidings from the SECR at Stonehall and the renewed sinking of Guilford's No. 2 shaft which had ceased again by July, the scheme was to prove abortive.

On a more positive note, the South Eastern Coalfield Extension commenced new borings at Trapham and Stodmarsh, a logical westward extension of its previous borings, and Extended Extension put down its first boring at Ripple near Walmer. An unidentified company in the Concessions Group, possibly Extended Extension, put down a boring at Maydensole, about mid-way between Guilford and Walmer, and entrusted the work to Société Trefor of Brussels. This seems to have been the speediest of all the borings as within the space of only 12 months a depth of 3,760 ft had been reached. A further boring, at Oxney which was mid-way along the main road between Dover and Deal, was begun by a new member of the Concessions Group, the Deal & Walmer Coalfield Ltd. The Oxney boring reached almost the same depth as that at Maydensole but took almost three times as long to complete. Deal & Walmer, under the management of Malcolm Burr, had been promoted by East Kent Contract & Financial to exploit this previously unpromising area in order to fend off possible competition here by a competitor that had recently appeared on the scene, the Channel Collieries Trust. This firm had been created in connection with developments then taking place at Dover Colliery and was later to evolve, under a different name, into the most hostile of a number of interests opposed to the East Kent Light Railways Company.

Two other new Concessions companies were registered in 1910. The Mines Construction Company, with Marley and Ritchie as Directors, was something of an enigma. With a nominal share capital of £100,000 it seems to have been intended to finance the sinking of collieries in the South Eastern Coalfield Extension area but only seven shares were ever issued during the Concessions

£20

Group period. It was destined to play a brief and litigious role in the early years of the East Kent Light Railways Company before lapsing into a long period of inactivity until revived under new ownership as a holding company in the 1920s. The role for which Mines Construction seems to have been originally intended was instead fulfilled by the other new company, Intermediate Equipments Ltd., but it was to be some time before this company had raised sufficient funds to get to work.

The East Kent Contract & Financial Company entered a new line of business by leasing the Telegraph Farm Brickworks near Tilmanstone and purchasing the Pluckley Brickworks. The latter was one of the few brickworks in the region which was capable of supplying the engineering bricks used for lining the pits. Both brickworks were later transferred to Kent Coal Concessions.

However, the biggest new enterprise to be contemplated by the Concessions Group in 1910 was its application to the Light Railway Commissioners for authority to incorporate and construct the East Kent (Mineral) Light Railways. The success of this application and another which followed on its heels form the subject of the next chapter.

Snowdown Colliery was to be the first Kent colliery to make a trading profit . . . but not for some time yet.

Holman Fred Stephens in military mode.   *Colonel Stephens Railway Museum*

Chapter Two

Genesis of the Railway -
The Engineer and the First Orders

The Engineer

In order to plan a railway and to submit those plans with any hope of success it is necessary to have an engineer. Wide as Arthur Burr's experience had been, he does not seem to have been previously involved with the construction or operation of railways and therefore turned to James Mathew of Hawthorn, Leslie & Co. for advice upon the choice of a suitably experienced engineer. Mathew recommended Holman Fred Stephens for the post and thus placed the future fortunes of the East Kent Light Railways in the hands of a man every bit as 'larger than life' as Arthur Burr himself.

Holman Stephens had been born in 1868 and was the son of Frederic George Stephens who, despairing of ever coming up to the standards of the Pre-Raphaelite artists in whose circle he moved, had abandoned painting and taken up an influential career as art critic of The Athenaeum. Holman proved to have more interest in things technical than artistic and studied Civil Engineering at University College under Sir Alexander Kennedy from 1887 to 1888. His next step was a period of practical training in railway engineering at the Neasden works of the Metropolitan Railway until 1890 when he was appointed Resident Engineer to the Cranbrook & Paddock Wood Railway. With the completion of that line he embarked upon a constantly busy career planning, building and managing railways throughout England and Wales. His speciality was the planning and construction of railways under the provisions of the Light Railways Act 1896, which had been passed to open rural areas to the benefits of railway services by simplifying authorisation procedures and reducing building and operating costs.

Stephens made economy of operation an article of faith and, in doing so, enabled railways to be built and to survive where others would have failed. He was aided in this by having acquired through his family or built up by his own energy a considerable body of influential personal contacts. His own modest personal fortune was often put at the disposal of the various railways in his care and his time was unstintingly devoted to his responsibilities. He required a similar devotion from those in his employment and could be merciless in his criticism of those who had fallen short of the standards he expected. He could also be generous to those who had fallen on hard times and was always ready to recognise and reward good practice.

James Mathew may have known Stephens personally but we have not been able to trace any evidence for this. However, Stephens would have been well known as a customer to Mathew as most of the new locomotives purchased by Stephens for his various lines came from Hawthorn, Leslie. It should be added that new locomotives were something of a rarity on the railways managed by Stephens where second-hand rolling stock was usual and fourth-hand stock was far from unknown.

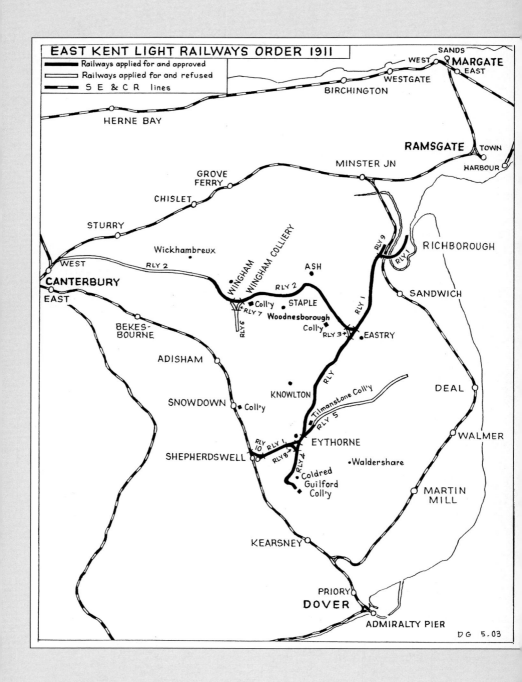

Stephens' other continuing interest was the Territorial Army in which he rose to the rank of Lieutenant Colonel during World War I. As a result of this rank the lines which he managed from his offices in Tonbridge came to be known as the 'Colonel Stephens Railways' and there was something of the air of an inspection from brigade headquarters whenever he visited one of his lines. However, he was plain Mr H.F. Stephens when he first set about the creation of the East Kent Light Railways and since the line was to have more than its fair share of ranking officers amongst those responsible for its affairs we shall usually refer to him as Stephens for simplicity.

The First Order

The earliest surviving record of Stephens' connection with the Concessions Group is a sealed agreement dated 9th May, 1910 between the various Concessions companies and Stephens, retaining his services as Engineer for an application to the Light Railway Commissioners for authority to construct a light railway. Since the application was actually advertised on 24th May, 1910 Stephens must have started work well before this agreement was made.

The statutory advertisement itself announced an intention to apply to the Light Railway Commissioners for an order incorporating the East Kent Minerals (Light) Railways Company and authorising that company to construct the following railways:

Railway No. 1 – From Shepherdswell to Stonar on the River Stour. [10 miles 2 furlongs]
Railway No. 2 – From Canterbury West Station to a junction with Railway No. 1 at Eastry. [11 miles 4 furlongs 6 chains]
Railway No. 3 – A short line providing a second junction between Railway No. 1 and Railway No. 2 at Eastry. [5 furlongs 1 chain]
Railway No. 4 – From Eythorne on Railway No. 1 to Guilford Colliery. [2 miles 3 furlongs 1.5 chains]
Railway No. 5 – From Eythorne on Railway No. 1 to Northbourne. [3 miles 7 furlongs]
Railway No. 6 – A short line from Wingham on Railway No. 2. [1 mile 6 furlongs 8 chains]
Railway No. 7 – A short line providing a second junction between Railway No. 6 and Railway No. 2. [2 furlongs 3.5 chains]
Railway No. 8 – A short line providing a second junction between Railway No. 1 and Railway No. 4. [1 furlong 8 chains]
Railway No. 9 – A short line at Richborough Castle on Railway No. 1. [1 furlong]
Railway No. 10 – A second junction between Railway No. 1 and the SECR main line at Shepherdswell. [2 furlongs 1.5 chains]

The promoters of the railway were cited as The Kent Coal Concessions Limited, The Sondage Syndicate Limited, The Fonçage Syndicate Limited, The Snowdown Colliery Limited, The South Eastern Coalfields Extension Limited, The East Kent Colliery Company Limited, The East Kent Contract & Financial Company Limited and The Extended Extension Limited. The solicitors for the promotion were Messrs F.C. Mathews & Company. This firm had been involved with several other railways under Stephens' control and was to play an active role in the future affairs of the East Kent.

The proposals made in this first application were clearly intended to safeguard as wide a range of options for the development of the coalfield as possible. Railway No. 1 would create a South to North axis from a junction with the SECR at Shepherdswell to the banks of the River Stour at Stonar. Railway No. 2 would establish alternative main line rail access at Canterbury West and then run eastwards through the South Eastern Coalfields Extension territories to join Railway No. 1 by a northwards-facing junction at Eastry. A southwards-facing junction would be provided here by Railway No. 3.

Railway No. 4 would have linked Guilford Colliery to Railway No. 1 at Eythorne by a northwards-facing junction. This would have been complemented by Railway No. 8 which would have created an additional junction between Railway No. 4 and Railway No. 1 facing towards Shepherdswell. Railway No. 5 would have struck away from Railway No. 1 north of Eythorne to serve Tilmanstone Colliery and then gone on to serve any collieries that might be developed in the future on Lord Northbourne's Estate. Railway No. 6 would have linked an intended colliery on the site of the Goodnestone boring by a westward-facing junction with Railway No. 2 at Wingham. Railway No. 7 would have provided an eastward-facing junction at the same place.

Railway No. 9 would have created a main line rail connection in the northern section of the system at Richborough Castle. Railway No. 10 would have provided a northern-facing junction with the main line at Shepherdswell to complement the original intention that Railway No. 1 would commence with a southern-facing junction into Shepherdswell goods yard.

It can be seen that this first application would have provided the collieries being sunk at Guilford and Tilmanstone with the means to bring in construction materials and, when mining commenced, to consign coal by rail through Shepherdswell, Canterbury or Richborough and by water from Stonar. Potential pits at Northbourne and between Eastry and Canterbury would be within easy reach of rail transport. Of the pits currently under construction only Snowdown was omitted from the scheme and, since this site adjoined the Canterbury-Dover main line, it could be considered well enough served already.

The task now facing the promoters was to satisfy the Light Railway Commissioners that there was a need for the railways proposed, that the company would be capable of constructing and operating the railways, that suitable arrangements would be made for operating the railways safely, and that any legitimate objections to the railways could be answered. In the event there were several major objections to be overcome and these led to some substantial modifications to the application even before the statutory public hearings were held.

The first casualty was the stretch of Line No. 2 between Canterbury and Wingham to which there were three influential objectors. The first of these was the South Eastern & Chatham Railway which not only objected to the East Kent gaining access to its system by running through its goods yard but was also firmly of the opinion that the logical place for a line from Wingham to meet its tracks was at Adisham. This could be achieved by a line of two miles instead of the six miles that would be involved in running to Canterbury. Moreover, a line from Wingham to Adisham could be routed via Goodnestone and thus do away with the need for Lines 6 and 7.

The second objection came from the War Office who objected on the grounds that the proposed line crossed through a large parcel of land recently purchased for cavalry training. This objection might have been met by diverting the route but was accompanied by a very resolute objection from the Ecclesiastical Commissioners, the main landowner in this vicinity, to any interference with their lands. The bad feeling between Burr and the Commissioners has already been mentioned. Although the Light Railway Commissioners would have judged the case for crossing the Ecclesiastical Commissioners' land on its merits it seems that Burr, anticipating a long and acrimonious dispute, preferred not to put the issue to the test. It may well have been that Burr, having failed to persuade the Ecclesiastical Commissioners to sell him their mineral rights in this area, had hoped to obtain their co-operation by acquiring railway rights instead. On finding that the Ecclesiastical Commissioners were prepared to fight, Burr abandoned the application for the section of Line No. 2 between Canterbury and the Wingham parish boundary.

A very similar situation arose in respect of Line No. 5 from Eythorne to Northbourne. Lord Northbourne was negotiating the sale of mineral options over his estate to interests outside the Concessions Group and had no wish to let Concessions control the transport of any coal that might be found. Whereas other lines could be justified by an intention by the Concessions Group to sink a colliery, no such case could be argued for Line No. 5 and it was accordingly abandoned, apart from the short length needed to connect the Tilmanstone sinkings with Eythorne. Even this section had led the Commissioners to wonder whether it might not just as easily have been served by taking the route of Railway No. 1 alongside the colliery.

The proposal for Lines 6 and 7 was also abandoned but this time for reasons of the Concessions Group's own making. The South Eastern Coalfield Extension Company had decided to sink the pit which it had originally intended to put down at Goodnestone closer to the proposed Line No. 2 at Dambridge Farm on the eastern edge of Wingham. These Lines were therefore no longer needed.

The final abandonment from the original plan was Line No. 3. This was the south-facing connection between Line No. 2 and Line No. 1 at Eastry. As originally planned this would have so thoroughly severed Wells Farm as to justify heavy compensation and long argument. It was accordingly dropped from the Light Railway application. Since this left only a Richborough-facing connection between Lines 1 and 2 it is surprising that no alternative connection was proposed in its place but there appears to have been no consideration of this problem at the time.

As a result of these various abandonments it was a somewhat less ambitious scheme that was put forward at the public hearings at the County Hotel, Canterbury on the 17th and 18th October, 1910. Much of the evidence on behalf of the promoters was concerned with establishing the need for rail transport to the pits being sunk and those planned for the future. The two main arguments used were that commercial extraction of coal was imminent and, conversely, that the pits could not be completed if they had to depend upon road transport

The narrow gauge rails in the foreground were purely for internal traffic at Tilmanstone Colliery. If the colliery was to make reasonable progress then a proper rail connection to the main line was essential.

for the delivery of construction materials. Arthur Burr was characteristically enthusiastic about the importance of the development of the Kent coalfield but seems to have been carried away by his own eloquence when he claimed that navigation coal from Kent would be 'of vast imperial importance' should England ever be cut off from Cardiff! More prosaically he dwelt upon the fine qualities of the fireclay which would also be extracted and called the attention of the Hearing to 'some fine examples of our potteryware at the back of this room'.

Considerable efforts were also made to establish that the Concessions Group was a fit and proper body to be entrusted with the construction and operation of the proposed lines. It was emphasised that there were 4,000 shareholders in the various concerns '. . . including many of the leading Coal Owners in the United Kingdom, also Directors of important Collieries in the Pas de Calais France' and that the Group was quite distinct from the developers of the Dover Colliery. Numerous references were made to the vast amounts already spent by the Group on exploring and developing the coalfield and to the large reserves available to the Group to complete its undertakings. A close examination of these reserves might have led to a more cautious estimate of the ability of the Group to achieve its aims but none of these claims was challenged.

This is not to say that there was no opposition to the Application. One major obstacle was the question of access to the River Stour at Stonar. The greater part of the land enclosed by the loop of the Stour on which it was proposed to terminate Line No. 1 was owned by Lord Greville and the actual site of the Line's proposed terminus was not, in his opinion, suitable for river traffic at present. Slightly beyond this point there were proposals by St Augustine's Links Ltd, a company which had originally been formed to develop a golf course here, to construct a port at the mouth of the Stour primarily for the export of coal. However, since St Augustine's Links felt that it would be premature to commence the port until they had a better knowledge of the quantities of coal likely to pass through it, Lord Greville suggested that Line No. 1 should terminate at a more southerly point from which it could be connected to an existing wharf of his on the Stour. If the new port were subsequently to be constructed Lord Greville would not object to Line No. 1 being extended. The connection to the Stour was to prove the subject of extensive negotiations and frustrations in the years to come.

Objections also arose at the other end of Line No. 1. The SECR raised no objections to the junctions between its line and the Light Railway but, upon leaving the vicinity of Shepherdswell station, Line No. 1 would cut through a building estate belonging to a Mr Dixon. Although the estate had been laid out some 10 years previously only one house had been built so far. A second plot had been sold but building had not commenced on it. Despite this somewhat inauspicious start Mr Dixon was convinced that if only the SECR were to run a more frequent service between Shepherdswell and Dover his estate would flourish as a country suburb for the Dover business community. If Line No. 1 had to be built through his estate, then he wanted far more substantial compensation than the promoters had been prepared to offer. This led to an intemperate outburst by Burr that he would never accept demands '. . . at the point of a bayonet'. The Commissioners were content to refer the matter for settlement through the normal compensation procedures.

The only other major point to be raised at the Hearing was by the Commissioners themselves who proposed that the word 'Mineral' be dropped from the title of the railway company. The brief prepared by the promoters had perhaps anticipated this: 'It is proposed to convey Goods, Minerals, Livestock and Parcels upon the Line and if any bona fide demand arises arrangements will be made for the carriage of Passengers'. The Commissioners believed that there was a local demand for passenger services and that the alteration to the name would provide some reassurance on this point. The promoters agreed to change their title to The East Kent Light Railways Company.

A number of questions remained to be resolved before the Commissioners were prepared to recommend the granting of a Light Railway Order. Formal agreements had to be reached between the promoters, Lord Greville and Saint Augustine's Links Ltd and relevant clauses inserted in the Light Railway Order. The upshot of this was that the proposed terminus of Line No. 1 on the Stour remained unchanged, but until the proposed port was built Line No. 1 would instead make a junction with an existing tramway between Lord Greville's Wharf and the SECR's Deal branch. This tramway had been used by the contracting firm Messrs S. Pearson & Son in connection with their construction of the new harbour at Dover. Lord Greville undertook to give Pearson's notice to quit their sole tenancy of the tramway, but retained the right to come to a new agreement with Pearson's if this was not inconsistent with the railway's use of the tramway. The railway could relay the tramway, add its own sidings and use Lord Greville's Wharf in return for an annual payment of £100 together with 50 per cent of carriage rates over the Tramway and 25 per cent of terminal rates at the Wharf with a minimum payment of £50 a year. As for St Augustine's Links the railway undertook not to build a port of its own but to retain the right to do so should St Augustine's Links fail to build its port within two years of the granting of the Light Railway Order, or within six months after the completion of Line No. 1.

A point not raised at the Public Hearing but requiring considerable negotiation afterwards was the nature of the bridge by which Line No. 1 would cross the Stour at Richborough. It was eventually ordered that this should be an opening bridge leaving an open channel of 30 feet and a headway of 11 feet above spring tide with footpaths on both sides of the river and on both sides of any central pier that might need to be built. This was for the control and operation of the 'blow boat' or dredger used by the Commissioners of Sewers to maintain navigation along the Stour. As far as the height of the river bridge was concerned this was to some extent fixed by the requirement to give a 15 feet headway to the adjoining bridge over the South Eastern & Chatham branch to Deal.

There was less controversy over the other bridges planned for the line. These were a bridge under the Eythorne to Coldred road on Line No. 4, a bridge over the Barville to Lower Eythorne road on Line No. 5 and a bridge over the Eastry to Selson road on Line No. 1. A planned level crossing through the centre of a crossroads on Golgotha Hill near Shepherdswell was to be avoided by realigning the roads as an 'H' rather than an 'X' and taking the railway under the centre 'span' of the 'H' which would be a road over-bridge.

With the exception of the level crossing over the road between Sandwich and Ash, which should be gated, it was agreed that cattle guards would be sufficient at road crossings. A 25 mph speed limit was specified in place of the 30 mph requested by the promoters. This was something the Light Railway Commissioners had come to expect in any Light Railway application submitted by Stephens.

After some lengthy consideration the Commissioners agreed to the promoters' request that motive power on the railway could be either steam or electricity. They were less easily convinced that the company needed powers to raise £200,000 capital with additional powers to borrow up to £100,000. Eventually the company's capital powers were settled at £160,000 and its borrowing powers at £80,000. Clauses empowering the East Kent to have unspecified running powers over the SECR and to erect platforms and other structures on that concern's property were rejected out of hand: 'We never grant such powers except by agreement and it is difficult to understand why Mr Stephens continues to insert them in his Draft Orders'.

Finally, the Directors were to be Sir Henry Edward Dering, Bart, Arthur Burr, Malcolm Burr, Augustus Montague Bradley and three others. The East Kent Light Railways Order 1911 was officially confirmed on 19th June, 1911 and the East Kent Light Railways Company joined the ranks of the Concessions Group.

The Second Order

Even before the first Light Railway Order had been granted Stephens had been set to work to produce a submission for a second order. Because the first order had not yet been granted and the East Kent Light Railways Company had yet to be incorporated, this application was promoted in the names of the various Concessions companies that had promoted the first order. The statutory advertisement for this application appeared on 26th November, 1910 and proposed four additional lines as follows:

> *Railway No. 11* – From Railway No. 1 at Eythorne to Mongeham. [4 miles 3 furlongs 4 chains]
> *Railway No. 12* – From Railway No. 4 to Maydensole. [2 miles 3 furlongs 4 chains]
> *Railway No. 13* – From Railway No. 4 to a junction with the London, Chatham & Dover Railway (LCDR) at Stonehall. [2 miles 7 furlongs 7 chains]
> *Railway No. 14* – From Railway No. 2 at Eastry to Hammill. [5 furlongs 3.5 chains]

Lines 11, 12 and 14 were planned to connect three newly proposed collieries to the East Kent system. Line No. 11, announced as a substitute for the abandoned portion of Line No. 5, would connect a proposed colliery at Great Mongeham to Line No. 1 near Eythorne, Line No. 12 would connect a proposed colliery at Maydensole with Line No. 4 near to Guilford Colliery and Line No. 14 would connect a proposed Goodnestone & Woodnesborough Colliery at Hammill to Line No. 2 about half a mile from the junction of Line No. 2 with

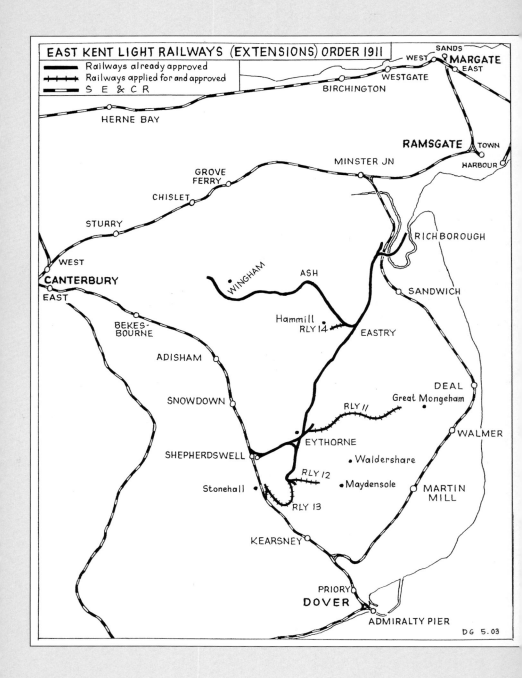

EAST KENT LIGHT RAILWAYS (EXTENSIONS) ORDER 1911

Railways already approved
Railways applied for and approved
S E & C R

DG 5.03

Line No. 1. Although much was made of the prospects of the collieries at Mongeham and Maydensole, there is little evidence that any serious effort was ever made by the Concessions Group to put down a colliery at either site. There is some evidence that the Concessions Group later tried to interest other parties in sinking a pit at Maydensole, but the site at Mongeham was suspiciously close to Lord Northbourne's estate and may have been speculatively intended as a springboard to tap traffic from developments arising there.

Whatever the prospects for the Mongeham and Maydensole sites, the Concessions Group were at least serious in their intentions to sink a colliery at Hammill on Line 14 though the inclusion of 'Goodnestone' is puzzling as it was a considerable distance from Goodnestone and it had already been decided to build the colliery originally intended for Goodnestone at Wingham. Later references to this colliery usually name it either as Woodnesborough or as Hammill.

Line No. 13 was the most curious of the lines projected under this Application. Whereas the other lines connected proposed collieries to the East Kent, Line No. 13 connected the East Kent to a proposed colliery the site of which was already on a railway. More specifically, Line No. 13 would have branched off Line No. 4 close to Guilford Colliery and looped back on itself to join the SECR line from Canterbury to Dover at the site on which it was proposed to build Stonehall Colliery.

The Public Inquiry for the Extensions Application was opened at the Lord Warden Hotel, Dover, on 17th February, 1911. Once again the Concessions Group was at pains to show its bona fides by reporting on the satisfactory progress being made with the pits already under construction. In answer to questions concerning the problems that had arisen from flooding, Malcolm Burr confidently announced, 'We have now bored through the whole of that water-bearing strata ; we have bored into the hard-coal measures that cannot possibly carry any water'. This confidence was to prove to be misplaced as were also hopes expressed at the Enquiry of attracting investment from the local authorities. The draft Order made provision for Kent County Council to subscribe £2,000 and for Dover Corporation and Eastry Rural District Council to subscribe £1,000 each. The local authorities were only too happy to support the venture to the extent that it would preserve the local roads from heavy colliery construction traffic, but their support fell well short of actual investment in the enterprise.

There were fewer objections from landowners to the extensions than there had been to the original Order. Much of the land needed for the planned new lines was the property of supporters of the railway, notably Henry Fitzwalter Plumptre and Mr F.L. Hamilton Morrice of Norfolk who owned land at Great and Little Mongeham and at Northbourne. Most of the landowners who did object were referred to compensation by the Light Railway Commissioners. The main exception was Mr H. Coleman, whose Woodville Estate was to be caught in the loop of Line No. 13, and who was able to extract an undertaking from the promoters that the view from his home would be preserved by running the line in a 77 yard 'covered way' and then screening it from sight by means of a belt of trees at least six yards deep.

Line No. 13 was the subject of much discussion at the Enquiry. Its avowed purpose in connecting Guilford to Stonehall was to relieve Shepherdswell of congestion when all the collieries were producing at full capacity. It would have been a very steeply graded line, up to 1 in 37 for much of its length, and would have required heavy earthworks. Surveying the line had proved far from easy according to Stephens who admitted that the surveyors had had difficulty standing upright at certain points! Understandably the Commissioners had readily agreed with a proposition from the SECR that this line at least should not be considered for the carriage of passengers.

One objection that was overruled in a somewhat cavalier fashion by the Commissioners was raised in relation to a bridge over one of the roads on Line No. 12. The Kent County Surveyor had suggested a headway of 16 feet instead of the 15 feet proposed and Mr Prosser, speaking for the County Council, urged the case in this way: 'There is only just this I should like to say, hay wagons, as you heard this morning, go along this road, and there is the double-deck motor 'bus , I am told, that will be over 16 feet with a passenger standing on the top'. Mr Steward, for the Commissioners, dismissed this objection: 'I think he must sit down when he comes to the bridge'.

All in all it could be said that the Commissioners viewed the Extensions application as a natural development of the original scheme and, apart from reducing the capital and borrowing powers asked for from £100,000 and £50,000 to £80,000 and £40,000 respectively, were happy to endorse the application. The East Kent Light Railways (Extensions) Order was confirmed on 7th September, 1911.

At or about the same date the first section of the East Kent Light Railways, a temporary line between Shepherdswell and Tilmanstone, was sufficiently complete for trains to start conveying construction equipment and materials to Tilmanstone. The East Kent Light Railways Company was in business or at least appeared to be. For a company that had raised only a nominal sum of capital so far, and spent even less, it was making remarkable progress.

Photograph published in a Kent Coal Concessions circular for October-November 1911 showing progress on the contractor's line at Shepherdswell. Locomotive No. 1 can just be made out in the distance.

Chapter Three

Finding Funds and Counting Costs

Financing the railway

Such progress as the railway had made by September 1911 was almost entirely attributable to Kent Coal Concessions and the East Kent Contract & Financial Company. By contrast the Board of the East Kent Light Railways Company had met exactly once. This meeting, at Castle Hill House, Dover, on 13th July, had established the Directors as Arthur Burr, Malcolm Burr, Sir Henry Dering, Mr H.W. Plumptre, Mr A. Loring and Mr W. Richmond Powell. The main business of the meeting was to appoint Arthur Burr as Chairman and Arthur and Malcolm Burr as joint Managing Directors, to appoint Mr Frank Wilkinson as Secretary during construction of the line, to appoint Holman Stephens as Engineer and Messrs F.C . Mathews & Co. as Solicitors. One curious feature of the proceedings was the absence of Arthur Burr himself. It was to be another 11 months before he actually put in an appearance at the company's meetings.

There was some mention at the meeting of negotiations between the East Kent Contract & Financial Company and the Mines Construction Company regarding construction and finance of the railways but no decisions were taken at this time. The Contract company, as it was known within the Concessions Group, was already in the process of constructing the temporary line to Tilmanstone but this had given rise to a problem in that the Directors of the railways company were not legally allowed to make a contract with a company in which they were shareholders. Therefore it was proposed to use Mines Construction as a conduit between the railways company and the Contract company. Until the details could be worked out Mines Construction had shared the costs of promoting the two Light Railway Orders. The work being done by the Contract company at this stage seems to have been financed with loans from various of the Concessions Group companies, primarily from Kent Coal Concessions. In the longer term it was envisaged that Mines Construction would finance construction and the Contract company would carry out the work but the urgency of getting colliery construction materials to Tilmanstone had forced the pace of events.

The Directors did not meet again until February 1912, by which date the temporary line to Tilmanstone had been in operation for some months. Work had actually been recorded in the *Dover Express* as commencing on Monday 10th July, 1911: 'On Monday a start was made on the construction of the mineral light railway that is to be constructed under the auspices of the Kent Coal Concessions Company. The railway will run from the goods yard at Shepherdswell Station through a meadow belonging to the Kent Coal Concessions, and across the fields to "The Firs". Already two thousand sleepers have been sent to Shepherdswell some of which have been deposited in the fields nearly opposite to "The Firs".'

Construction was sub-contracted by the Contract company as two contracts. The first of these, covering the line from Shepherdswell to Eastry and the lines from Eythorne to Tilmanstone and Guilford, went to William Rigby & Company. This firm had in 1911 just completed a contract for the construction of Hither Green Sidings for the SECR and had previously widened the line from St Johns to Orpington and opened an office at Grove Park. This latter place is mentioned since several locomotives were delivered there. William Rigby was well known to Holman Stephens and had carried out a number of contracts for him. These included the Sheppey Light Railway, the Headcorn Extension of the Kent & East Sussex Railway and the refurbishment of the Shropshire & Montgomeryshire Light Railway.

Amongst the lines covered by Rigby's contract was the northern connecting curve at Shepherdswell, Railway No. 10. It was for this line that the embankment known afterwards as North Bank had to be built. During its construction a locomotive is rumoured to have toppled over the side of the embankment. There was always a strong belief amongst the older railway staff that the owners were unable to retrieve the locomotive due to the waterlogged nature of the ground and that it remained buried in the embankment. Similar tales are told concerning the Paddock Wood & Cranbrook Railway engineered by Stephens where the embankment north of Horsmonden was reputed to contain a number of abandoned vehicles. If one carries research deep enough one finds that tales of remarkable similarity abound on many of the Stephens lines, and some commentators have even made so bold as to suggest that it was Stephens who started them!

To link Shepherdswell with Tilmanstone as quickly as possible, a rough standard gauge surface line was carried around the north-west side of Golgotha Hill. This left the permanent course of the line just beyond where the points to Shepherdswell platform siding would later be installed and swung to the right on a low embankment before climbing through a small orchard and passing close to a small house bearing the name 'Shamrock'. The line crossed the Shepherdswell to Eythorne Road several hundred yards closer to Shepherdswell than the level crossing used by the permanent line. Still climbing steeply and curving to the north the track crossed the route of the permanent line and ran parallel to the public road round and over the top of the hill. Some idea of the gradients involved can be gained from the fact that trains were confined to four wagons in length.

Progress with the surface line was fairly rapid. In July Arthur Burr reported that a mile of rails had been laid and that Tilmanstone would be reached before the end of August. In saying this he was being typically optimistic, but by 18th August the *Kentish Express* was able to announce: 'Good progress is being made with the light railway between Shepherdswell and Tilmanstone Colliery, which is to take over the heavy traffic which previously had to go over the main road, causing the road at the time to be in a terrible condition. Where the line crosses the main road a level crossing is being made, and two signal posts have been erected, whilst there is now a long stretch of rails down.' At the end of September Arthur Burr was prophesying that, '. . . the line itself will be into the colliery within two or three weeks.' But it is believed that Tilmanstone was not actually reached until the end of October.

The second construction contract, for the remainder of Railway 1 beyond Eastry and for Railway 2 from Eastry to Wingham, was let to Stephens himself and he in turn sub-contracted this to Mr John Brenchley who had worked for Stephens on the Kent & East Sussex. This was to prove a rather unhappy arrangement for both Stephens and Brenchley as the Contract company seems to have felt less need to pay Stephens than Rigby. In consequence there were times when Stephens had no money to pay Brenchley and Brenchley had no money to pay his workmen. This led to considerable distress amongst the workforce and to at least one attempted suicide. Brenchley remained on this contract until 1915 and obviously remained on good personal terms with Stephens as he later worked for him on the construction of the Edge Hill Light Railway. It was on this line that his strength of character showed itself. In June 1922 this railway acquired *Sankey*, a small Manning, Wardle 0-4-0 saddle tank locomotive, to work the line at the head of a steep rope-worked incline. It was necessary for *Sankey* to mount the incline under its own steam albeit with assistance from the winding cables and counter-balanced by two wagons. The duty driver refused to undertake this risky task and, no other volunteers being forthcoming, Mr Brenchley climbed into the cab, motioned his son, Mr F. Brenchley, to join him and drove the engine straight up the incline without a hitch.

Construction work progressed well in the first six months. In April 1912 it was said that the contractor's temporary line had been operating for nearly five months, which would put the date of opening at some time in November 1911. A letter from Stephens to Dover Council in October 1911, proposing that wagons be propelled up hill to the Eythorne Road level crossing instead of providing catch points, suggests that the line was already in use at that time but probably only for construction traffic. Certainly Dover Council were concerned at the operation of the line at this point and somewhat sceptical that, if permitted, the contractors would keep to this arrangement. Soon after the arrival of EKR* locomotive No. 1, in late September 1911, a number of photographs were issued to the railway press purporting to show the first official goods train. A copy of this photograph appeared in the December 1911 *Railway Magazine*, but neither here nor anywhere else is an actual date given for this event.

All this work had been put in hand even though the only shares in the EKR to have been issued were the £250 qualifying shares held by each of the six Directors. The EKR had even employed its own traffic superintendent, Mr Harry Springgay. Yet the only identifiable source of finance to date had been a temporary loan of £4,500 by Mines Construction Company to pay the statutory deposits. Since Mines Construction does not itself appear to have issued more than a nominal handful of shares it appears that this money was itself borrowed.

At the February 1912 Board Meeting the nature of the financial arrangements proposed by Mines Construction were outlined; it would take up £50,000 EKR shares at par with an option to underwrite a further £50,000 at 10 per cent commission. The EKR would pay Mines Construction £25,000 for work completed to date, with one exception dealt with later, and Mines Construction would issue a Prospectus for the underwritten shares and meet any claims against the EKR that might be made by the East Kent Contract & Financial Company.

---

* For simplicity the railway company will be referred to from here on as EKR – strictly the initials should be EKLR but EKR was the form chosen by the company on its locomotives.

John Brenchley at the controls of 0-4-0ST *Sankey* on the Edge Hill Light Railway in June 1922.

The Board met again in March 1912 to learn that Mines Construction had under-estimated its expenses and now found it necessary to increase its quotation to £30,000. Since the EKR had still not made a public share issue and could not even make use of its borrowing powers until it had done so, there was no question of the Board being able to make a payment of any sort at this stage.

A further request for agreement to a cash payment of £30,000 was received from Mines Construction at the Board's April meeting together with more detailed proposals to underwrite the EKR's share issues. However, on 1st April Kent Coal Concessions had issued a Prospectus to its own shareholders for EKR shares. The Prospectus mentioned that Mines Construction had paid the costs of promoting the Light Railway Orders but that East Kent Contract & Financial was guaranteeing the obligations of Mines Construction.

There then occurred a curious sequence of events in which one of the shareholders in the Contract company, Mr E.B. Dawson, brought an action on 17th May against the EKR to restrain it from paying £30,000 to Mines Construction. The Judge ordered the matter to stand over for some days on the understanding that the money would not be paid. On 22nd May Mr Dawson applied for the injunction to continue. Against him it was argued that shareholders with a much greater holding than Mr Dawson in the Contract company opposed his application. Mr Justice Eady refused to grant any further injunction and stood the matter over until the next sittings. This was followed by an extraordinary general meeting of the Contract company shareholders '. . . for the purpose of considering and passing a resolution expressing unqualified support and confidence in the conduct and management of the company's businesses by Mr Arthur Burr and Dr Malcolm Burr, and disapproval of certain action brought against them and others by Mr E.B. Dawson purporting to act on behalf of himself and all other shareholders of this company'.

The meeting was chaired by Dr Malcolm Burr who apologised for his father's absence for the benefit of his health at Droitwich. The shareholders were warned that Mr Dawson's action would paralyse the Contract company in constructing the railway which was essential to the development of the '. . . 15 to 20 collieries that were proposed.' Mines Construction had made no profit from its involvement in the railway and simply existed as a conduit between the EKR and the Contract company. Mr Dawson's 150 shares contrasted unfavourably with the 31,211 shares held by shareholders who had sent in proxies in favour of Arthur Burr. Not surprisingly the motion was carried unanimously and was followed by speeches congratulating Arthur Burr. It was suggested that since it was his birthday a telegram of congratulations should be sent to him. The jubilant mood of the meeting may be judged from the following extract from the *Dover Express*:

> Dr Burr, in giving a few details of the recent progress of the Kent Coal undertaking, said it had always been their custom when they were gathered together as they were then to receive a telegram announcing another seam of coal having been struck (laughter). He was sure they would not like him to disappoint them then. He had received a telegram but not while the meeting was in progress, it had arrived 20 minutes beforehand, and announced that another new seam of 6 ft 9 in. had been struck at a boring in which they had already proved over 90 ft (applause).

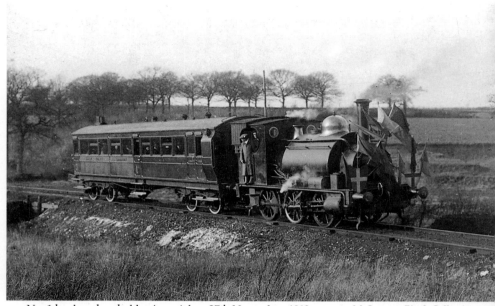

No. 1 hauls a shareholders' special on 27th November, 1912.   *M. Lawson Finch Collection*

No. 1 shunting at Tilmanstone in 1912 with its wooden cab extension as also seen in the top photograph. Unusually No. 1 is facing away from Shepherdswell.   *Ralph Gillam Collection*

For an issue that had so preoccupied both the EKR and the Contract company there is disappointingly little further to record. The legal action petered out, the legal difficulties preventing direct relations between the Contract company and the EKR seem to have been overcome and, apart from some later references to litigation against Mines Construction, there appears to be no further mention of that company in the EKR records.

In August 1912 a contract was finally sealed between the EKR and the Contract company. It was an ingenious agreement and its obvious intention was to lock the EKR securely within the grip of the Concessions Group. East Kent Contract & Financial undertook:

(1) to construct the railways authorised by the 1911 Order and the 1911 Extensions Order (2) to provide the necessary engines rolling stock machinery works and equipment for such railways (3) to provide the money for the purchase of all land rights and easements required and all compensation payable to landowners and others and for all expenses payable by the company (4) to redeem the land tax and procure the apportionment of all tithe rent-charges (5) to meet the cost of administering the affairs of the company until the said railways had been passed by the Board of Trade and opened for public traffic (including office accommodation and Directors' fees and salaries for the company's officers) (6) to pay all interest upon debenture stock issued by the company accrued due prior to the date of the passing of all the said railways by the Board of Trade and (7) to provide the company with a cash working capital of £5,000 as and when the said railways should be opened for public traffic. [The obligations of the EKR were] . . . to pay to the Contract company the sum of £325,000 as to £205,000 in cash as the works proceeded and as to the balance in debenture stock . . . and that so long as the Contract company should carry out the Agreement no shares or mortgages or debenture stock should be issued except to or with the consent of the Contract company.

The works should be completed and the railways ready for public traffic on or before 30th June, 1914.

Had all gone as intended the EKR would have effectively become a wholly owned subsidiary of East Kent Contract & Financial. Even if events did not proceed as intended there were some useful provisions in the small print that would prevent the EKR courting patronage elsewhere. The chief of these was that the Contract company should have an automatic extension of time to complete the works should there be any exceptional financial depression, any suspension of the development of the East Kent coalfield preventing the public from subscribing capital, any strike by the employees or any event in which an arbitrator or court might prevent the Contract company from raising money.

One other safeguard within the agreement that might not have passed objective scrutiny was that all claims for construction expenses made by the Contract company had to be passed by the EKR Engineer. This was, of course, Holman Stephens but as he was also responsible for supervising the work being done for the Contract company and, through Mr Brenchley, for doing part of that work, the end result was that Stephens was certifying the quality and cost of his own work. On Stephens' behalf it must be remembered that his supervision of the works was somewhat remote as he was also heavily engaged in the refurbishment of the Shropshire & Montgomeryshire and the Weston Clevedon & Portishead Light Railways at this time, besides managing

Right: Cutting shored up on the approach to Golgotha tunnel workings.
M. Lawson Finch Collection

Below: A steam crane raises spoil from the central shaft of Golgotha tunnel workings.
M. Lawson Finch Collection

the Kent & East Sussex Light Railway and the Hundred of Manhood & Selsey Tramway.

Finance for the railways apparently guaranteed and construction well under way, the Directors must have thought the future of their enterprise assured. This was just as well as the EKR had already put in hand two further developments. The first of these concerned Railway No. 1 of the original Order.

As originally proposed and approved in the 1911 Order Railway No. 1 would have left Shepherdswell by climbing and then descending Golgotha Hill. This would have created an inconveniently heavy gradient for loaded coal trains from Tilmanstone to tackle. It was therefore decided to tunnel through Golgotha Hill instead. Whilst this would involve a great deal more work and expense than the surface route it would considerably ease the gradient and create savings in the motive power and fuel needed to work the line.

Strangely we have found almost no documentary evidence for this major change of plan. There seems to have been no application to the Light Railway Commissioners for approval or even comment on the substitution of a tunnel in place of the approved route, not even an application to raise additional capital to meet the increased costs that must have been involved. Nor is there any record of the matter being discussed by the Board. In fact the only evidence of an approximate date for the decision to use a tunnel is that in February 1912 Mines Construction had specifically excluded the tunnel costs from its estimate of the amount to be paid to it by the EKR for works already in hand, and a statement by Malcolm Burr at a public hearing in April 1912 that work had started on the tunnel.

This tunnel, although only 476 yards long, is noteworthy for the methods used in its construction. A vertical shaft was put down at the top of the hill and two horizontal bores were dug outwards at the bottom. The spoil from these was placed on the top of a narrow gauge skip truck, used in lieu of a bucket, and hauled up the vertical shaft by a steam crane. Cuttings were excavated on each side of the hill and from these bores were driven into the side of the hill. This enabled four faces to be worked simultaneously. Inside the tunnel only enough material was excavated to allow for the insertion of a brick arched roof but without brick sidewalls. At track level only half the floor was cleared to allow a single track along the north-west side. The remaining material along the other side was left as large neatly squared blocks of chalk which might be removed without too much trouble if the track needed to be doubled.

The public hearing at which Malcolm Burr had announced the start of work on the tunnel concerned the second new development of 1912, an application for yet another Light Railway Order. The advertisement for this appeared on 28th November, 1911 and proposed two extensions:

Railway No. 15 - from Railway No. 2 at Wingham to Wickhambreux. [3 miles 4 furlongs 8 chains]

Railway No. 16 - from Railway No. 11 at Little Mongeham to Sutton Vale. [1 mile 5 furlongs]

Both extensions were planned to connect new collieries to the EKR system. No. 15 was to serve a colliery at Stodmarsh or Wickham Court, a third of the

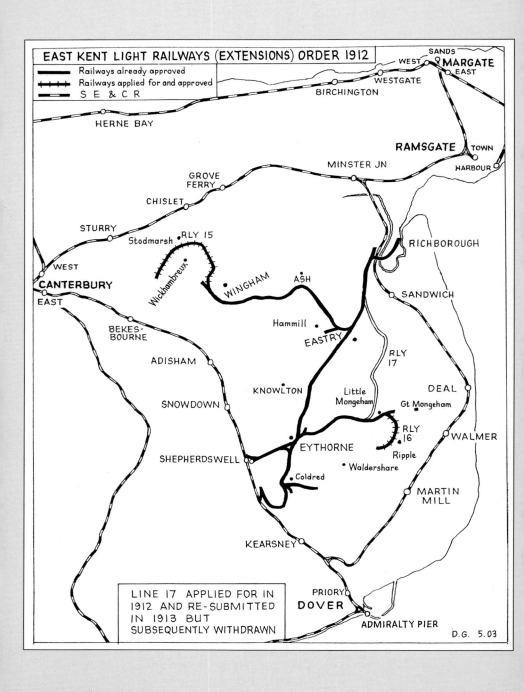

Widening out the cutting to Golgotha tunnel entrance. *M. Lawson Finch Collection*

Locomotive No. 1 rests at Shepherdswell after duties on the contractor's line over Golgotha Hill.
M. Lawson Finch Collection

way between Wingham and Canterbury and almost exactly on that part of the route of Railway No. 2 of the 1911 Order that had been abandoned. However, whereas Railway No. 2 would have gone directly from Wingham to Wickham Court, Railway No. 15 travelled in an enormous northerly semi-circle in order to avoid the lands and objections of the Ecclesiastical Commissioners.

Railway 16 also ran in a semi-circle but this was due to a logical preference for going around an intervening hill rather than over or through it. It branched off Railway No. 11 at Little Mongeham shortly before its terminus and curved round the flanks of Sutton Hill before terminating on the lands of Mr Morrice where it was proposed to build the Sutton or Ripple Colliery.

The public hearings were held at the Bell Hotel, Sandwich, on 13th April, 1912 at which the Commissioners were presented with a revised route for the greater part of Railway No. 15. The original route had followed the eastern bank of the Wingham River up to its junction with the Little Stour, and the Marquis Conyngham, on whose land most of the original route would have run, had objected to being severed from the river. It was therefore now proposed to take the line to the west of the Wingham River and onto the land of the Ecclesiastical Commissioners. Surprisingly, agreement had been reached with the Ecclesiastical Commissioners possibly because the new route was virtually on the boundary of their lands and Marquis Conyngham's. Upon reaching the Little Stour the line changed from being on the inside of its original semi-circle to going somewhat on the outside of its original route. This was to meet further objections from Marquis Conyngham, but by taking the line onto lower ground this new route also enabled two roads to cross the line by bridges rather than by level crossings to which Bridge Council had objected. Two other roads still retained level crossings but Bridge Council's objections to these were overruled by the Chairman, the Hon. A.E. Gathorne-Hardy, 'We can't really, at this time of day, refuse to sanction level crossings, simply because they are level crossings'.

There were no real objections to Railway No. 16 but one significant point emerged in the evidence in favour of this line. Mr Crundall, speaking for the railways company, was reported in the *Deal Walmer and Sandwich Mercury* as saying, '. . . the promoters were applying for powers to build the railways before the collieries were put down. They had learnt wisdom since the first application and intended getting all the materials and machinery to the site by railway and not by road'. This was emphasised in Malcolm Burr's evidence when he reported that, 'With regard to the Wingham line only last week we paid the Kent County Council £2,300 in respect of damage on the roads by extraordinary traffic'.

It was in Malcolm Burr's evidence that it was reported that the temporary line between Shepherdswell and Tilmanstone had been in operation for some '. . . four or five months' and that work had been begun on the tunnel and on Railway No. 4 to Guilford Colliery. He went on to explain that an electric power station had been completed at Tilmanstone and, now that the flooding in the shafts had been drained by the new electric pumps, the colliery was within 30 feet of the coal measures. All the Group's efforts were being concentrated on Tilmanstone and they would '. . . mark time at all the other works till the railway is built'. With an optimism characteristic of his father he concluded with the remark, 'Our difficulties are vanishing away before us'.

In their report to the Board of Trade the Light Railway Commissioners recommended approval of the application including capital and borrowing powers of £40,000 and £20,000. They also reported that the EKR was retrospectively requesting permission to hold its first annual shareholders' meeting later than the prescribed date. The meeting should have been held within six months of the granting of the original 1911 Order but, as no shares had been issued to the public until April 1912, it was hoped that it would be in order to substitute 31st December, 1912 as the latest date by which the meeting had to be held. The Board of Trade saw no need to object to this request and confirmed the East Kent Light Railways (Extensions) Order 1912 on the 8th November, 1912.

The bills come in but hope prevails

From June 1912 the EKR Directors met every month, sometimes twice a month. The main concern at these meetings once the agreement with the Contract company had been finalised was to consider the various claims made under that agreement. These had begun even before the contract was sealed with a request in June for £4,500 from the Contract company to pay Mines Construction's loan for the statutory deposit. It was decided to make a 5s. call on shares issued and to pay the £4,500 when funds permitted. By the July meeting the call on shares had raised £4,753 but a further £2,694 was still outstanding, £1,250 of which was for shares issued to the Contract company. At the same time the latter was asking for a further £5,000 on account. It was resolved to pay '. . . when funds permitted'.

August 1912 saw the sealing of the contract at last and a brief respite from calls for more money. It was, however, the month in which the EKR claimed its first victim. A boy named Charles Williams had been knocked from his bicycle on the Eythorne Road crossing and half of his foot had been amputated. As the accident was reported to have been the boy's own fault the Directors decided to take no action. A later meeting in the same month saw a further refinement in the art of inactivity: 'The Secretary read a letter from Mr J.S. Fraser, Solicitor, Ashford (Kent), in which he asked whether the shares in the company were earning any dividend at the present time. After discussion it was decided to put off answering the letter till he wrote again when he was to be informed that till the railways were completed, no dividends would be declared'. The same meeting did, however, see a decision to make a second 5s. call on shares.

September's meeting raised a wide variety of issues. Mr C.J. West was planning to claim for injuries to his son '. . . run over by one of the trucks at the level crossing at Eythorne'. The Light Railway Commissioners wanted to know what the prospects were for completing the remaining works. They were to be informed that land was being purchased between Tilmanstone and Eastry. General E.F. Marcille of Rennes had bought £100 shares paid up to 15s.; he was the first of many small investors from France to be attracted to the possibilities of the EKR. Stephens wanted to know whether the Directors wished to save four to five months by lining the tunnel with cement mortar rather than concrete and could the Contract company have a further £5,000? The question of the tunnel lining was referred back to the Contract company and it was agreed to pay the £5,000 as soon as possible, by borrowing if necessary.

By October 1912 the £5,000 had been paid but there was now a request for £19,942 which had risen by November to £25,711. This so far exceeded the resources of the EKR that it could only be discharged by issuing £25,711 fully paid shares to the Contract company. This was to prove to be the pattern for settling its future claims but revealed a fundamental weakness in the Agreement to which the EKR was committed. In theory the Contract company would have had sufficient funds to complete its side of the Agreement while the EKR gathered sufficient capital to pay off the Contract company when it was able to hand over the completed railways. In practice the Contract company was itself desperately short of funds and could only carry out the Agreement by constantly demanding payment from the EKR. Once these payments began to be made in shares the ability of the Contract company to complete the railways depended on its ability to sell those shares at full value. It was the start of a dangerously slippery slope.

At least one claim at the October meeting was easily resolved. Malcolm Burr asked whether the EKR would pay half of the cost of a motor car purchased by the Deal & Walmer Coalfield Company. He was firmly directed to address his request to the Contract company. The same response attended the news that James Buttifint, a brakesman, had suddenly died leaving a wife and seven children: 'It was resolved that the Board heard with regret of this man's death but that this matter should be referred to the Contract company for them to do what they felt disposed'.

The Directors' Meeting was followed by the EKR's first Annual Shareholders' Meeting but it would have been difficult to have guessed this from comparing the records of the two meetings. Whereas the mood of the Directors' Meeting was of a company living beyond its means there was little evidence of this at the Shareholders' Meeting.

For most of the shareholders the day had begun with a trip over the completed section of line. Arthur Burr had not been able to join the shareholders, 'Unfortunately, I am not able to walk and we only purchased the coach which you travelled in today a few days back'. He had therefore only been able to view the works where they were visible from a car but he was sure that the company's future was assured. He estimated that the £30,000 that it would take to finish the lines to Tilmanstone and Guilford would earn £70,000 pa when both mines were in full production. The costs of construction had been very much reduced by the very reasonable terms for land purchase being reached under the compensation procedures ; one estate originally valued by its owner at £150 per acre had been eventually purchased at £10 per acre. Nevertheless, economy was not everything, 'In return for the statutory powers which we have received we have to serve the public and our intention is to serve in no mean spirit'. To this end the Engineer had been instructed to start work on the Wingham line at both the Tilmanstone and Stodmarsh ends.

Fearing that the SECR might prove unco-operative Arthur Burr had a typically extravagant warning to give that concern, '. . . in his opinion the guarantee of the EKR's traffic to London alone would justify a competing line with the Chatham and Dover and South-Eastern railway companies to the outskirts of London. He had not the smallest doubt that if they found themselves treated in the future as they had been in the past, and they put the matter fairly and squarely before Parliament, that they would get their powers'. Fortunately, the EKR never made an application for a London extension and Arthur Burr's threat appears to have owed more to bravado than to serious intention.

Only one discordant note was struck at the Meeting. This was when a shareholder asked about the 30,000 tons already carried over the line. Arthur Burr replied that this was over the contractor's temporary railway and therefore did not affect the EKR. Closer questioning would have revealed that until the lines were handed over to the EKR any revenue that might be earned was the property of the Contract company.

No sooner had the General Meeting closed than a Special Meeting was opened to approve an application for a further extension to the railways between Little Mongeham and Eastry. The fate of this application will be discussed later but approval was obtained *nem. con.* Lest the shareholders should feel that they had not yet heard enough of the prospects of the company, or of Arthur Burr's voice, the business of the meeting was extended by an account from the Chairman of his introduction to Holman Stephens and the proposal of a vote of thanks to the Engineer for his services. This was followed by an account of the prospects at Snowdown, Tilmanstone and Guilford and of the developments at Wingham and Goodnestone. Intermediate Equipments were developing both these sites and the surface equipment at Wingham was considerably advanced. Wingham now boasted the tallest chimney in Kent and had been privileged not only to have been visited by Lord Desborough, the local landowner, but had even been climbed by the noble lord. It was hoped that Wingham would be producing coal within a year. At Goodnestone, i.e. Hammill, the works were claimed to be only three months behind those at Wingham.

The shareholders must have left their first meeting in a mood of advanced optimism. It is doubtful whether the same could be said for the Directors. There was to be worse to come before the year ended. The final meeting of 1912 took place on 30th December and had as its business to consider how to pay the Contract company's latest demand for £25,600 which, added to existing liabilities, brought the EKR's debt to the former to £38,811. It was decided to make use of the EKR's borrowing powers and to issue up to £80,000 debentures. The Contract company could then be paid with £25,000 debentures and £10,000 shares leaving a balance of £3,811 to be found.

If 1912 ended with a faltering in the fortunes of the EKR how was the rest of the Concessions Group faring?

Originally supplied to Lucas & Aird for the construction of the Suakin-Berber Railway in the
Sudan, this Manning, Wardle 0-6-0ST (959/1886) was instead employed at Dover Colliery.
M. Lawson Finch Collection

Dover Colliery seems to be a hive of activity in this pre-1914 view. The South Eastern main line
is in the foreground.   *M. Lawson Finch Collection*

Chapter Four

Concessions in Crisis -
The Kent Coalfield 1911-1918

To understand the erratic career of the EKR up to the end of World War I it is necessary to return to the equally erratic story of the Kent coalfield from the close of 1910. Developments in the coalfield took place at such a rapid rate and in such a convoluted fashion that we have found it impossible to combine them with the equally complicated story of the EKR during this period. Since the story of the EKR makes little sense without the story of the coalfield we must tempt the reader's patience and fill in this background first.

1911

The situation in the coalfield at the start of 1911 was that the Concessions Group, under-financed and over-committed, controlled the mineral rights to the greater part of the coalfield within the triangle between Canterbury, Sandwich and Dover with the exception of those areas owned by the Ecclesiastical Commissioners and by Lord Northbourne who had his own plans for mineral development. The Group had begun pits at Tilmanstone, Snowdown and Guilford and the EKR had been promoted to link the pits at Tilmanstone and Guilford with the SECR at Shepherdswell and with Lord Greville's Wharf on the Stour at Stonar pending completion of a more ambitious harbour at Richborough. Other lines of the EKR would open up the area between Eastry and Wingham, connect potential pits at Hammill, Ripple and Maydensole to the system and link Guilford with Stonehall.

Elsewhere in the coalfield the only significant development to date had been the slow and expensive sinking of the Dover Colliery at Shakespeare Cliff, where Mr Tilden Smith's Share Guarantee Trust had enabled work to resume by under-writing the issue of new preference shares. Before the end of 1910 the Share Guarantee Trust transferred its holdings in the Dover Colliery to the Channel Collieries Trust formed by two major figures in the iron industry, Sir Hugh Bell of Bell Bros and Arthur Dorman of Dorman Long & Company. In return for Share Guarantee Trust's interests in the Dover Colliery, Mr Tilden Smith acquired a substantial holding in the Channel Collieries Trust and a seat on its Board. Work now resumed in earnest at Dover though an attempt by the Channel Collieries Trust to interest the Belgian Government in financing a new ferry port alongside the colliery proved unsuccessful.

The Channel Collieries Trust was not the only new participant in the development of the coalfield. In 1910 the Ebbsfleet Coal Syndicate had been incorporated by the company formed to build the new harbour at Richborough, Saint Augustine's Links Limited. During 1911 they began a boring at Ebbsfleet. In the Northern section of the coalfield the Anglo-Westphalian Kent Coal Syndicate, with substantial backing from German commercial interests, acquired extensive mineral rights from the Ecclesiastical Commissioners in the area to the east and north-east of Canterbury.

For the Concessions Group 1911 was a year of mixed fortunes, particularly at Tilmanstone. While awaiting the completion of the power station and the arrival of electric pumps the steam pipe to the No. 2 pump burst twice and shafts 1 and 2 were flooded to 600 ft in March. By November the first of the Sulzer electric pumps was ready and shafts 1 and 2 had been drained to 983 ft revealing damage to the brickwork in No. 2 shaft. Work had continued in the interim on the new No. 3 shaft which had reached 814 ft when it was decided to halt further sinking while a connecting road was cut at 760 ft to link it with No. 1 shaft. It was also decided that any further sinking of No. 1 and No. 2 shafts through the junction beds should be lined with tubbing. The good news was that within four months of the granting of its first Light Railway Order the EKR temporary line had reached Tilmanstone and by the end of November 1911 had already carried 3,000 tons of materials to the colliery.

Work at Snowdown during 1911 was hampered by the slow delivery of tubbing but better progress was made at Guilford where No. 2 and No. 3 shafts reached 900 ft and steam pumps had at last been installed together with 'modern' winding gear. Further progress was halted pending the arrival of the EKR.

Meanwhile Intermediate Equipments had started two new collieries. The first of these, the Wingham & Stour Valley Colliery, had actually been promoted by Mines Construction who had undertaken to sink two 18 ft shafts to 1,500 ft. In the event the colliery's shares were actually issued to Intermediate Equipments and East Kent Contract & Financial. The site chosen for this colliery was on land belonging to Lord Desborough to the east of Wingham alongside the projected line of Railway No. 2.

The second new pit was the Goodnestone & Woodnesborough Colliery and was located at Hammill at the termination of Line No. 14 of the 1911 Extensions Order. No subsidiary company was set up to develop this pit which remained the direct responsibility of Intermediate Equipments. It was intended that at both pits Intermediate Equipments would do little more than erect and equip the surface buildings until the EKR arrived. There had as yet been no attempt to develop the pits at Mongeham, Maydensole and Stonehall which had been cited as justifying railway connection in the application for the 1911 Extensions Order.

1912

The improvement in the fortunes of the Dover Colliery in 1911 seemed destined to continue in 1912 with the Channel Collieries Trust planning to erect steel and cement works on the cliffs overlooking the colliery, with which they would be linked by a 20 ft diameter shaft. It was proposed to extract both coal, said to be ideal for coking, and ironstone, said to be of much better quality than that found in the Midlands, from the colliery. Unfortunately progress with the colliery itself suffered further setbacks. First the workmen joined in a six week national coal strike and then an overwinding accident in September badly damaged the winding and pumping equipment. Meanwhile the capital raised by the preference issue was beginning to run out. There was at least some consolation from the raising of the first coal from the colliery, enough to fill twelve 10 ton wagons. There would have been less consolation had it been known that this would also be the last coal to be raised from the colliery.

The misfortunes of the established colliery companies do not seem to have deterred newcomers from setting up in Kent. Lord Northbourne's lands were at last opened to exploration by the incorporation of the Betteshanger Boring Company whose Board not only included one of Lord Northbourne's sons but also several representatives of established coal interests from the North. The company was to prove a strong ally to Lord Northbourne in resisting attempts by the EKR to secure railway powers in the vicinity of Betteshanger and Northbourne.

Taking advantage of the Concessions Group's shortage of funds, the Adisham Colliery Company was incorporated to negotiate the establishment of a pit in the vicinity of Goodnestone Park, mid-way between Wingham and Snowdown. The company's first registered address was in Chesterfield where one of its Directors, Arthur Capel, already had coal interests. The moving spirits behind the company were, however, two Parisian bankers, Jules Bernard and Mathieu Goudchaux, and their interest in the Kent coalfield was but the first of a number of French initiatives in the area.

Foreign interests of quite a different sort lay behind the third of the new enterprises to be incorporated in 1912. This was the Canterbury Coal Company whose finances involved both the West African Exploring Company and the New Rhodesian Mines. The exact nature of this company's interest in the coalfield is not entirely clear but the Marquis of Winchester, who was one of its Directors, is known to have been jointly involved with Arthur Burr in a boring begun in 1912 at Chilton in the Alkham Valley . This boring was completed at 3,346ft in June 1913 and revealed seven bands of coal but these were only between 8 in. and 1 ft thick. Despite this unpromising start it was expected that the company would develop at least one pit in this area of the coalfield. In the event the company soon faded from the scene but its interests in this area led to the promotion of a branch of the EKR along the Alkham Valley.

As for the Concessions Group itself 1912 was to prove a relatively quiet year. Sinking at Snowdown was delayed by the effect of the national coal strike on the delivery of tubbing but by the year's end was making rapid progress towards the coal measures. At Guilford, Wingham and Woodnesborough sinking still awaited the arrival of the EKR, although at Wingham it had been possible to install the boilers and the winding engines had been delivered. At Tilmanstone an issue of debentures had produced sufficient capital to clear the last of the sand from No. 2 shaft, to prepare No. 1 shaft for its final 30 ft descent to the coal measures and to bring No. 3 shaft to 1,095 ft.

One development whicht would have had a major effect on the EKR was the proposed incorporation by the Concessions Group of a major new enterprise. This would have been the United Coalfields of Kent and its capital of £1,000,000 would have been sufficient to take responsibility for completing the EKR, developing the power station and brickworks and to take over the undeveloped areas of the coalfield. Unfortunately the necessary finance was not forthcoming.

1913

For the Concessions Group 1913 began with triumph but ended with serious doubts. The first success of the year was Snowdown Colliery's entry into the coal measures in January when the 'Beresford' seam was reached at 1,490 ft. Allegations that the pit had in fact been 'salted' with coal from elsewhere were allayed by conveying shareholders, journalists and local dignitaries to the coalface to inspect the workings. In case the public needed any further convincing, the proceedings were filmed by the Topical Film Company.

This inspection was part of a day-long celebration on the 4th February, which culminated in a banquet chaired by the Marquis of Winchester at which Arthur Burr was presented with the freedom of the City of Dover. The celebrations also included a trip over the EKR from Shepherdswell to Tilmanstone and an inspection of the Miners' Village at Elvington. At the banquet Arthur Burr was forced to keep to his wheelchair but his speech of reply was in the grand Burr tradition. Commenting on the fact that the evening's meal had been cooked with Snowdown coal and that the Dover evening papers were that night being printed by the power of Snowdown coal he prophesied that Tilmanstone too would soon be producing coal. Guilford would not take long now to reach coal, Wingham and Woodnesborough were nearing completion of their surface works and work had begun at Stonehall. Soon Dover would be amongst the first six towns in the land and, 'In twenty years there would be no unemployment, or poverty or hardupness in Dover'.

Tilmanstone did reach the coal measures in March but, as had by now been discovered at Snowdown, the coal in the 'Beresford' seam proved friable and unsuitable for domestic use. At both Snowdown and Tilmanstone it would be necessary to raise additional capital to sink to the next seam which borings had proved to contain a harder grade of coal.

Good and bad news attended the other Concessions pits in 1913. The EKR reached Guilford in February and the Wingham and Hammill Collieries in July. This should have greatly reduced construction costs at these pits but funds for construction were now extremely limited. At Guilford it was decided to bring No. 2 shaft down to the same level as No. 3 and then suspend work until a buyer could be found for the colliery. The shortage of funds also affected construction of the EKR, on which Burr was forced to order work to be suspended when within half a mile of the wharf at Sandwich Haven.

Two complementary strategies began to emerge for salvaging the Concessions Group at this stage. One was to amalgamate Kent Coal Concessions, South Eastern Coalfield Extensions, Extended Extension, Deal & Walmer and Sondage into a single reconstructed company to hold the Group's mineral rights. This would have still left the various construction and operating companies to survive as best they could; but the scheme foundered in a heated atmosphere of suspicion and Burr's reluctance to give way to a Board of Directors for the new company that would be entirely independent of his influence.

The second strategy was to find buyers for the undeveloped pits. In July 1913 agreement was reached for the Adisham Colliery Company to purchase a site for their colliery in the Goodnestone area. In the same month the same parties formed the Stonehall Colliery Limited to purchase the Stonehall site where a boring begun the previous year had now proved the existence of coal. The Stonehall boring seems to have been the richest ever found in Kent ; in its 3,691 ft a total of 112 ft 11 in. of coal was found in 18 seams with an average thickness of 6 ft 3 in. The richness of the boring was suspected to be due to the presence of overthrow faults which had resulted in most seams being bored through twice. The Stonehall Colliery Company therefore began a second boring to verify the findings of the first but felt sufficiently confident to start work on constructing a colliery pending those results.

Not for the first time in his life Arthur Burr was now the subject of unwelcome attention by the press. The *Pall Mall Gazette* ran a particularly sustained attack on his business practices to which Burr, frequently confined to bed by illness, was unable to respond effectively. These newspaper attacks and Burr's own state of health undermined confidence in the Concessions Group and share prices began to fall. Since shares still remained the main source of income and exchange within the Group this inevitably further hindered the Group's progress.

In November Sir Arthur Conan Doyle, who had long supported Burr and the Concessions Group, came to Burr's defence in the *Joint Stock Companies Journal*: 'When the commercial history of this age comes to be written his name will, I believe, take a high place as being the prime mover in a development which is destined to shift the whole industrial centre of gravity of England'. Burr also wrote to the same *Journal* defending his policies with the Concessions Group:

> We have done more than has ever been done before, and done it with a relatively small amount of capital. If we had been content with 5,000 or 10,000 acres we should probably be paying 100% on our capital by now, but we did not see why we should prove the field for other people. We spent £180,000 on boring alone. No coalfield in this country has ever been bored to the same extent, and it is surely evidence of the character of what we have got that the big Continental people, advised by the leading experts, are willing to pay such large premiums as have never before been heard of. If only the shareholders could afford to wait, and my policy were continued, with ample capital, there are no limits to the fortunes that are in it.

There was one comfort for Burr and the shareholders before the year ended. On 23rd December, 1913 Snowdown reached the 3 ft seam of hard coal at 1,898 ft. Even the 'Beresford' coal, from both Snowdown and Tilmanstone, was finding buyers so that some income was being made at last.

Elsewhere in the coalfield 1913 produced plans for the future but little tangible success. The Ebbsfleet Syndicate and the Betteshanger Boring Company joined forces to put down a boring at Lydden Valley. In the north of the coalfield the borings made by the Anglo-Westphalian concern had proved the existence of coal measures and it was decided to sink a colliery at Chislet alongside the SECR. To boost the credibility of this enterprise Sir Joseph Shaw, the Chairman of Powell Duffryn, was appointed as Chairman of the Anglo-Westphalian Company. The Concessions Group no longer had the coalfield to itself.

Photograph published by Kent Coal Concessions showing new houses constructed for colliery workers alongside the SECR main line at Stonehall.

Stonehall colliery under construction. Work ceased with the outbreak of war in 1914 and was never resumed.

At Dover the Channel Collieries Trust, having made borings that proved the existence of good seams of ironstone at Dover and Folkestone, came to an agreement with Kent Collieries Ltd to work the ironstone and chalk on the Kent Collieries lands for five years and for Kent Collieries to supply 100,000 tons of coal annually to them for 20 years. On lands of its own between Dover and Kingsdown the Trust proposed to sink a chain of four collieries, two of which would exploit coal reserves beneath the sea bed. It was further proposed to construct a Dover, St Margarets & Martin Mill Light Railway to link these collieries. This scheme would have included use of the disused Martin Mill Railway that had been constructed for the contract to extend Dover Harbour.

1914

Arthur Burr had always feared that any danger to the Concessions Group would come from the outside. At the end of 1913 he had said: 'The assets of our shareholders are not only ample and complete, but safe and immune from attack, thanks largely to the "Burr Finance", which, if now obsolete and unnecessary, protects them like the quills on the porcupine, for to wreck a company or companies outside creditors are essential, and they are non-existent with regard to some of our companies and few and far between with others'. What Burr did not foresee was that the Concessions Group could collapse from the inside. This was what was to occur in 1914.

The year began well enough. Tilmanstone was recorded as producing 2,000 tons each week in January. In February the sale of Stonehall to the French-financed Stonehall Colliery Ltd was agreed and work begun on the colliery. In May agreement was reached to sell Guilford Colliery to a group of six French iron and steel firms led by Compagnie des Forges du Chatillon Commentry et Neuves Maisons for £150,000 to be divided between Kent Coal Concessions and the Guilford Syndicate. Meanwhile Burr had been able to obtain additional finance for Tilmanstone from a stockbroker named Myers who advanced £30,000 to the East Kent Colliery Company on the security of debentures at 75 per cent face value.

Unfortunately water broke into one of the Tilmanstone headings at the end of March and mining had to be suspended for six weeks. Myers was sufficiently alarmed by this to transfer his debentures at 40 per cent face value to Mr Tilden Smith who already held a substantial interest in the rival Channel Collieries Trust. More importantly in the short-term this incident highlighted the chronic lack of reserve funds to cope with such problems. At Tilmanstone this led to the appointment of a Receiver in July and an unsuccessful attempt to sell the colliery to the Government in September as a source of fuel for shipping at Dover. By December the colliery's funds were exhausted and mining at Tilmanstone was suspended.

In the past such incidents had been overcome by financial support from the other Concessions Group companies. But by July it had become apparent that all the companies in the Group had reached their limit and that the affairs of East Kent Contract & Financial, the financial power house of the Group, were in a particularly complete muddle. As far as the auditors were able to determine it appeared that the company had raised £49,947 in cash and £33,183 on share premiums. It had additionally borrowed £63,859 from various Group companies but had lent £166,550 to others. It claimed to have spent £190,660 on constructing the EKR but had received payment, mostly in shares, of £201,694 owing to a miscalculation by Stephens. It had lost £35,429 in re-selling EKR shares. It owed £6,167 for land purchased for railway construction but not yet paid for, £5,146 for Stephens' fees and expenses, and £1,674 for interest due on debentures. It was in turn owed £22,007 by Kent Coal Concessions for the brickworks alone, £14,702 by East Kent Colliery, £20,016 by Snowdown Colliery and £42,508 by the Guilford Syndicate. Apart from debts and shares its only tangible assets appear to have been £201 worth of railway plant and £15 1s. 9d. for the typewriter and stove in the Shepherdswell office! Most significantly the company estimated its claim against Arthur Burr at £51,030.

In terms of assets, either working collieries, surface plant, mineral rights, leases or freeholds, few of the other Concessions Group companies were quite as badly off as the East Kent Contract & Financial but, company by company, it became apparent that Burr's robbing of Peter to pay Paul, often without security and frequently without adequate records, had hopelessly confused their affairs. Led by Sir John Dewrance of the engineering firm Babcock & Wilcox shareholders' committees took over the management of their companies from Arthur Burr's personal control and installed boards of Directors. The process was a slow one as with some of the companies, like the Fonçage Syndicate, it made little difference who controlled the debts and worthless securities that remained. It fell to the South Eastern Coalfields Extension Company to bring legal proceedings against Arthur Burr for misappropriation of funds but the eventual award to them of £16,681 with costs was a hollow victory. Burr's own assets were also exhausted and for the second time in his life he was adjudged bankrupt.

Arthur Burr died of cancer in September 1919 aged 70. His had been a grand design but too grand for one man to attempt on his own ; with foresight and better fortune he might have succeeded. Dr Malcolm Burr was to gain considerable respect for his wartime service in Macedonia and as a renowned entomologist. He was to renew his interest in mining in various parts of Africa before eventually settling down as Professor of English in the School of Economics at Istanbul. He died in Turkey in 1954.

The outbreak of war in August 1914 at least gave some respite to the Allied Companies as the Concessions Group now styled itself. Under wartime conditions it proved possible for schemes of arrangement to be drawn up with the holders of bonds, shares and debentures to postpone payments of interest and dividends until six months from the conclusion of hostilities. This was of particular advantage to East Kent Contract & Financial but was to be a mixed blessing for the EKR.

The outbreak of war also interrupted the operations of the French colliery concerns. Although the sale of the Adisham and Stonehall sites had been agreed it had not been completed and now had to be postponed. Three shafts had actually been started at Stonehall, one had reached 183 ft and was serving as a reservoir to supply the five boilers that had been installed, the second had reached 273 ft and the third had only managed 75 ft. Considerable trouble had been met with inrushes of water which the company had attempted to halt by the cementation process. Large quantities of tubbing had been ordered but had not been delivered and were eventually sold for scrap at the manufacturer's premises. Sinking immediately ceased on the outbreak of war and all the loose tools and portable equipment were commandeered shortly afterwards by a contingent of the Royal Naval Division on its way to France.

The site of Adisham Colliery had not even been selected and all thought of work on this colliery was postponed. As it was difficult for French citizens to invest outside the country during the war it became necessary for Stonehall to be mortgaged back to Kent Coal Concessions with a number of mineral leases as security. Similarly the Forges du Chatillon group were unable to proceed with their purchase of Guilford and work was not resumed here until after the war. Intermediate Equipments also stopped work on the collieries at Wingham and at Woodnesborough for the duration. Two shafts had been begun at Wingham of which one had reached 60 ft and the other 75 ft. No sinking at all had taken place at Woodnesborough.

The onset of war had varying effects on the other parties developing the Kent coalfield. Plans by the Ebbsfleet Syndicate and Betteshanger Boring Company to sink their own pits were shelved but Anglo-Westphalian continued sinking at Chislet. It did, however, become necessary for the German Directors to retire, and for the company to change its name to the Chislet Colliery Company, when rumours swept Canterbury that the colliery workings were actually the foundations for gun emplacements to shell the city!

Work continued at the Dover Colliery but the Channel Collieries Trust was now more interested in the development of the area between Dover and Kingsdown which had attracted investment from the steel enterprise of Bolckow Vaughan. Additionally the Trust now controlled over 9,000 acres to the north of Folkestone and Hythe where iron deposits had been proved by further borings.

1915

This was essentially a year of consolidation for the Allied Companies, although a bond issue enabled further sinking to take place at Snowdown to develop the deeper and more remunerative seams. At Tilmanstone an offer to buy out the colliery by the Channel Collieries Trust was resisted by the local Directors on the basis of the low price being offered to the debenture holders. An appeal by the Directors to the holders of shares and debentures secured £1,500 which enabled them to keep the pit drained. It was then decided to approve the issue of £75,000 second mortgage debentures. By December this had raised £50,000 and enabled the pit to discharge the Receiver and to resume operations. One point of significance is that the Directors, mostly local businessmen, who took over the management of the East Kent Collieries Company on behalf of the shareholders were quite distinct from the group led by Sir John Dewrance who took control of most of the other Allied Companies. Some financial assistance for Tilmanstone was initially forthcoming from Dewrance and his colleagues but gradually the East Kent Collieries Company went its own way.

At Dover work was continued in 1915 with a further loan from the Channel Collieries Trust but increasing problems with flooding led to the suspension of further sinking. Rather than abandon the pit entirely a road was cut through the ironstone seam between No. 2 and No. 3 shafts and 2,350 tons of iron ore were extracted. After this the pit was closed, initially for the duration but in practice for ever.

1916

Although an important year for the EKR, 1916 saw relatively little change in the coalfield. Snowdown Colliery won the honour of being the first to show a trading profit while at Tilmanstone the East Kent Colliery Company acquired its power station in a tidying up of debts between the South East Kent Electric Power Company, Kent Coal Concessions and the colliery.

1917

Snowdown Colliery had by now reached a satisfactory seam at 3,007 ft and it was decided that further sinking was unnecessary. The colliery was still in profit but at a lower level than in 1916. Tilmanstone also recorded its first net profit of £2,848 in 1917.

The giant French steel and engineering concern Schneider was now taking an interest in the coalfield and investigating the possibilities offered by the undeveloped properties held by the Allied Companies. In July a combined meeting of South Eastern Coalfield Extension, Kent Coal Concessions and Extended Extension took place at which the assets of the three companies were valued on the basis of the price Schneider was prepared to pay for an option to purchase the Allied Companies' acreage. On this basis South Eastern Coalfield Extension would have had a surplus of assets over liabilities of £304,242. The others were not so well off, Extended Extension had assets of £224,063 and liabilities of £91,692 leaving a surplus of £132,371. The possibility of Schneider entering the coalfield on a large scale must not only have excited the shareholders in the Allied Companies but must also have brought renewed hope to the EKR. Equally encouraging was the establishment of the Guilford & Waldershare Colliery Company by the Forges du Chatillon group. This confirmed that the group was still interested in proceeding with the purchase of Guilford Colliery as soon as circumstances allowed.

At Woodnesborough and at Wingham there was less encouraging news. The site at Woodnesborough had been taken over for a cavalry re-mount unit shortly after the outbreak of war and had been given over to stabling large numbers of horses. Intermediate Equipments had now begun to dispose of what remained of the surface equipment installed before the war. At Wingham some of the boilers and various other items of plant had been requisitioned by the Government. If work at either of these collieries was to be resumed it would mean starting from scratch.

After considerable problems with manpower shortages and severe weather conditions the Chislet Colliery finally reached coal measures at 1,432 ft. Elsewhere, the Channel Collieries Trust and Kent Collieries Ltd were amalgamated to form the Channel Steel Company. Mr Tilden Smith took this opportunity to part company with the concern whilst the Dorman Long part of the enterprise extended its interests in the coalfield by taking over the Betteshanger Boring Company.

1918

The final year of the war saw Snowdown trading at a loss again, though both here and at Tilmanstone the position was salvaged by payments from the Government's Coal Controller on the basis of a 9 per cent return on investment. Schneider went as far as to buy a two month option to take up the second mortgage debentures in Tilmanstone but did not in the event exercise the option. A similar interest that it had expressed in taking over the Wingham Colliery area and sinking two new pits was also to fall through, but for some time the Allied Companies lived in hope of salvation from this source.

The situation at the end of the war may be summarised as follows:

a)   Two collieries, Snowdown and Tilmanstone, were operating but were in a weak financial position;
b)   Guilford Colliery was ready to be taken over by a French company and should be able to start producing coal without too much difficulty;
c)   Chislet Colliery was being prepared to start producing coal and would do so in 1919;
d)   Sinking had been begun at Wingham and Stonehall but much of the equipment at both these pits had been removed during the war;
e)   Surface buildings and some equipment existed at the Woodnesborough Colliery at Hammill but sinking had not started here;
f)   Work had ceased at Dover Colliery and would not be resumed;
g)   Dorman Long & Company and the Channel Steel Company held considerable mineral rights in East Kent and were still seriously interested in developing collieries, iron ore mines and steelworks in the area;
h)   Most of the companies that had formed the Concessions Group, now known as the Allied Companies, were still trading under the leadership of Sir John Dewrance but were in a poor financial position and unlikely to be able to exploit the mineral rights they held;
i)   Various French industrial combines were still interested in investing in the Kent coalfield.

The subsequent history of the coalfield becomes considerably simpler and can be dealt with in the history of the EKR to which we now return.

Chapter Five

So Near and Yet So Far -
The East Kent Light Railways 1913-1916

1913

The Dover Express and East Kent News, 7th February, 1913:

The occasion of the honouring of Mr Burr by the shareholders and the Borough of Dover on Tuesday evening at the Town Hall, gave an opportunity for the large number of shareholders who were in Dover for the purpose to visit Snowdown and Tilmanstone Collieries. Fortunately very fine weather was enjoyed and the large numbers who visited the collieries had a very pleasant and instructive time. Parties were made up at both Dover and Canterbury, and these were taken to Shepherdswell Station, from where they journeyed to Tilmanstone by the East Kent Railway. The temporary line is still in use, but those who travelled over it had a good opportunity of seeing the great progress being made with the permanent line, on which a large number of men were at work as far as nearly a couple of miles to the north of Eythorne. The accommodation for passengers was quite good, some of the smaller carriages used on the railways formerly, being converted into comfortable corridor carriages. The railway itself will extend from Shepherdswell as far as Sandwich. It already is constructed at Tilmanstone and Guilford Collieries, and by Easter it is expected to reach Wingham.

Celebrations like these did much to maintain confidence in all the Concessions enterprises but the main pre-occupation for the EKR in 1913 continued to be the continual calls for payment from the Contract company. These were now running at an average of £10,000 every month and, although temporary lines reached Guilford in February and Woodnesborough and Wingham in July, there was little immediate prospect of any part of the system reaching a sufficient state of completion for the EKR to be able to take it over from the Contract company. Until that day arrived all revenue from the railway went to the latter.

The EKR was also beginning to receive complaints from landowners that accommodation works agreed with them were not being completed. It was becoming apparent that effective supervision of the works required more time than Stephens was able to give to the task. The Directors therefore agreed in May to the appointment of a Mr Harrisson, currently working in South Africa, to the post of Resident Engineer under Stephens. Harrisson's wages would be the responsibility of the Contract company until the line was open to public traffic.

Despite a severe shortage of funds to complete the lines for which it had already obtained authorisation, the EKR embarked upon an application for 10 additional lines in May 1913. An application had actually been made for the first of these in May 1912 as follows (*see map page 50*):

Railway No. 17: A line from Little Mongeham on Railway 11 to a junction with Railway 1 in the parish of Woodnesborough. [4 miles 4 furlongs and 7 chains]

The alleged purpose of this line was to provide a more convenient route between the proposed Ripple Colliery, for which Line 16 had been approved, and the wharves on the Stour. Since the junction of Line 17 with Line 11 faced Eythorne it would have been necessary for trains from Ripple to reverse direction at this point. This rather calls into question its 'convenience' and it was clearly the view of Lord Northbourne and the newly formed Betteshanger Boring Company that the line was yet another attempt by the Concessions Group to get into their territory. As a result of their objections the EKR had postponed pursuing its application for Line 17 until May 1913 when it could be considered with an application for Lines 18 to 28.

Although this application was postponed it was certainly not forgotten and Stephens continued to negotiate with the various road authorities and landowners along its route in order to meet objections that they might make when the application was eventually heard. This included a major deviation of the line at Finglesham where the original route would have caused substantial severance of farmland there. However, when Railways 18 to 28 were presented in 1913 the railways company found that Lord Northbourne was still resolutely opposed to Line 17 and it was again withdrawn '. . . without prejudice to its being redeposited at a future time when a satisfactory route can be agreed'. This was to be the last that was to be heard of Line 17. It might be mentioned that had the line been built it would have passed through the parish of Ham on its way to Sandwich!

The actual application of May 1913 was for the following lines:

Railway No. 18: A line starting from an end-on connection with Line 14 at Hammill to a junction with the SECR at Snowdown Colliery. [4 miles 6 furlongs and 8½ chains]

Railway No. 19: A line from Little Mongeham on Railway 11 to Deal. [2 miles 6 furlongs and 2.5 chains]

Railway No. 20: A spur from Railway 19 to the SECR at Deal. [2 furlongs and 5.75 chains]

Railway No. 22: A line from Wickhambreux on Railway 15 to the SECR sidings at Canterbury West. [4 miles 1 furlong and 6 chains]

Railway No. 23: A line from Coldred on Railway 4 to Drellingore in the Alkham Valley. [7 miles 2 furlongs]

Railway No. 24: A line linking Railway 13 to Railway 23. [7 furlongs and 3 chains]

Railway No. 26: A spur from Railway 11 to Telegraph Farm Brickworks. [4 furlongs 6½ chains]

Railway No. 27: A line from Railway 2 to Wingham Colliery. [7 furlongs]

Railway No. 28: A spur from Railway 1 at Stonar to Lord Greville's Wharf. [2 furlongs and 2 chains]

To authorize the Company to construct, re-construct, maintain, work and use as a Light Railway a Tramway in the parish of Stonar and a wharf adjoining the River Stour connected therewith.

Before discussing the proposed lines what of the missing Railways 21 and 25? Although there is no definite identification of either of these lines in the available records there is evidence of what the EKR may have had in mind. In the Public Record Office File MT58/428, which relates to the eventual granting

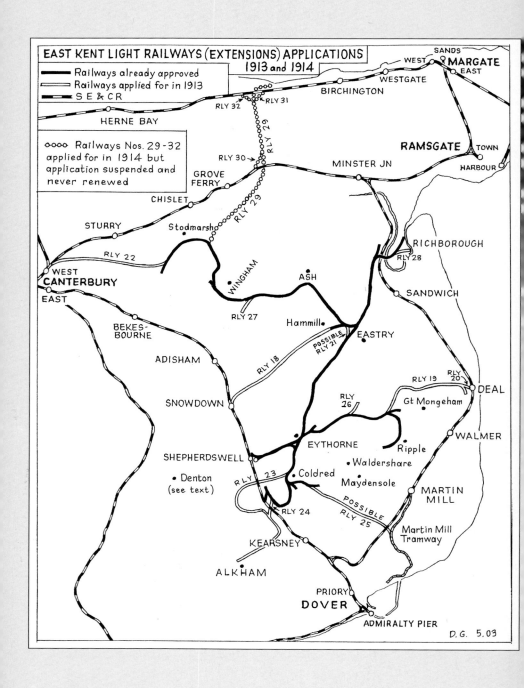

of an Order for the 1913 application, there is a map upon which two proposed lines have been crossed out. One of these is an almost exact repetition of Railway No. 3, the southern connection between Railways 1 and 2, which had been dropped from the original application in 1910. This may have been included on the map in error or there may have been a serious intention to re-apply for this line. It should be noted that Railway 2 had actually been built with a south-facing junction with Railway 1 but on a much tighter alignment than the original Railway No. 3 would have followed. This had avoided the objections that had been raised to Railway 3 and, being within the limits of deviation, never gave rise to official objection.

The second deleted line on the map is of even greater interest as it shows a line diverging in a south-easterly direction about half-way along Railway No. 12 from Guilford to Maydensole. This line maintains a south-easterly course passing to the north of Wingfield, crossing the Dover to Deal line of the SECR to the north of Guston and then swinging south to join the tracks of the disused Martin Mill Railway. This would have given it access to the Eastern Harbour at Dover, for the construction of which it had originally been built by the contractors S. Pearson & Sons. It is unlikely that this intended use of the Martin Mill Railway would have been welcomed, as the Channel Collieries Trust had their own plans for this line as part of their Dover, St Margarets and Martin Mill Light Railway and would hardly relish the arrival of a Kent Concessions interest here. If this was to have been Railway 21 or 25 it is easy to see why the railways company abandoned it even before lodging their application.

There is one other possible indication of the whereabouts of Railways 21 and 25. In a statement by Holman Stephens as to debts owing to him by the Contract company there is a reference to unpaid fees for 'surveying the lines to Denton and Tilbury'. Denton is not far from the old Ropersole boring which had shown evidence of coal though in somewhat unpromising quantities. If there had been an intention to build a line here it would probably have been best achieved by a branch from Railway 23. We have been unable to identify any location in the coalfield area known as Tilbury, but is it too fanciful to imagine a coded reference to the Admiralty Harbour at Dover to be reached by the Martin Mill Railway?

The lines for which approval was sought in the 1913 application were an extremely mixed assortment. No. 18 would obviously enable coal from Snowdown to reach Richborough for shipment by sea but a number of other arguments were advanced in its favour. Its course would also serve the proposed Adisham Colliery near Goodnestone Park and mention is also made by Malcolm Burr to a 'Goodnestone Colliery' to be built by a separate but otherwise unidentified syndicate. It should be noted that this was distinct from the earlier Goodnestone Colliery for which Railways 6 and 7 had been proposed in the original application, and which had subsequently become Wingham Colliery, and was also distinct from the Goodnestone & Woodnesborough Colliery at Hammill. Next it was argued that Railway 18 would enable coal from Snowdown and any other collieries on its route to reach a processing centre where the Concessions Group would produce '. . . coke and benzol and aniline dyes and all sorts of by-products'. When questioned on this point at the public hearings, Mr Crundall, counsel for the railways company, had to confess

Digging out Pedding cutting. Foreman Jack Hougham can be seen in the right foreground.
M. Lawson Finch Collection

The 'Morrison & Mason' Andrew Barclay 0-4-0ST, presumed to be the property of William Rigby, on a spoil train in Pedding cutting between Ash and Hammill on Railway No. 2.
M. Lawson Finch Collection

that no site had yet been chosen for such a processing centre. The final argument for Railway 18 was that its junction with Railway 14 at Hammill would enable gravitation sidings to be built alongside the line to serve the Woodnesborough Colliery. Whilst this might not seem a very good reason for building an entirely new line, it can be explained by the fact that an application for additional land at Hammill for this purpose had formed part of the postponed 1912 application for Railway 17 and was now combined with the proposal for Railway 18.

Railway 19 extended Railway 11 from Mongeham to bring the Light Railway close to the centre of Deal and Railway 20 was a short spur linking Railway 19 to the SECR line through Deal. When Lord Northbourne and the Betteshanger Boring Company had originally objected to Railway 17 they had indicated that if they wanted a railway branch at all it would be a branch to Deal that they wanted and not one to Stonar. The railways company now solicited their support for Railways 19 and 20 but also argued for the lines on other grounds. The lines would encourage the development of a harbour at Deal through which coal might be shipped. They would enable miners, for whom local accommodation was limited, to live in Deal and would also enable any miners who had managed to find accommodation in the coalfield to shop in Deal. Similar arguments were also advanced for Railway 22, which would have completed the connection to Canterbury withdrawn from the proposal for Railway 2 in the original application of 1910. The course of Railway 22 would have been slightly to the north of the original proposed course of Railway 2 and, by laying down very narrow limits of deviation, had avoided the previous stumbling block of the cavalry training grounds. The prior approval of Railway 15 had removed the opposition of the Ecclesiastical Commissioners by replacing the section of Railway 2 to which they had objected.

Railway 23 produced a route even more tortuous than that of the combined Lines 2, 15 and 22 but with slightly more justification as it produced the most level route possible through a district of particularly difficult contours. Even so, a tunnel would still have been needed beneath Scotland Common and the gradients, earthworks and bridges required by the line would have made it expensive to construct and operate. Its stated purpose was to link Railway 4 with the Canterbury Coal Company's proposed collieries in the Alkham Valley. Given the rather doubtful state of these proposals it is more likely that the application for this line was intended to enhance the value of the Concessions Group's mineral rights in the area than with any immediate intention to construct the line. At various times, even after the powers for this line had lapsed, reference was to be made to the proximity of its terminus at Alkham to the possible starting point of a new Channel Tunnel.

Railway 24 was a bizarre high level spur linking Line 23 with Line 13 which would have enabled coal from the Alkham Valley to reach the SECR at Stonehall and would have required a substantial bridge across the SECR's tracks. Had Lines 13 and 23 ever been built, or the collieries opened that they were intended to serve, it seems unlikely that the limited site at Stonehall could have coped effectively with the combined output of Guilford, the Alkham Valley and Stonehall.

Railway 26 was a short spur from Railway 11 giving a railway connection to the Telegraph Farm Brickworks owned by Kent Coal Concessions and was an entirely straightforward proposition. Railway 27, a similar short spur connecting Wingham Colliery with Railway 2, would have extended beyond the colliery and partly climbed the slopes of Blackney Hill in order to create a gradient suitable for the construction of gravitation sidings.

The final line proposed, Railway 28, was to create the necessary link to Lord Greville's Wharf at Stonar and to give formal authority to the EKR agreement with Lord Greville. Although a mineral tramway already existed along much of the alignment of Railway 28, and only a short length of entirely new track would need to be built, it was felt necessary to acquire powers to rebuild the line to the eastern side of the Sandwich to Ramsgate road in order to give the company authority to cross that road.

Of all the lines for which powers were applied in 1913 only Railway 26 to Telegraph Farm was to prove uncontentious. Railway 18 aroused opposition from Henry Fitzwalter Plumptre on the grounds that it ran too close to his estate at Goodnestone Park and from the Adisham Colliery Company on the grounds that it interfered with the proposed site of its colliery. Railway 19 was strongly opposed by Mr Gilbert Elliott because it not only ran too close to his Tudor house at Hull Place, which he had recently renovated at a cost of £15,000, but would also spoil his view across the marshes to Ramsgate. At Deal the Council and the SECR objected to the course of both Railways 19 and 20 on the respective grounds of interference with roads and closeness to the level crossing in Western Road. It should be added that Deal Council generally supported the lines, though their conversion to the idea of building a port for coal exports seems to have been too sudden to convince the Railway Commissioners.

Railway 22 was also the cause of both local authority and railway objections. Canterbury City Council and the County Council both wished the line to cross the increasingly busy road between Canterbury and Sturry by a bridge rather than a level crossing. The SECR was still not convinced that its sidings at Canterbury West were the best location for a junction with the EKR. Sturry Council felt that the line should join the SECR at Sturry rather than running all the way into Canterbury.

Railway 23 aroused a number of objections relating to bridges and level crossings and gave particular cause for concern to the Ministry of Agriculture with regard to proposals to pile excavated spoil on common land at Scotland Common. Railway 24 was not opposed in principle by the SECR but reassurance was wanted as to the design and specifications for the bridge over their tracks.

Railway 27 was opposed by the two principal landowners over whose property it would have passed. St John's College, Cambridge, claimed that it would seriously interfere with a particularly prosperous portion of farmland, that the company had as yet failed to fence Railway 2 alongside this farmland, and that Railway 27 was not needed as a branch to Wingham Colliery already existed. This latter certainly existed but must have been built under the Concessions Group's mineral rights which usually included a specific right to lay down tramways to serve any exploitation of those minerals. Presumably the line had been built by East Kent Contract & Financial when they were constructing Railway 2 and would have been considered to all intents and purposes as part of the EKR at that stage. Lord Desborough objected to the need to extend the line onto Blackney Hill.

Railway 28 was acceptable to Lord Greville but was opposed by the highways authority on the grounds that it created yet another level crossing on a stretch of busy road over which several level crossings already existed. Since the proposed level crossing simply replaced the existing level crossing used by Lord Greville's Tramway this objection is surprising, but the main cause for concern seems to have been that the EKR already had powers for another level crossing on this road to carry Railway 1 to the port proposed by St Augustine's Links.

The combined effect of so many objections was to delay final approval of the 1913 application until 1920 by which date some of the lines were no longer needed. It was the objections to Railways 18, 19, and 27 which initially caused difficulties. In the case of Railways 18 and 19 the Light Railway Commissioners insisted upon substantial deviations which themselves generated new objections. With Railway 18 the objections from Mr Plumptre were met by moving the course of the line to the east, only to find that the Adisham Colliery Company had also moved the site of its proposed colliery to sit slap in the middle of the new alignment. This led to the opening of protracted negotiations for the waiving of the rights of support that the EKR could expect from the colliery company.

On Railway 19 the Commissioners insisted that the EKR should apply for a more direct route avoiding Hull Place but cutting through the centre of the village of Sholden and considerably interfering with the grounds of Sholden Lodge. The railways company had originally considered this route, which was more direct than that for which they actually applied, but had rejected it on the advice of their Land Agent, Mr Elgar. It was probably mere coincidence that Sholden Lodge belonged to the Mayor of Deal whose support for the line must have been considered fairly essential. The route proposed by the Light Railway Commissioners not only aroused the opposition of the villagers but also created problems with the highway authority over the width of the bridge under which the railway would cross the main road through the village. The Commissioners remained adamant that their route was the best and therefore approved Railway 19 in a form that pleased nobody but themselves and Mr Elliott.

With Railway 27 the Commissioners overruled the objections of St John's College on the grounds that these might be remedied by compensation but refused to approve compulsory purchase powers for the section of line on Lord Desborough's land. Instead the EKR would have to come to a mutually acceptable arrangement with him. They were unable to do so and Railway 27 was eventually dropped from the application.

The various negotiations relating to these three lines were still proceeding when war broke out. For the duration of the war the application was continued with varying degrees of urgency but no sooner was one problem overcome than some new difficulties arose elsewhere. This was particularly true of Railway 28. We shall therefore have to return to the progress of the 1913 application at a later stage.

Track laying near Wells Farm in 1913. Brenchley's ganger, Ernest Northcote, on the left, and Brenchley's son sitting on the trolley. *M. Lawson Finch Collection*

Construction work in the Prince of Wales cutting between Eastry and Woodnesborough. It is hoped that its owner retrieves the jacket hung on wagon No. 3 before the train departs! *M. Lawson Finch Collection*

Meanwhile the EKR had entered into a further agreement with the Contract company on 28th March, 1913, this time for the construction of Railways 15 and 16, the Stodmarsh and Ripple extensions respectively, on identical terms to those agreed in respect of Railways 1 to 14. Some work was begun on Railway 15. Fencing was erected and various light earthworks were executed for the first mile or so from Wingham but beyond this point only isolated pockets of land were purchased and it is unlikely that much work was done at the Stodmarsh end. There is no evidence that any work was ever attempted on Railway 16. Work was, however, continued on Railways 1, 2 and 4 and upwards of 300 men were employed in a number of gangs at different points along these lines.

Whilst work was proceeding on the cutting at Selson, between Woodnesborough and Eastry, an incident occurred which might have ended very tragically. The men engaged here were surprised one day to hear the furious whistling of a locomotive which was approaching with unusual haste from Eastry. The engine, one of Rigby's and reputedly driven by a George Bassett, came to a halt and the driver shouted for ganger Mathews, in charge of the team working here, to climb into the cab. No sooner had Mathews mounted the footplate than the engine immediately reversed towards Eastry. The cause of all this excitement was that a spark from a passing locomotive had set light to the house in which Mathews and his family were lodging and where Mrs Mathews was lying in bed with her four-day-old baby. Luckily, although '. . . burned out of house and home', Mrs Mathews and the baby were rescued safely.

Despite such setbacks there was real progress in the construction of the line during 1913. On 5th May, 1913 the Wingham branch was sufficiently complete for driver Tom Hambrook to take locomotive No. 1 and several wagons on an inaugural trip as far as Ash. Beyond Ash, Mr Jack Hougham, the ganger in charge of constructing the mineral branch to Wingham Colliery, remembered that it was completed during the first half of 1913. Certainly a report in the *Dover Express* for 20th June, 1913 claimed that the railway had been 'connected up' to the Wingham pit. This would indicate that construction from Ash to Wingham was fairly rapid. This is quite feasible as this length of line posed no major difficulties and seems to have been laid down as a temporary surface line at first.

Elsewhere, temporary works were giving way to more permanent construction. On 27th June the *Dover Express* reported that planning consent had been granted to divert the road at Coldred for three months during the building of a bridge under that road for the Guilford branch. Presumably the temporary line already in use crossed the road on the level. Of much greater significance though, was a report in the same paper for 31st October that the first train had passed through the Golgotha tunnel on 24th October. Trains to and from Tilmanstone would no longer be restricted to the four wagons at a time permitted over the temporary line.

On the financial front the Board of the EKR was continuing to conceal its worries from the shareholders. This was particularly true at the Annual General Meeting in July 1913 when a glowing picture of progress on all fronts was presented. Golgotha tunnel had nearly been completed, having been lined with

Locomotive No. 1 on construction work near Prince of Wales cutting in 1913.

M. Lawson Finch Collection

bricks from the Group's own Pluckley Brickworks. It is significant that the shareholders were not told that it was only the tunnel roof that had been lined. Tilmanstone Colliery was reported to be producing 1,000 tons each week and the railway had by now carried more than 70,000 tons of traffic. Sufficient track had been laid to start serving the sites of the pits at Guilford, Woodnesborough and Wingham and work was in hand on completing Railway 1 to Sandwich and Railway 15 to Stodmarsh. It was now planned to link Snowdown Colliery to the company's system and also to serve the proposed Adisham Colliery which Arthur Burr had sold to a French syndicate. The shareholders were reassured that they should have no worries about the recent sale by the Ecclesiastical Commissioners of mineral rights north of the Stour to the Anglo-Westphalian Company ; Arthur Burr stated that he had never been interested in buying mineral rights in this area even if they had been offered to him.

The Annual Meeting was followed by a Special Meeting to authorise the Directors' application for Lines 18 to 28. The main interest of this meeting was in Arthur Burr's concluding words, 'As for myself, I am worn out. My work will be passed on to a large extent to other and younger men'. With the proposed amalgamation of the Concessions Group companies he intended to take a holiday and to content himself with light duties in the future. The affairs of the railways company would be entrusted to '.'. . a very able experienced General Manager'. In the absence of any other obvious candidates this must be presumed to be a reference to Holman Stephens.

The western end of Golgotha tunnel shortly after its completion in 1913.

M. Lawson Finch Collection

Meanwhile the bills continued to come in. In June 1913 the EKR had agreed to take over a hire purchase contract with Wagon Finance for 50 wagons originally ordered by Snowdown Colliery, but insisted that the Contract company remained responsible for payments and maintenance until the line was ready for public use. The EKR similarly considered the Contract company to be responsible for dealing with claims arising from the death of the railway storekeeper, Mr A. Bradley, due to a haemorrhage and, on a less serious note, from Mr W. Gordon Martin for harm to his tandem caused by damage to the road at Eythorne and from Lord Guilford as Secretary to the West Street Harriers for interference with their sport arising from railway construction.

More positive news for the Directors came in the form of an enquiry in September 1913 from the Compagnie des Forges du Chatillon as to the rates for carrying coal from their proposed colliery at Waldershare. Taken together with various other references to a Waldershare Colliery this seems to indicate that, rather than taking over Guilford Colliery, this concern originally intended to sink a completely new colliery. This may have been intended to be located at the Waldershare boring beside Railway 4 on the western side of Lord Guilford's Waldershare Park.

Another piece of positive news came in November 1913 when it was reported that the SECR had agreed to an easement across their tracks for the bridge taking Railway 1 to Stonar. As Burr had prophesied in May that coal would be being dispatched from Stonar by the end of the year, it is clear that difficulties in reaching agreement over the site of this bridge had played a part in preventing this from happening. A more fundamental problem had been shortage of funds. Shortage of cash throughout the Concessions Group had forced Burr to order work to be suspended on the Sandwich branch earlier in the year. The EKR resolved to remedy its own shortage of funds in November 1913 by authorising an issue of 40,000 debentures under the 1911 Order and 20,000 debentures under the 1912 Order. Blaming the company's financial position on a '. . . disgraceful conspiracy against the line', Arthur Burr urged the case for further borrowing as being vital to completion of the railway which would then command the transport of '. . . four-fifths of the coal in this great coalfield'. Once the money was raised, '. . . the whole of the railways will be completed as rapidly as engineering science will permit, under the skilful guidance of our friend Mr Stephens'.

One casualty of the financial crisis was Mr Brenchley, the sub-contractor for the Wingham and Sandwich lines, upon whom the burden of the money shortage fell most directly. He had eventually fallen ill and was unfit for work for several months. When he eventually returned to work he relinquished his former position and assumed the less worrying position of ganger in charge. Meanwhile Holman Stephens seems to have taken responsibility for financing the works from his own pocket.

1914

Evidence of East Kent Light Railways Company at the Public Enquiry into deviations of proposed lines 18 and 19 held at Upper Deal, 15th July, 1914:

> Hitherto Snowdown has only been connected with the one railway, the South Eastern & Chatham Railway, but it is essential, absolutely essential to the success of the undertaking, that this colliery should be connected with our system for this reason: The collieries in this coalfield produce many different sorts of coal. Some of the coal is soft and suitable for gas and coking, other coal is hard and suitable for house use and steam raising purposes. Now with regard to some of the coal a very great deal of it will no doubt be converted into coke and benzol and aniline dyes and all sorts of by products and in order to avoid the duplication of the plant for converting the coal into these by products, it is essential that there should be a connection between all these collieries and some central plant which will deal with the coal and the by products . . .

1914 opened with the Directors proposing that Holman Stephens should be promoted to the post of General Manager. It took some time to work out the details but in May it was agreed that Stephens would be appointed as General Manager, Engineer and Locomotive Superintendent as soon as the line was open for public traffic. His annual salary as Engineer and Locomotive Superintendent would be £250 and as General Manager £350. Additionally he would receive 250 guineas for organising the staff and traffic prior to opening. Arthur and Malcolm Burr would retire as Joint Managing Directors as soon as Stephens took over as General Manager. The influence of the Burrs was dwindling in the EKR even before it was rudely overthrown elsewhere in the Concessions Group.

Contemporary with the negotiation of Stephens' proposed employment as General Manager there occurred a development which might have completely altered the future course of the EKR. The key elements in this development were the incorporation of The Birchington Development Company and an application for a further Light Railway Order (*see map page 70*). The Birchington Development Company, incorporated in May 1914, had as its aim nothing less than developing an entirely new town on the North Kent Coast at Coldharbour Sluice adjacent to the established resort of Birchington on Sea. The aims of the Development Company were extremely comprehensive. It would not only buy land and lay out that land for housing but it would also develop 'factories, railways, tramways, roads, reservoirs, electric power heat and light supply works, telephone works, hotels restaurants, clubs, baths, places of amusement, piers, jetties, quays and wharves . . .' At the heart of the scheme lay a plan to build a very long pier out into the Thames Estuary, from which Kent coal could be loaded onto sea-going ships rather than the barges and lighters that would have had to be used at Stonar. The Engineer to this ambitious undertaking was to be Holman Stephens.

It would be necessary for the EKR to apply for a Light Railway Order to connect its system to Birchington. The Application was published in May 1914 and specified the following lines:

Railway No. 29: A line from Railway 15 to the Thames Estuary at St Nicholas-at-Wade.
Railway No. 30: A spur linking the SECR Ramsgate line to Railway 29.
Railway No. 31: An east-facing spur linking Railway 29 to the SECR Kent Coast line.
Railway No. 32: A west-facing spur linking Railway 29 to the SECR Kent Coast line.

Powers were also sought to authorize the company to enter into and carry into effect agreements with the owners, lessees and occupiers of lands adjoining the termination of the railway (No. 29) with reference to the construction, maintenance, purchase or leasing by the company of wharves, quays, jetties, sidings and works upon such lands or upon lands of the company, together with all necessary buildings, machinery, works, tramways, ropeways, approaches and conveniences connected therewith and to charge dues and tolls.

The application was solely concerned with the 'Birchington Scheme', consisting straightforwardly of the main extension by Railway 29 and its three very short spurs. From its initial junction with Railway 15 the course of Railway 29 first followed the Little Stour then cut northwards to cross the Great Stour and the South Eastern & Chatham line from Canterbury to Ramsgate to which Railway 30 made a trailing connection. Railway 29 then crossed the Chislet Marshes to bridge the SECR Kent Coast Line close to its crossing of the River Wantsum and would then have turned eastwards and run parallel to the Kent Coast Line to reach the area designated for development. Shortly before reaching the Kent Coast Line the two spur lines, Railways 31 and 32, fanned out to make connection with that line in each direction.

Railway 29 would have run across predominantly flat terrain but its bridges across the Great Stour and the two SECR lines would have required substantial engineering work. The marshy nature of much of the terrain and its many streams and ditches would have required firm foundations and numerous culverts. The only real peculiarity of the application was the trailing connection made by Railway 30 with the Canterbury to Ramsgate line. This would have been of no real value to the rest of the EKR but would have enabled coal from Chislet Colliery to run onto Railway 29 for dispatch by sea at Birchington.

Although the application for the Birchington Extension was lodged in May 1914 little had been done towards pursuing the application when war broke out in August. Arrangements were made to suspend the application for the time being. It was not specifically suspended 'for the duration' but the Light Railway Commissioners were prepared to let it rest while the war continued. This led to some bitter complaints from landowners who feared that the value of their properties would suffer with the threat of a possible railway line hanging over them.

If the 'Birchington Scheme' shows nothing else it was of major significance in being the first enterprise involving the EKR that was not solely concerned with the coalfield and the Concessions Group. One sign of the increasing independence of the EKR from the Concessions Group was that the Contract company was willing to surrender its right to undertake the construction of Railways 29 to 32 to the Birchington Development Company. The Contract company did try to insist on its right to undertake the construction of Railways 18 to 28, but was rebuffed on the grounds that it was somewhat premature to consider building these lines when they had not yet been authorised.

Meanwhile the question of coal rates for Waldershare Colliery was being satisfactorily settled with the Compagnie des Forges du Chatillon who now asked for similar rates to be settled for Guilford Colliery. A Belgian concern was also asking for settlement of coal rates for the Sutton Concession, i.e. Ripple Colliery. This seems to be the first mention of an actual proposal to develop a pit at Ripple and reflects the very active policy being pursued to find buyers for those pits that the Concessions Group were unable to develop themselves.

Under the original contract with the Contract company, Railways 1 to 14 should have been completed and handed over to the EKR by 30th June, 1914 at the latest. The actual state of construction was that Railways 1 and 5 had been completed in 'permanent' form as far as Tilmanstone Colliery and 'temporary' lines had been laid over the greater part of the remainder of Railway 1 and over Railways 2, 4 and 14. Little seems to have been done on Railways 9, 10, 11, 12 or 13 apart from some purchases of land. The state of Railway 8 at this date is unclear but it may have been laid out in temporary form for construction work on Railway 4. It was agreed to allow the Contract company a further six months to complete the contract. Whilst this would clearly have been insufficient to complete the lines on which no work had been done, it might have been possible to complete at least a temporary line to Stonar and to bring some of the 'temporary' lines up to 'permanent' condition. The alternative of forcing the Contract company to hand over the work in its uncompleted state would have left the EKR with the problem of finding the funds to complete the lines itself. Legally, it might have been possible to obtain damages for breach of contract from the Contract company but it was at this stage that the catastrophic state of the latter's finances was becoming apparent. There would be little point in suing the Contract company for damages they could not pay.

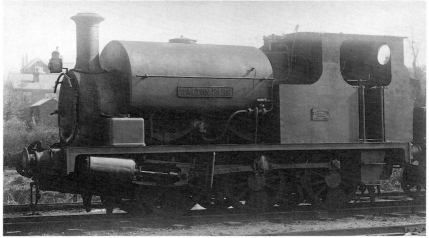

Hudswell, Clarke 0-6-0ST *Walton Park* arrived on the EKR in 1913 having previously served on two other 'Stephens' lines - the Weston, Clevedon & Portishead and the Shropshire & Montgomeryshire railways.   *Colonel Stephens Railway Museum*

Arthur Burr attended his last EKR meeting in June 1914 and Malcolm Burr attended his last in August. By now the company's main concerns were finding the means to complete their lines and establishing a new relationship with the Contract company where the new Board of Directors had taken over on 4th August. Effectively the EKR was seceding from the Allied Companies as the Concessions Group was now known. Although there was inevitably some overlap between the shareholders in the EKR and the shareholders in the Allied Companies, there were many EKR shareholders who held no shares in the Allied Companies. The EKR also differed from the Allied Companies in that it had always had a Board of Directors of its own. Four of these Directors, Sir Henry Dering, Henry Western Plumptre, Arthur Loring and Mr W. Richmond Powell, had been closely involved with the direction of the EKR but had had little or no role in relation to the Allied Companies. It was to be these four, with the aid of Holman Stephens, who were to steer the EKR through the troubled years ahead.

The outbreak of World War I in August 1914 had little immediate effect on the railway. Work was already virtually at a standstill as a result of the Contract company's shortage of funds. The abandonment of work on the collieries at Wingham, Woodnesborough and Stonehall would have its effect on the railway in due course but does not seem to have been discussed by the Directors at this time.

October 1914 saw the first serious altercation between the EKR and the Contract company. The latter had dismissed the Resident Engineer, Harrisson, and the traffic superintendent, Springgay. The EKR could do nothing to help Harrisson, who was an employee of the Contract company, but Springgay was an EKR employee. The EKR Secretary was instructed 'to suggest to the Contract company that should they desire a change in any of the officers of the railway company they should communicate with the Board giving their reasons for any such change'.

A more serious problem arose in December when the Contract company proposed that the payment of all debts in excess of £100 should be postponed until six months after the end of hostilities. A rapid calculation of the Contract company's debts relating to the EKR showed them as owing £7,249 to the EKR, £4,085 to the railway's solicitors, F.C. Mathews & Co., and £9,255 to Holman Stephens whose fees and expenses had not been paid for a considerable time. Counsel's opinion was obtained as to the EKR's legal position and gave little cause for cheer. The EKR was advised that it should not agree to the proposal unless the Contract company agreed to indemnify them against any action by its own creditors. Unfortunately, the Contract company could now legitimately use the exclusion clause in the original contract that allowed it to claim indefinite extensions of time to complete the contract during any period of financial depression preventing it from raising capital. The EKR could therefore choose between insisting on payment of its debts, and risk bankrupting the Contract company, or allow the debts to stand over and risk its own bankruptcy. In neither case could the Contract company be forced to complete the contract. In the event the Directors chose a middle course. They would not vote in favour of the Contract company suspending payment of its debts, but they would not actively seek to enforce payment of those debts. In this way the Contract company might stay afloat and some work might yet be done to complete the contract.

1915

Directors' Report to Shareholders: The report of the company's engineer is attached and indicates the extent of the progress which was made with the construction of the railways during the year under review. The progress was not sufficient to enable any part of the railway to be opened for traffic under the order of the Board of Trade and during the year in question the whole of the railway remained in the hands of the contractors who are responsible for the maintenance of the property. Your Directors much regret the delay in completion of your railway, but the contractors have been faced not only with the difficulty of raising capital in the present financial circumstances but with the current shortage of labour caused by the War. The question of the contractors' failure to complete the work within the contract time is occupying the earnest attention of the Board.

1915 began with little prospect of progress from the Contract company and a threat of legal action from Lord Greville if the railways company did not complete certain purchases of land from him. The Contract company should have been responsible for these purchases but was unable to do so. If the EKR wanted its railway completed it would have to find a means of paying such essential expenses itself. The best hope that counsel could offer was that the company should hope for a reasonable judgment. Given the delays of the English Legal System it would at least be some time before the case came up in court.

By March the Directors had obviously decided to get their affairs into as good order as possible. Arthur Burr and Malcolm Burr were relieved of their positions as Joint Managing Directors since they had done no work for the company since June and August 1914 respectively and Malcolm Burr was reported to be in Petrograd, '. . . from which it appeared that he was now in Russia and apparently proposed to remain there for some time'. It was also proposed that any further land purchases should be put off until the war ended. This would ease part of the company's financial burden but would not solve the continuing drain on the company's resources imposed by payments of tithes, quitrents and the like. It was feared that such work as had been completed on the railway might become dilapidated as Stephens had to report that '. . . the men earmarked for the maintenance of the railway had been employed for the removal of timber between Snowdown and Wingham Collieries.' With Tilmanstone Colliery out of operation and work suspended at Guilford, Woodnesborough and Wingham there was little incentive for the Allied Companies to find the means to enable the Contract company to press ahead with railway construction.

In May 1915 the company received formal resignations from the Burrs which were announced to the shareholders at the Annual General Meeting held that month. A lengthy report from Stephens then catalogued the many respects in which the line fell short of readiness for inspection by the Board of Trade. The earthworks and permanent way were only complete on the section from Shepherdswell to Eastry and on the branch to Tilmanstone Colliery. Temporary lines had been laid as far as Dambridge Road on the Wingham Line, as far as Gosshall Sluice on the Sandwich Line and to the Guilford, Woodnesborough and Wingham collieries. The temporary line over Golgotha Hill had been taken up and the lands involved reinstated. Earthworks for about a mile of the Stodmarsh Line had been started, as had some of the earthworks beyond Gosshall Sluice on the Richborough Line and on the Mongeham Line where half a mile of fencing had been erected. Platforms had been erected at Woodnesborough & Hammill, Ash Town and at Staple & Ash. Two new locomotives that had been announced as under construction at the 1914 AGM had not been delivered and it was believed that they had now been sold to other purchasers. In answer to a call from Mr Solley, a past Mayor of Sandwich and associated with St Augustine's Links, for the line to Stonar to be completed, Stephens replied that this was too costly for the company at present as the bridge alone would cost at least £4,000.

The Directors were taken by surprise by a motion pressing for the two vacant seats on the Board to be given to Sir John Dewrance and to Mr Greig, the leading Directors on the Boards of the Allied Companies. Although a motion to elect them there and then was ruled out of order due to lack of notice, a second motion requesting the Directors to appoint Dewrance and Greig was passed convincingly. The Directors subsequently met on their own and resolved that it would be undesirable for two Directors of the Contract company to become Directors of the EKR when the interests of the two companies were so much at variance. Despite the company's financial difficulties a Special Meeting was held immediately after the General Meeting to obtain the shareholders' approval for an application for the Birchington Extension.

The Directors subsequently invited Dewrance and Greig to join the Board but only if they first resigned their positions on the Contract company's Board. This successfully shelved the issue for the time being but the relationship with the Contract company continued to occupy the Directors' minds. The 50 wagons purchased from Wagon Finance had now been sold by the Contract company and the Directors were anxious to recover their share of the proceeds. £200 was eventually recovered. More fundamental was a suggestion by the company's solicitor, Mr Mathews, that the EKR should terminate its contract with the Contract company for non-performance and take over the railway itself. There should be sufficient traffic from Tilmanstone to meet running expenses and to generate enough income to enable the company to open as much of the system as could be readily completed. The remainder of the system could be completed when funds permitted.

In October a possible saviour of the EKR appeared. This was a Mr Phillips who seems to have been particularly interested in the possibilities of the Birchington Scheme. He had made an offer to buy the Contract company's shares in the EKR at 12s. 6d. a share and to buy land owned at Birchington by the former. The Contract company had agreed to this offer but Mr Phillips had then found that it had already sold a significant number of its EKR shares and debentures to its own shareholders. This would have given Mr Phillips fewer shares than he wanted and he began to have second thoughts at this stage. He was, nevertheless, prepared to pay for the land at Stonar over which Lord Greville had begun legal proceedings. The Directors now began to have doubts about Mr Phillips' reliability and decided that the better way of paying for Lord

Greville's land would be to take over the railway and earn some money of their own.

The year closed with the Directors receiving information that Mr Phillips had agreed to purchase 30,000 EKR shares and the lands at Birchington. Hopes that this would lead to further investment in the railway from this source were soon dashed. January 1916 saw three appointments arranged with Mr Phillips and three appointments broken.

With or without Mr Phillips' assistance, the EKR was now determined to take over the lines as soon as possible. An initial setback was the news that the Contract company had sold the bulk of its stocks of sleepers to the War Office and that £660 worth of permanent way materials had been used to lay out the sidings at Tilmanstone Colliery. Stephens did point out that this would increase the route mileage over which Tilmanstone coal would travel and that this would entitle the EKR to charge a higher rate for this traffic. This would not, however, of itself solve the problem of finding replacement permanent way materials which were extremely scarce by this stage of the war. For years to come surplus rails or unused pointwork laid in one place would be lifted and relaid elsewhere in order to overcome this shortage. This went on long after permanent way materials had again become freely available and the lines of the EKR were to be notorious for the economy of their track layouts.

1916

Bradshaw's Railway Manual 1916:

EAST KENT LIGHT RAILWAY - Incorporated under the Light Railways Act by order of 1911 to construct a line 35 miles 4 furlongs. Period for construction expires in September 1917. Temporary lines (20 miles) connecting four collieries had been completed at the end of 1914, and the permanent lines were in course of construction.

In March 1916 the company's Secretary since 1910, Mr F. Wilkinson, was given three months' notice. His place was taken by Mr S. Pettifer and the company's office was moved to 110 Cannon Street, E.C., where the company's solicitors, F.C. Matthews & Company, had their offices. At the same time Stephens, for the first time referred to as Colonel Stephens, waived his own entitlement to remuneration until the declaration of peace. He was now carrying on the construction of the line directly for the EKR and it was in this role that he made the following report to the Directors on 1st June:

I beg to report for your information on the construction and progress of the various lines as follows:
No works of any moment have been done by the Contractors during the past year towards the completion of the railways.

SHEPHERDSWELL & RICHBOROUGH LINE. Between Shepherdswell and Eythorne the line has been strengthened and ballasting partially completed.
Small Station works were also put in hand.

Two views of the loading screens at Tilmanstone Colliery with a wide range of pre-Grouping wagons on display, together with some of the colliery's own wagons.

From Eythorne to Eastry certain banks have been widened and ballasting and strengthening this section are now in hand. Beyond Eastry earthworks have been practically completed as far as Woodnesborough Road and partially so to Sandwich Road. Ballasting has been carried out on the first mile from Eastry.

EASTRY TO WINGHAM LINE. Earthworks between Wingham Colliery Branch Junction and Dambridge Road have been continued to a certain extent and the line between Eastry and Ash partly strengthened and finished off.

Nothing further has been done beyond Dambridge Road towards completion of the works.

Tilmanstone Colliery Branch and Sidings have been maintained in running order.

No further works have been carried out on Guilford, Hammill, Wingham Colliery, Mongeham, or Stodmarsh Branches.

Agreement was finally reached with the Contract company on 10th May for the EKR to take over that part of the system that had been constructed so far. The EKR would allow the Contract company access to the lines that had not yet been constructed and would carry goods and materials for any construction carried out by the latter at 60 per cent of normal rates. The lines to be handed over were Line 1 from Shepherdswell to the Sandwich road, Line 2 from Eastry to Wingham, Line 4 to Guilford , Line 14 to Hammill Colliery 'so far as constructed' and Line 10, the northern connection at Shepherdswell. The Tilmanstone and Wingham Colliery branches and sidings were to be handed over 'as at present partially constructed'. The Contract company would hand over all rolling stock, tools and equipment and pay £650 towards working expenses. The EKR would bring the various lines up to a sufficient standard to be passed by the Board of Trade and when these were passed the Contract company would pay the EKR £1,000 on account towards the £5,000 due under the original contract. For railways that had not been constructed the EKR would pay proportionately reduced interest on the debentures that had been issued, as far as the company's earnings would allow, once Lord Greville and other landowners had been paid from the operating revenues. The Contract company would remain responsible for paying for lands that had been purchased but for which payment had not yet been made.

On 22nd June the Contract company formally handed the railways over to the EKR. On 2nd August Stephens was able to report, '. . . the stations have arrived and are being erected'! He hoped that the line could be open within the month but it was not until 26th September that Colonel Pringle was ready to inspect the railway for the Board of Trade. Colonel Pringle's report gives such a detailed account that it is worth reproducing in full.

27th September, 1916

Sir,

I have the honour to report for the information of the Board of Trade, that in compliance with the instructions contained in your Minute of the 14th September, I made an inspection on the 26th instant of portions of Railways Nos. 1 and 2, authorised by the East Kent Light Railways Order 1911, as follows:

Railway No. 1. Length 5 miles 57 chains, commencing at Shepherdswell and terminating by a junction with Railway No. 2.

Railway No. 2. Length 4 miles 50.66 chains commencing at the junction with Railway No. 1 and terminating at Wingham, about 1 mile 20 chains short of the authorised termination.

The railways are laid single throughout, with passing places or siding loops, on a gauge of 4 ft 8½ ins. The ruling gradient 1 in 60 is near Shepherdswell. The sharpest curves have a radius of 9 chains, with one exception. At a point 28 chs. from Shepherdswell there is a curve with a radius of 7½ chains with a length of 1.35 chains. It would not be difficult, I think, to flatten this curve to one of 9 chains radius and I understand that the company are prepared to do this, otherwise it will be necessary to provide a check rail on this curve.

The formation is almost entirely of chalk on Railway No. 1 and sandy clay on No. 2. The maximum depth and height in cutting and embankment are 43 ft and 13 ft 5 ins. respectively on Railway No. 1 and 19 ft and 12 ft respectively on Railway No. 2. No retaining walls have been necessary. There is one tunnel, length 476 yards on Railway No. 1. This is cut for double line, with the lower lift taken out for one line of rails only. It is half lined throughout with four rings of bricks. The side walls are unlined except at the ends, where a blue brick facing has been built for a length of 100 ft as a protection against the effects of frost. Recesses at one chain intervals have been given.

The only bridge is one with a span of 21 ft 4½ ins. on the skew, which carries the railway over a public road at Eastry Station. Timber rail bearers are used to carry the rails as a temporary measure, the steelwork for the permanent bridge having been delayed. Each rail bearer consists of four 12 ins. by 12 ins. pitch pine beams, and the deflection (½ in.) under engine load (9-ton axles) is greater than would be acceptable for a permanent structure, but may be accepted in this instance in the case of a temporary bridge. There are no viaducts or other engineering works on either railway.

Permanent Way. There are four varieties of flat bottom rails used, varying from 60 lbs. per yard to 90 lbs. per yard. These are fixed to cross sleepers by dogspikes and fangbolts. The sleepers consist of creosoted Baltic fir, and measure 9 ft by 9 ins. by 4½ ins. The ballast is colliery refuse, shingle and ashes, laid to a stated depth of 11 ins. below the under side of the sleepers.

The line is fenced throughout with wire fencing 4 ft high, which consists of seven galvanised iron wires, with T iron standards and oak straining posts. No difficulty has been met with as regards drainage.

The following stations and platforms exist on Railway No. 1:

Shepherdswell Station. There are two siding loops at this station. Platform 294 ft long by 12½ ft by 3 ft with a small shelter.

Eythorne Station, with a siding loop and single platform, 200 ft long by 8 ft by 3 ft with a small shelter.

Tilmanstone Platform, 100 ft by 6 ft by 3 ft.

Eastry Platform, 170 ft by 10 ft by 3 ft, with a small shelter.

Railway No. 2:

Woodnesborough and Hammill Platform, 200 ft long by 12 ft by 3 ft.

Ash Platform, 200 ft by 9½ ft by 3 ft.

Staple and Ash Platform (temporary) at present termination, 100 ft by 6 ft by 3 ft, with a small shelter.

Wingham (temporary) single platform, 100 ft by 6 ft by 3 ft with small shelter.

The company propose to work these railways on the staff and ticket system between Shepherdswell and Eythorne, and under the one engine in steam or two engines coupled together system between Eythorne and Wingham. I attach an undertaking to this effect.

Signalling arrangements exist at:

Shepherdswell Station where there are up stop and down starter signals worked from a ground frame with three levers. One of the levers releases the loop points which are worked by hand balance weight lever in each case after being unlocked by the key on the train staff. The interlocking is correct.

Eythorne. Here there are stop and starter signals in each direction worked from a ground frame with 4 levers, and 2 Annett's keys, which control the loop points at each end of the station. The interlocking is correct. Telephone boxes have been established for controlling the working at Shepherdswell and Eythorne.

The present termination at Wingham is with a single road and a passenger train, in order to reverse the position of the engine, will have to be propelled about 500 yards into the Wingham Colliery loop, where the engine will run round. This arrangement is not very satisfactory, but pending the completion of the line it may be accepted as sufficient, for a section worked by one engine in steam.

In addition to the loops at Shepherdswell and Eythorne Stations, there are the following connections:

Tilmanstone Colliery siding loop
Sandwich branch connection
Hammill Colliery branch
Farm siding connection
Wingham Colliery loop

All these connections are controlled by the key on the train staff, the points being worked by hand lever. There are no facing point locks except at Eythorne.

Level Crossings. There are 6 public road level crossings on Railway No. 1, where cattle guards have been fitted in accordance with the Order. In addition there are 17 private or occupation crossings, fitted with gates which do not close across the railway, and 5 footpath and 3 bridle level crossings, the former fitted with stiles and the latter with gates.

On Railway No. 2 there are 4 public road level crossings fitted with cattle guards, 22 private and 3 foot way crossings.

I have the following observations to make:

Permanent Way. The expansion joints are irregular and require attention. The top ballasting in places is incomplete. This is particularly so at the level crossing at 27.5 chains from the commencement of Railway No. 1. The triangular timbers of the cattle guards on both sides of the level crossing at 2 miles 1.50 chains on Railway No. 1 require lengthening.

At the level crossing at 5 miles 11.50 chains on Railway No. 1, there is a bad view from the road approach from the south. An additional warning board should be fixed 100 to 150 yards from the crossing on this approach road. Speed of trains approaching the crossing from Eythorne should be reduced to 5 miles an hour at a point 100 yards from the crossing, and the necessary speed post erected.

Level crossing at 68.53 chains from the commencement of Railway No. 2. The view obtainable of trains approaching this crossing from Eastry is not good. Speed should be reduced to 5 miles an hour 100 yards from the crossing, and the necessary speed post erected. Level crossing at 2 miles 79.22 chains on Railway No. 2. Trains approaching from Ash are not clearly seen from the road approaches. Speed should be reduced to 5 miles an hour 100 yards from the crossing, and a speed board erected.

At some of the stations, e.g. Eastry, the posts which have been erected for carrying lamps for lighting purposes have been fixed unnecessarily close to the edge of the platform. They should be moved back to the line of fence. The same remark applies in the name boards in some cases.

The side path planking on the bridge at Eastry requires securing.

Additional strapping is necessary to secure the timbering to which the locking apparatus at many of the hand-worked point connections is attached.

The key on the staff of the section for Eythorne to Wingham requires correction by the substitution of the word 'Wingham' instead of 'Eastry'.

There is insufficient clearance at one of the platforms on Railway No. 2, between the edge of the platform and the footboard. The line should be pulled to provide the necessary clearance.

"Support the Local Line."

EAST KENT RAILWAY.

TIME TABLE.

OCTOBER 16th, 1916,

AND UNTIL FURTHER NOTICE.

DOWN TRAINS. **WEEK DAYS.**

MILES.		a.m.	a.m.	p.m.	p.m.
	S.E. & C.R. London, Victoria.........dep.	5 50	10 45	2NS15	1SO34
	S.E. & C.R. Canterbury East .... „	8 10	12 32	4NS31	3SO51
	S.E. & C.R. Dover Priory .... „	9 35	1 10	4 45	
	S.E. & C.R. Deal .... „	8B42	11 15	3 5	
—	Shepherdswell Jn., E.K.Rly.dep.	10 10	1 32	5 10	
1¾	Eythorne .... „	10 17	1 38	5 17	
2½	Tilmanstone Colliery .... „	10 20	1 41	5 20	
—	Tilmanstone Village & Knowlton „	10 24	1 45	5 24	
5¾	Eastry, for Sandwich .... „	10 31	1 52	5 31	
6½	Woodnesborough & Hammill „	10 35	1 56	5 35	
8	Ash Town........ .... „	10 40	2 1	5 40	
8¾	Staple .... „	10 44	2 5	5 44	
10¼	Wingham ....arr.	10 50	2 11	5 56	

UP TRAINS. **WEEK DAYS.**

MILES.		a.m.	p.m.	p.m.	p.m.
—	Wingham.......................dep.	10 55	2 14	6 0	
1½	Staple .... „	11 7	2 25	s	
2¼	Ash Town......................... „	11 11	2 29	6 13	
3¾	Woodnesborough & Hammill „	11 15	2 33	6 16	
4½	Eastry, for Sandwich .... „	11 20	2 38	6 21	
—	Tilmanstone Village & Knowlton „	s	s	s	
7¾	Tilmanstone Colliery .... „	11 30	2 48	6 31	
8½	Eythorne .... „	11 35	2 53	6 36	
10¼	Shepherdswell Jn., E.K.Rly. arr.	11 41	2 58	6 42	
	S.E. & C.R. Deal .... „	—	B *5NS42	7 17	
	S.E. & C.R. Dover Priory .... „	1 14	3 17	7 3	
	S.E. & C.R. Canterbury East .... „	12 25	3 49	6 29	
	S.E. & C.R. London, Victoria......... „	2 47	6 12	8 37	

B—via Dover Priory. N.S.—Not Saturdays. S—Stops by signal to pick up or set down passengers. S.O.—Saturdays only.

*—On Saturdays arrives 5-2 p.m.

Special arrangements for quick and cheap delivery of parcels and goods. **Special trips arranged as required.**

Every effort will be made to connect with the trains of S. E. & C. Rly. as shewn, but the same will not be guaranteed.

TONBRIDGE,
October, 1916.

H. F. STEPHENS,
General Manager.

I understand that the economical facing point locks will be fitted at the connections in due course, in place of the hand-worked levers.

Subject to this understanding, and to the early completion of the minor works and alterations above-named, and to the improvement of the curve above noticed, I recommend the Board of Trade to approve these portions of single-line Light Railways for passenger traffic on the method of working indicated in the undertaking attached.

I have, &c,

(Signed) J. W. PRINGLE,
Colonel.

Considering the difficulties under which the lines had been completed, Colonel Pringle's report might have been much worse. Apart from the over-sharp curve at Shepherdswell it really only identified minor improvements to be made before the lines could be opened.

The Report raises a number of interesting issues. Colonel Pringle makes no reference to the various branches apart from the existence of connections to Tilmanstone Colliery, Sandwich, Woodnesborough Colliery and Wingham Colliery. It seems that he must have failed to notice the connection to Guilford Colliery or else that it had been temporarily disconnected. His failure to refer to either Line 8 or Line 10 cannot therefore be taken to confirm that these lines had not been commenced by this date. It is noteworthy that he did not inspect the Tilmanstone Colliery branch, where there was not only a bridge that might well have warranted inspection, but along which workmen's trains are known to have been run to Tilmanstone Colliery Yard.

Another omission amongst Colonel Pringle's observations was that he seems to have failed to notice that the connection between Railways 1 and 2 at Eastry faced south rather than north as stipulated in the original Order. Reference has already been made to the fact that this may have been excused as being within the limits of deviation and laid out on the company's land but it is strange that Colonel Pringle made no reference to it at all.

Colonel Pringle's acceptance of the wooden beams on the Eastry bridge and the lack of run-round facilities at Wingham Platform is also unusual. It is unlikely that they would have been accepted in peacetime. Although the girders for the Eastry bridge were subsequently delivered and fitted it seems that the operation at Wingham continued for much longer than Colonel Pringle had anticipated and was ultimately succeeded by an even more hazardous operation when the line reached Canterbury Road. The description of Staple & Ash Platform as 'at present termination' would seem to be a straightforward typographical error. It is unfortunate that the 'Farm siding connection' is not identified by name as two such sidings existed on the line and it is not clear whether the one described was at Moat Farm or at Poulton.

Stephens lost no time in setting right the various faults found by Colonel Pringle and the railway opened to the public on 16th October. There seems to have been little or no attempt to celebrate the opening but under wartime conditions this is not entirely surprising. The only newspaper report that has so far been traced was the following paragraph in the *Dover Express* for Friday 20th October:

EAST KENT RAILWAY.

NOTICE.

Special Workmen's Trains will run as under every Weekday :—

DOWN TRAINS		N.S.	S.O.
	a.m.	p.m.	p.m.
Shepherdswell .... dep.	5 13	9 30	7 20
Eythorne .... ,,	5 20	9 37	7 27
Tilmanstone Colliery .... ,,	5 23	9 40	7 30
Tilmanstone Village & Knowlton ,,	5 27	Stop.	7 34
Eastry .... arr.	5 34		7 41

UP TRAINS		N.S.	S.O.
	a.m.	p.m.	p.m.
Eastry .... dep.	5 42	- -	7 50
Tilmanstone Village & Knowlton ,,	5 49	---	7 57
Tilmanstone Colliery .... arrive	5 53		8 1
dept.	6 20	10 20	
Eythorne .... ,,	6 24	10 24	8 6
Shepherdswell .... ,,	6 30	10 30	8 12

N.S. Not Saturdays.   S.O. Saturdays only.

FARES :— 3rd Class.

Shepherdswell to Eastry or Tilmanstone Colliery - - **2d.**
Shepherdswell to Eastry or Tilmanstone Colliery & return 3d.
Tilmanstone Colliery to Shepherdswell - - - **2d.**
Tilmanstone Colliery to Eastry & return - - - **4d.**
Eastry to Tilmanstone Colliery & return - - - **4d.**

These Fares are only available for Workmen travelling by above Special
Trains. Ordinary Fares will be charged by ordinary Trains.

Tonbridge,
October, 1916.

H. F. STEPHENS,
General Manager.

EAST KENT LIGHT RAILWAY - Open for passenger traffic from Shepherdswell to Wingham.

The East Kent Light Railway was, on Monday, opened for traffic from Shepherdswell to Wingham. The stations on the line are Shepherdswell, which is close to the South Eastern & Chatham Railway Station, but at the present time it has to be approached by a rather roundabout route round the 'Whitehall' Inn; Eythorne (Just below the Chapel); Tilmanstone Colliery Halt; Eastry; Drenold's Drove; Ash; Durlock and Wingham (by Dambridge Farm). Three trains run daily each way as follows: 10.17 am, 1.38 pm, and 5.17 pm, and they return at 11.35 am, 2.33 pm, and 6.36 pm. At the present, there is only one coach in use. A permanent truck station is in course of erection at Eythorne.

Although the titles of East Kent stations tended to change over the years this seems to be the only reference to Woodnesborough as Drenold's Drove or of Staple as Durlock. The reference to 'only one coach in use' presumably refers to the size of individual trains as the company had at least four carriages and one passenger brakevan available at this time. The reference to 'permanent truck station' seems to mean that the company were now installing a goods siding at Eythorne.

In addition to the trains referred to in the newspaper there was also a service of workmen's trains for Tilmanstone Colliery some of which continued to Eastry. Since there was no run-round loop at Eastry at this time trains terminating here probably travelled the short distance up the Sandwich branch to Eastry goods station, later known as Poison Cross, where there was such a loop for the locomotive to run round its train.

Special workmen's fares were available on these trains only at the following rates:

Shepherdswell to Eastry or Tilmanstone Colliery	2*d*.
Shepherdswell to Eastry or Tilmanstone Colliery & return	3*d*.
Tilmanstone Colliery to Shepherdswell	2*d*.
Tilmanstone Colliery to Eastry & return	4*d*.
Eastry to Tilmanstone Colliery & return	4*d*.

It is curious that a return from Shepherdswell to Eastry should have cost less than the shorter return from Tilmanstone Colliery to Eastry.

It was reported to the Directors on 16th October that the initial traffic was 'satisfactory' and on 30th November that through rates had at last been agreed with the SECR. The same meeting also explained the termination of Mr Wilkinson's appointment as Secretary. He had left the Debenture Books in a mess and had failed to record many of the transfers of debentures to the Contract company. It was agreed that these should be entered in the presence of the EKR auditors.

Presumably traffic continued to come up to expectations as in December it was agreed to extend Line No. 2 to Wingham Village and to move Wingham station to the new railhead. There is some doubt as to when this actually took place but the decision can be taken as a sign that the EKR was well and truly in business in its own right.

Chapter Six

Seven Years Hard Labour - 1917-1923

Between 1917 and 1923 the EKR faced severe difficulties. Although it was now earning money in its own right it also had debts to pay for the lines already constructed. The fact that these should have been paid by the Contract company was an irrelevance to the landowners and authorities who expected payment. Since it was also generally expected that development of the coalfield would resume after the war, the company also needed to find money for the completion of the lines already authorised and to undertake the construction of the lines for which authorisation was still being sought.

An additional problem was that the War Office had occupied most of Lord Greville's lands between Stonar and Richborough and was in the process of establishing a port there together with numerous supply depots and camps.* Had the EKR already reached Stonar the railway would undoubtedly have shared in the massive traffic that developed here but this was not the case. Instead the railway's efforts to safeguard its access to the Stonar Wharf were seen as an unwelcome intrusion into what had become a military zone.

1917

> *Locomotive Magazine* 16th July, 1917: The passenger service comprises four trains a day each way between Shepherdswell and Wingham, with two additional short trips in each direction between Shepherdswell and Eastry. A curious method of working exists at Wingham, a temporary terminus only, where, at present, no accommodation is provided for running the engine round the train. There is, however, a passing loop about 300 yards towards Staple and up trains starting from the latter station are propelled to the loop, where a stop is made to enable the engine to get round to the front of the train.

The first Directors' Meeting of 1917 actually raised some hope of the railway profiting from the developments at Richborough. Mr Richmond-Powell tabled a request from the War Office desiring completion of the line to 'the works at Richborough' so as to relieve the SECR main line. Stephens was requested to draw up estimates for reaching Richborough either by a junction with the SECR, presumably by completing Line 9, or by completing Line 1 to join up with Lord Greville's Tramway. There is unfortunately no record of these estimates and although the question of alternative temporary access to the Tramway was again raised at the May meeting nothing came of these proposals.

---

* The port was begun in 1916 when work began on a new deep channel leading to extensive new wharves from which 1,000 ton barges carried massive quantities of military supplies across to France. In February 1918 these were supplemented by a train ferry service. To serve the port and its associated military establishments a number of marshalling yards were set up and an extensive railway system was developed capable of handling 1,500 wagons daily. It has been estimated that some 70 locomotives worked at the Port at one time or another during the period that it was open.

Meanwhile the Directors had sealed the company's bye-laws in February. These appear to have been copied from the bye-laws of the Shropshire & Montgomeryshire Light Railway and were fairly standard. They were to occasion some difficulty at Nationalisation when it had to be pointed out that there was no statutory provision for the EKR upon which the British Transport Police could base a claim for jurisdiction. The same problem arose with the Kent & East Sussex Railway.

Although the railway had not yet been able to cross the Stour to make connection with Lord Greville's Tramway it was still liable to pay Lord Greville for the use of his wharf. More accurately the Contract company was liable to make these payments, but had not done so for some time and was unlikely to be able to do so for the foreseeable future. The EKR therefore agreed to meet these payments, initially on the basis of meeting current liabilities at £50 every six months, '. . . pending recovery of the amount from the Contract company'. If these payments could be kept up the company would retain some standing in pressing its claims for authorisation of Line 28. This was of particular importance in view of the news in July that the War Office were negotiating the purchase of a considerable amount of Lord Greville's land including the wharf and the tramway. The question of outstanding liabilities for rent unpaid in the past was left for further discussion. One other item of bad news reported in July was the occurrence of a fatal accident to an employee outside the engine shed. The coroner's jury recorded a verdict of death by misadventure but the exact details of the accident went unreported.

Better news came in October in the form of an undertaking by the Contract company to pay over a sum of £7,287 5s. 3d. This included £4,500 of the EKR's own money which had been advanced to pay the deposits required under the 1911 Light Railway Order and which had been released by the Board of Trade upon the opening of the line to the public. Unfortunately the bank had paid the money to the Contract company instead of to the EKR. The prospect of ready cash seems to have cheered the Directors sufficiently for them to instruct Stephens to continue construction of the Wingham line as far as the premises of the Wingham Engineering Company.

A similar infusion of confidence may have prompted the company to renew its attempts to obtain confirmation of the Light Railway Order for Railways 18 to 28 which had been hanging fire since the outbreak of the war. In August 1917 Stephens wrote to the Light Railway Commissioners asking to revive the powers for purchase and completion of works for Railway 11, which he had inadvertently allowed to lapse during an absence on service in France. Railway 11 from Eythorne to Mongeham was, of course, essential to the application for Line 19 from Mongeham to Deal. Customarily a fee was charged where such powers had to be revived but Stephens persuaded the Commissioners to waive this. It is possible that the Commissioners took into account the fact that it had been their own insistence on a deviation of Railway 19 away from Hull Place that had contributed to the long delays this application had suffered.

Initially Stephens had intended to revive the powers for Line 11 as an application in its own right, the East Kent Light Railways (Renewal of Powers & Extension of Time) Order, but was persuaded by the Commissioners to include it as part of the continuing application for the lines first sought in 1913.

Views of both ends of the collision near Eythorne involving locomotives Nos. 1 and 2 and the ex-Kent & East Sussex Railway carriage, No. 13. George Rogers, an EKR platelayer, was the only passenger and remarkably escaped unscathed, though he later lost a leg in another accident on the line. These photographs were taken by Bert Clarabut, the Eythorne station agent.

At the same time he informed the Commissioners that the company wished to discontinue its application for Line 27, the improved branch to Wingham Colliery. Having failed to come to agreement with Lord Desborough there was little point in persisting with the section across the land belonging to St John's College that the Commissioners were prepared to approve. If it had not been for new difficulties arising from the War Office's occupation of Lord Greville's lands it is likely that the 1913 application would have been approved in 1917.

Before leaving 1917 it would be appropriate to mention a potentially disastrous accident that has variously been described as occurring in 1917, 1918 and 1919. Our attribution of this accident to 1917 is based on the recollections of those surviving members of staff who could be interviewed in the last years of the railway. Curiously, there is apparently no official record of the accident and it has therefore proved impossible to ascertain a definite date for it.

One morning the miners' train to Tilmanstone Colliery Halt, which normally continued to Eastry, set off as usual consisting of locomotive No. 1 and an ex-Great Eastern carriage acquired from the Kent & East Sussex where it had ominously borne the number 13. Driver G. Buttifint and fireman R. Hills were in charge. They had arrived safely at Tilmanstone Halt when a bad leak was discovered in one of the boiler tubes. Having deposited their passengers they looked to their charge and were able to effect a temporary but very uncertain repair. Since there was no means of calling up any help from the Halt it was decided to try to get back to Shepherdswell as quickly as possible. Mr G. Rogers, who was then a platelayer, had picked up some tools at the Halt which had to be returned to Shepherdswell and was thus able to accept a most welcome lift back as the sole occupant of the carriage which had, in the absence of run-round facilities at the Halt, to be propelled in front of the locomotive.

Half-way back, just past Eythorne, at a spot known as 'Dung Maxell Crossing', they were run into by a train of 15 empties destined for Tilmanstone Colliery hauled by locomotive No. 2 *Walton Park*. This second train was in the charge of driver Billy Harbuckle and fireman Fred Ash, neither of whom were expecting to meet another train on a routine run up to the pit. The site of the collision was on a bend and at the end of a shallow cutting so that visibility was limited. There was a resounding crash which echoed loudly in the still morning air and the carriage, as can be seen from the photographs taken by Eythorne station agent Bert Clarabut, was smashed to pieces. Surprisingly, little damage seems to have been suffered by either locomotive. Even more remarkable was the fact that Mr Rogers, the only passenger, had chosen the moment before impact to look out of the carriage window and had been able to leap from the carriage. He escaped the accident almost completely unharmed although, as he later recalled, he was 'a bit shaken up'. When interviewed many years later he carried a very clear memory of the first four words spoken as the noise of the impact subsided. These were, 'I expect he's killed' and were spoken by fireman Hills who was naturally overjoyed when the suspected corpse pronounced himself alive.

How this event was kept from the ears of the Board of Trade, what was said by Stephens if and when he learned of this breach of the operating rules and how the destruction of the carriage was explained has gone unrecorded. Obviously some things could avoid notice in wartime conditions that would have called for searching enquiry in peacetime.

Hernden siding was installed in 1918 but is short of custom in this 1926 view. Eastry South Halt is on the left, just beyond the level crossing.

Locomotive No. 3, acquired in 1918, has steam to spare between duties at Sherperdswell.
Colonel Stephens Railway Museum

1918

MINUTES OF THE LONDON & SOUTH WESTERN RAILWAY LOCOMOTIVE AND CARRIAGE AND WAGON COMMITTEE 10th October, 1918: The General Manager reported an arrangement made with the East Kent Railway Company for the hire to them of one of this Company's 6-wheeled coupled type locomotive engines (with tender) No.0394 for a term of 5 years from the 1st August, 1918 at a rent of £200 for each year by monthly payments of £16 13s. 4d.

In January 1918 the Directors authorised a further £50 payment of rent to Lord Greville '. . . so as to keep open the company's rights with regard to the wharf'. Otherwise the only business discussed at their meetings in the first half of this year consisted of discussion of a report that certain parties were negotiating to buy the EKR shares still held by the Contract company, and the granting of authorisation to Stephens to purchase an additional locomotive. This was to lead to the acquisition of locomotive No. 3 from the London & South Western Railway and brought the number of locomotives available to four as another engine, the eight-coupled tank locomotive *Hecate*, was already on hire from the Kent & East Sussex Railway.

January 1918 had seen one positive development, although it does not seem to have merited any record in the company's Minutes. Stephens had written to the Board of Trade on 16th January requesting permission to install a short siding at Hernden, later better known as Eastry South, which had been requested by the local farmers '. . . to save cartage which is difficult to arrange for owing to the crisis.' Stephens was anxious to forestall any objections that the Board might raise and hastened to add that no additional material would be required as the siding would be constructed with '. . . the material now in use at a disused connection at Hammill Colliery.' The work would not require the employment of a contractor as it could be carried out by the company's own staff. The Board replied to Stephens on 21st January authorising construction of the siding, subject to inspection and the provision of some means of preventing vehicles running away unless it was only to be served by trains working from Shepherdswell to Eastry.

The siding seems to have been installed shortly afterwards, though no firm date for this has been found nor any record of a Board of Trade inspection. What is known is that one week after the opening of the siding it was the site of an accident. Locomotive No. 3 and driver Reuben Griffin were running a mixed train to Wingham when they found themselves derailed on unexpectedly entering the siding. The cause appears to have been interference with the point levers by the youngsters of the locality. The derailment effectively blocked the line from Friday to Sunday and No. 3 was only returned to the tracks after a long stint of continuous labour made lighter by copious supplies of free ale.

A very similar tale was recounted when interviewing in a public house at Eythorne shortly after the closure of the line. An elderly local man told how a locomotive had once toppled over on its side but as to the exact location he was not sure. He thought it was Poison Cross. He added that it had taken 47 hours to right the locomotive and that during this time the management had supplied free beer. It is possible that this was the same incident but it is not unknown for good story tellers to prolong or embroider their tales when being interviewed on licensed premises.

In June it was decided to tender a cheque for the £50 that would have been due to Lord Greville to the War Office instead. Presumably the War Office had completed their purchase of Lord Greville's lands at Stonar by this date. As there was no subsequent mention of this cheque being returned it would seem that the War Office were prepared to consider the question of EKR access to Stonar as still being open.

By August 1918 a considerable amount of money was owed to Stephens, Mathews and the Directors for their fees and expenses. Accordingly £10,000 in shares was allotted to a specially formed company, Stock Debentures Limited, to be held on their behalf in the following proportions: Stephens £3,085 12s. 0d., Mathews £1,322 8s. 0d., Loring £143 9s. 0d., Plumptre £99 5s. 6d. and Richmond-Powell £99 5s. 6d. With the ending of hostilities the following month came renewed interest from abroad in the development of the coalfield. Initially this took the form of a request from Forges du Chatillon for confirmation of its traffic agreement and serious consideration of the early revival of powers for Railways 11 and 16 in order to serve the Ripple Colliery site in which Schneider seems to have been showing an interest. Strangely the Directors' Minutes continued to refer to the Forges du Chatillon consortium by that name rather than by their English title, the Guilford & Waldershare Colliery Company.

Although the war had ended there was no immediate prospect of the Contract company renewing its payments of interest and other obligations that had been suspended at the start of the war. There seems to have been some question as to whether the suspension of payments was valid for six months after the end of fighting or for six months after the signing of a peace treaty. Since the affairs of the Contract company were in little better condition than when payments had been suspended, it made little difference to the company's creditors whether their debts were payable or not. However, as the EKR now hoped to renew construction of the railway it became necessary to issue an ultimatum to the Contract company in November. If the latter did not propose to do any further work to complete the contract then it would be considered at an end. Schneider was interested in taking over the Wingham and Woodnesborough sites and the EKR needed to be able to construct any lines that might be needed unfettered by the threat of intervention by the Contract company. Proof that Schneider was serious in its intentions to invest in the coalfield at this time may be gained from the fact that it had entered negotiations with the EKR so as to relieve Schneider from obligations in respect of vertical or horizontal support to the company's tracks. The price for such an agreement was that Schneider should buy 10,000 EKR shares and guarantee that all its traffic would be carried by the railway.

1919

DIRECTORS' REPORT: During the year there have been no developments on the Coal Field with the exception of some renewed activity at Guilford Colliery which has caused a certain amount of traffic over the line.

In January 1919 the Directors allotted a further £10,000 in shares to their own account in Stock Debentures Limited before putting a price on a possible settlement with the Contract company. For £7,000 the EKR would consider the obligations of the Contract company as discharged. Stephens had not been consulted and in February protested that £7,000 was insufficient with the result that the offer was withdrawn. Instead Loring and Stephens were authorised to negotiate with Mr Moens of the Contract company for whatever sum in excess of £7,000 that could be obtained. At the same meeting a letter was unexpectedly received from Arthur Burr offering to meet the calls on his shares in the EKR if the company would waive the interest he owed on the shares. Burr died in September without taking the matter any further and it is therefore impossible to say what impact his renewed interest in the railway might have had. It is clear that he still had serious hopes of rescuing something from the wreck of his grand design.

The Directors were now confident that a revival in the coalfield's fortunes was imminent. The third major item of business at the March 1919 meeting was a report by Stephens that he had agreed with Forges du Chatillon for that company to carry out major works on the Guilford branch '. . . which would enable part of the temporary line to be abandoned and would enable the company to run to the Guilford Colliery considerably heavier trains'. Forges du Chatillon would be paid in EKR shares at 15s. a share. Work had now been resumed at Guilford, the shafts having been drained in March, and sinking having begun again with the help of the cementation process.

The resumption of work on Guilford Colliery was an exception to the general trend in 1919. The mines had been under Government control during the war and the prospect of a return to private ownership had led to considerable discontent amongst the miners. To defuse the situation the Government had set up a commission in January 1919 under Sir John Sankey to advise on the future of the mining industry. The Government had effectively committed itself to implementing the decisions of the Sankey Commission and there was a widespread fear amongst the mine owners that the Commission would recommend nationalisation of the mines. Against this background it is not surprising that there was no immediate rush to invest in the development of the Kent coalfield. When the Commission finally reported in June 1919 it was divided over the merits of nationalisation; the Government was able to take advantage of this lack of unanimity and decided to return the mines to private ownership.

This did not take effect until April 1921 and the period preceding this saw continual unrest as the mining unions sought to protect the better wages and conditions they had enjoyed under Government control. At Tilmanstone, where a comparatively harmonious relationship had existed between the miners and

EKR No. 3, still bearing its LSWR identity as No. 394, at Shepherdswell on 23rd January, 1919.

Ken Nunn/LCGB Collection

the Burrs, this harmony did not extend to the management that had succeeded the Burrs. In 1919 this led to a strike in support of a claim to reduce the working day to 6½ hours from 7½ hours which was eventually resolved by a reduction to 7 hours. Any stoppage at Tilmanstone had a direct effect on the income of the railway, but relief at the ending of the strike may have been matched by equal concern at a settlement that would further weaken the finances of the colliery.

One promising development in the coalfield in 1919 was the start of coal production at Chislet Colliery. Although this would not directly benefit the railway any development that encouraged confidence in the prospects of the coalfield was to be welcomed.

In May 1919 Stephens became a Director of the EKR and in September he requested permission from the Board of Trade to carry out a long overdue improvement. This was the installation of a passing loop at Eastry. It does not appear to have occurred to anyone in authority to ask how trains terminating at Eastry had been handled hitherto but Stephens' request was approved without question.

The War Office was now beginning to run down its operations at Richborough Port. Although considerable quantities of stores and salvage were still being returned here from Europe there was nothing like the same amount of activity as there had been during the final years of the war. It was clear that the War Office would soon have no further use for the port. They were therefore better disposed to recognise the railway's right of access to the Stonar Wharf and meetings were held between the Board of Trade, the War Office and the EKR in London in July and at Richborough in August. The end result was a withdrawal of the War Office's objections to the granting of the long-delayed Light Railway Order though certain details would still require negotiation. These mainly stemmed from the fact that much of Lord Greville's Tramway had been lifted by the War Office and new lines on different alignments had been laid in its place. There had also been substantial alterations to the Stonar Wharf.

With the granting of the Light Railway Order in prospect there was a need for additional motive power and the Directors authorised Stephens in August to obtain an additional engine by hire or hire purchase. They were presumably encouraged to contemplate such additional expenditure by an approach by a Colonel Standen '. . . and certain friends of his' who were prepared to reconstruct the Sandwich branch as far as Poison Cross or Ash Road in return for the right to purchase an undisclosed quantity of ordinary shares at 10s. a share. At the December meeting Colonel Standen's 'friends' were revealed to be the Invicta Coal & Shipping Company who were now prepared to buy 1,000 shares at 9s. each provided that the proceeds be dedicated to completing the line to Ash Road where they wanted siding facilities. Invicta also wanted an option to purchase an additional 30,000 shares at 11s. each on or before the 31st March, 1920 the proceeds of which would be used to complete the line to 'the Government Sidings at Richborough.'

Wingham Colliery Halt, though the nameboard simply reads Wingham in this 1919 view. The buildings were moved on when the terminus moved to Wingham Town the following year.

1920

DIRECTORS' REPORT: During the year there have been no material developments on the Coal Field. The traffic of the Railway, having regard to the present development of the Coal Field, compares satisfactorily with that of the previous year.

The railway's business suffered a brief setback when a further strike took place at Tilmanstone for three weeks in February 1920 over the dismissal of a winding man. There was better news in March. Not only had a draft agreement with Invicta been drawn up but Dewrance and Moens, representing the Allied Companies and a significant section of the shareholders, were prepared to recommend acceptance of this agreement to the debenture holders. This encouraging progress was short-lived as Invicta promptly lapsed into silence.

Not long after this the Channel Steel Company announced definite proposals to sink the pit at Betteshanger which had been frustrated by the outbreak of war in 1914. It was estimated that the pit would produce more than a million tons each year. Although it would take some time before the pit would start producing coal it must have heartened the EKR to know that the coalfield was being taken seriously again. There might even be traffic from the pit to justify building Railway 19 to Deal for which authorisation was expected soon.

The East Kent Light Railways (Extensions) Order 1920 (*see map page overleaf*) was finally confirmed on 21st August, 1920. Amongst preliminary details it reduced the maximum number of Directors from nine to five and then went on to authorise construction of the following railways: Line 18 (Snowdown to Hammill), Line 19 (Mongeham to Deal), Line 20 (Junction with SECR at Deal), Line 22 (Wickhambreux to Canterbury), Line 23 (Coldred to Alkham), Line 24 (link between Line 23 and Line 13 at Stonehall), Line 26 (branch from Line 11 to Telegraph Farm Brickworks) and Line 28 (link to Stonar Wharf). The powers for Line 11 were revived on the same basis as for the newly approved lines, three years for purchase and five years for construction. Curiously there was no extension of powers for Railway 13 with which the new Railway 24 was meant to connect.

The Order was subject to a number of conditions. Seventeen roads were to cross or be crossed by bridges rather than level crossings. The War Office training area at Fordwich on Line 22 was to suffer as little interference as possible and the War Office were to be entitled to Railway Clearing House rates for their traffic, regardless of whatever rates the railway was empowered to charge their other customers. The junctions with the SECR at Deal and Canterbury were to be double line junctions to the satisfaction of the SECR, who had a number of other powers including the right to specify through rates over lines competing with their own ; this would presumably have affected rates between Canterbury West and Deal or Shepherdswell. The SECR also had the right to demand that the EKR erect platforms for the exchange of passengers where the lines of the two companies met. Any spoil left on Scotland Common in connection with the tunnel there for. Line 23 was to be levelled and sown with grass seed as soon as practicable. Line 28 might only use its level crossing on the Sandwich to Ramsgate road as long as Line 1 was not continued across the same road.

As to finance the Order empowered the EKR to raise £240,000 in shares and to borrow up to £120,000 in the proportion of £1,000 for every £2,000 shares

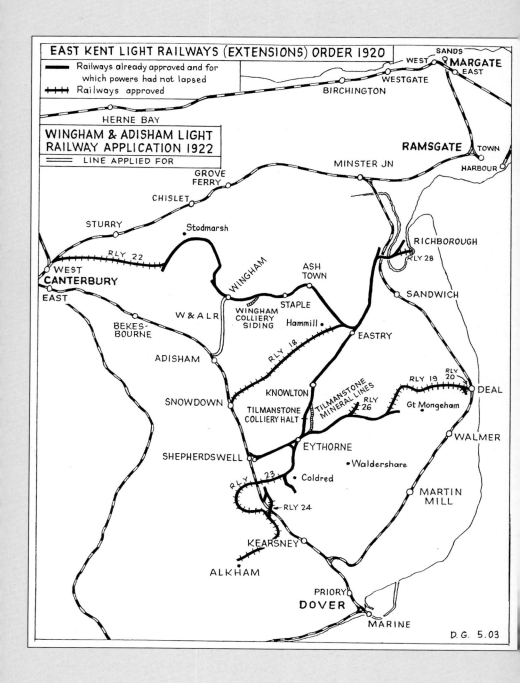

EAST KENT LIGHT RAILWAYS (EXTENSIONS) ORDER 1920

— Railways already approved and for
which powers had not lapsed
┼┼┼┼ Railways approved

WINGHAM & ADISHAM LIGHT
RAILWAY APPLICATION 1922
═══ LINE APPLIED FOR

SANDS
WEST MARGATE
EAST
WESTGATE
BIRCHINGTON
HERNE BAY
RAMSGATE TOWN
HARBOUR
GROVE
FERRY
MINSTER JN
CHISLET
STURRY
Stodmarsh
RICHBOROUGH
RLY 22
RLY 28
WEST
CANTERBURY
WINGHAM
ASH
TOWN
SANDWICH
EAST
STAPLE
W & A L R
WINGHAM
COLLIERY
SIDING
Hammill
BEKES-
BOURNE
RLY 18
EASTRY
ADISHAM
RLY 19 RLY
20
SNOWDOWN
KNOWLTON
TILMANSTONE
MINERAL LINES
RLY
26
Gt Mongeham
DEAL
TILMANSTONE
COLLIERY HALT
RLY 23
EYTHORNE
WALMER
SHEPHERDSWELL
•Waldershare
•Coldred
MARTIN
MILL
RLY 24
KEARSNEY
ALKHAM
PRIORY
DOVER
MARINE

D. G. 5.03

issued. This, of course, presumed that a market for EKR shares existed. Regrettably, as the slow progress of the negotiations with Invicta Coal & Shipping was making evident, there was no great onslaught of investors eager to snap up shares in the railway. As a result little or no attempt was made in 1920 to start work on the newly authorised lines.

One piece of additional construction had taken place by 1920. This was the extension of the Wingham line to Wingham Town where a proper run-round loop and a short siding were installed. This extension does not seem to have been inspected or approved but is clearly shown in the Railway Clearing House (RCH) Map of Southern England published in 1920. The company's timetables continued to refer discreetly to the terminus of the Wingham line as either Wingham Colliery or simply Wingham.

The RCH Map (*see overleaf*) shows a number of other interesting features. Both the Wingham Colliery and Woodnesborough Colliery branches are shown and Tilmanstone Colliery is clearly shown to be connected to Line 1 both north and south of the colliery. The Sandwich branch is shown as open as far as Sandwich Road and it is to be presumed that this branch was available for goods traffic. This point is supported by the fact that the station later known as Poison Cross is shown as Eastry (Goods) to distinguish it from Eastry (Passenger) at the junction of the Wingham and Sandwich branches. The later Roman Road station is shown as Woodnesborough Road and the station then being shown in the timetables as Woodnesborough is shown as Woodnesborough Colliery. The station at Eastry South had not yet been opened but it is surprising that the siding here is not shown.

A positive step forward in 1920 was an agreement made in August with the East Kent Colliery Company and the Guilford & Waldershare Colliery Company for the hire purchase of an additional locomotive which would be used exclusively for the coal traffic of those two companies. This was locomotive No. 4 and further details of its acquisition are given in Chapter 16. The Guilford & Waldershare Colliery Company did not as yet actually have any coal traffic but was still engaged in sinking at Guilford Colliery. By November the work it was undertaking for the EKR on the Guilford branch had been satisfactorily completed and it was paid by the allotment of 2,342 ordinary shares. At the same time a further £11,795 in debentures was paid into the holding account in payment of the fees of the EKR Engineer, Directors and Solicitors.

Whilst the lure of payment in shares and debentures of increasingly marginal value can hardly be regarded as a significant incentive it did not prevent a new member from joining the Board of the EKR in December 1920. This was Lt Col Charles Edward Gore Vesey R.E. of The Camp, Longmoor, Hampshire. Longmoor was well known for its Military Railway though Vesey's role at Longmoor was as Commandant of the R.E. Bridging Training Centre. Nevertheless he would have found the EKR's one and only bogie carriage a familiar sight as its two sisters from the Kent & East Sussex had long formed the mainstay of Longmoor's passenger fleet. Vesey was a good choice to join the East Kent's Board. Not only did he later become the company's Chairman and remain so until Nationalisation, but he was one of the few Directors to make it his business to visit the line with any regularity.

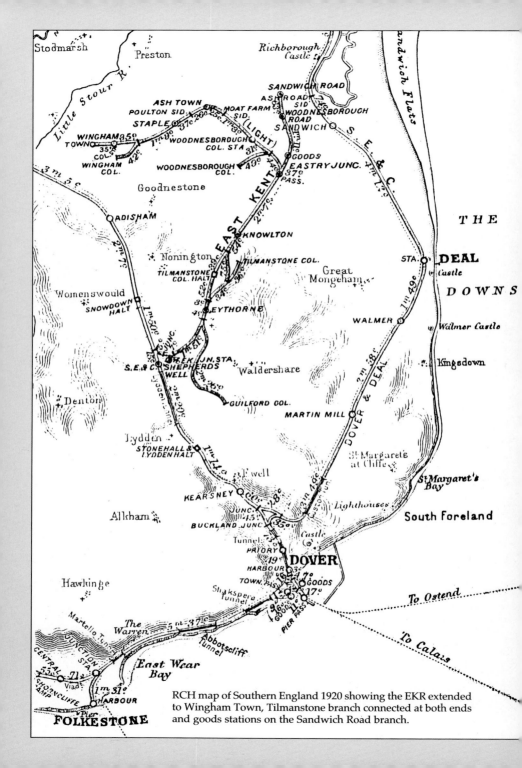

RCH map of Southern England 1920 showing the EKR extended to Wingham Town, Tilmanstone branch connected at both ends and goods stations on the Sandwich Road branch.

Work was evidently still in progress when this undated photograph of Guilford Colliery was taken.

Kerr, Stuart 0-6-0T jointly purchased from the Inland Waterways & Docks Department at Richborough by Tilmanstone and Guilford collieries for sale to the EKR on hire purchase terms. A fine locomotive, but the hire purchase agreement proved less than satisfactory.

"SUPPORT THE LOCAL LINE."

EAST KENT RAILWAY.

TIME TABLE.

JULY 11th, 1921.

AND UNTIL FURTHER NOTICE.

DOWN TRAINS. **WEEK DAYS.**

	a.m.	a.m.	a.m.	a.m.	p.m.	p.m.	p.m.
					so	N	
London, Holborn Viaduct ....dep.	—	—	7 30	—	—	—	5 10
„ Victoria .... „	—	—	—	10 45	1 25	2 5	—
Canterbury East................ „	—	6 26	10 26	12 44	3 24	4 12	7 4
Dover Priory .... „	—	6 44	11 30	12 55	4 42		7 10
Deal .... „	—	—	11 2	11 2	4 12		6 8
Shepherdswell Jn., E.K. Rly. .... „	5 58	7 20	12 0	1z22	5 5		8z 0
Eythorne for Guilford Colliery.... „	6A 7	7 27	12 7	1A29	5 12		8 9
Tilmanstone Colliery Halt .... „	Stop	7 32	12 14	Stop	5 17		8 12
Knowlton .... „		7 36	12 18		5 20		8 16
Eastry for Sandwich .... „		7 41	12 35		5 28		8 24
Woodnesborough Colliery .... „		7 44	12 39		5 31		Stop
Ash Town .... „		7 49	12 45		5 36		
Staple .... „		8 2	1 17		5 40		
Wingham Colliery .... arr.		8 7	1 23		5 45		

UP TRAINS. **WEEK DAYS.** **N** **SO**

	a.m.	a.m.	p.m.	p.m.	p.m.	p.m.	p.m.	p.m.
Wingham Colliery ....dep.	—	8 50	—	—	1 45	5 50	5 55	—
Staple .... „	—	8 56	—	—	1 53	6 0	6 2	—
Ash Town .... „	—	9 0	—	—	1 56	6 5	6 6	—
Woodnesborough Colliery .... „	—	9 9	—	—	2 7	6 25	6 20	—
Eastry for Sandwich .... „	—	9 22	—	—	2 15	6 30	6 26	9z10
Knowlton .... „	—	9 30	—	—	2 22	s	6 33	9 1
Tilmanstone Colliery Halt .... „	A	9 34	so	N	2 25	s	6 38	9 2
Eythorne for Guilford Colliery.... „	6z21	9 37	12zA51	2zA1	2 30	6 50	6 46	9 2
Shepherdswell Jn., E.K. Rly. .... arr.	6 30	9 46	1 0	2 10	2 40	7 5	6 53	9 3
Deal .... „	7 47	11 45	2 10	3 37	{4so7 / 3s37}	8 5	—	—
Dover Priory .... „	7 9	11 16	1 32	2 32	{3so36 / 3s17}	7 45	—	11 1
Canterbury East................ „	7 18	10 27	1 38	2 37	3 32	7 51	—	—
London, Victoria .... „	—	1 33	4 39	4 39	5 26	10 18	—	—
„ Holborn Viaduct...... „		1 0	—	—	—	—	—	—
„ Cannon Street............ „	9* 6	—		—	—	—	—	—

so—Saturdays only. N—Not on Saturdays. z—Colliers' Cheap Tickets available by these trains.
*—No luggage allowed by this train.
A—Provisionally starts from or runs into Tilmanstone Colliery yard. s—Stops by signal to pick up or set down passengers.
Special arrangements for quick and cheap delivery of parcels and goods. Special trips arranged as required.
Every effort will be made to connect with the trains of S. E. & C. Rly. as shewn, but the same will not be guaranteed.

Tonbridge,
June, 1921.

H. F. STEPHENS,
General Manager.

In December the railway submitted its return to the Light Railway Investigation Committee set up by the Government to gather data on the costs and operations of light railways. Stephens was far from happy to comply with the committee's request for information:

> They are a non-controlled line with, of course, no money to spend from public funds on this sort of thing . . . It hardly seems fair that *non-controlled* companies should not be recompensed for obtaining the information desired by your authorities. It seems hardly a 'British' proceeding.

Stephens was, however, able to provide most of the information requested except, significantly, 'the cost of land and total cost of construction which I am unable to give accurately'. One point seems to have caused a little head scratching, initially the return claimed that the line had two stations and seven halts, but this was corrected to read six stations and three halts. It would be interesting to learn what criteria were used to distinguish between a 'station' and a 'halt'.

1921

> DIRECTORS' REPORT: This decrease is due to the coal strike which caused an almost complete cessation of coal traffic on the railway for some months. The output from the Tilmanstone pit has not yet reached its pre-strike volume.

1921 must have been a frustrating first year of Directorship for Gore-Vesey. No further construction is recorded as having taken place which is not surprising in view of the company's increasingly fragile financial position. A gleam of hope briefly twinkled in August when a formal agreement was sealed with what was now named the Invicta Coal & Iron Company but was soon extinguished. It was reported in December that Invicta was already in default and its agreement with the EKR seems to have lapsed entirely shortly afterwards.

A further setback had already been suffered with the suspension of sinking at Guilford while more powerful pumps were obtained. It looked as though the railway would have to continue depending on Tilmanstone for the bulk of its income for some time yet and all was not well at Tilmanstone. The East Kent Colliery Company's Report for 1921 makes grim reading: 'A period of comparative prosperity came to a sudden end at the close of the year 1920 and was succeeded by a period of unparalleled depression coupled with the disastrous strike of 3 months which followed the withdrawal of Government control. During that fateful year our output tumbled down through lack of demand to an average of only about one-half of what it had been in 1920 and most of our output was sold at unremunerative prices in order to keep the pits open'. To safeguard its main source of traffic, the EKR revised its traffic agreement with the colliery by introducing a special rate of 9d. a ton for coal for export provided that 1,000 tons were dispatched each week. This rate was also subsequently applied to coal sent to Cement Works at Snodland, Halling and Cuxton and to coal sent to Lloyds Paper Mills at Sittingbourne, though this last was subject to a minimum weekly tonnage of 1,500 tons. Unfortunately for both the colliery and the railway tonnages of coal sufficient to qualify for the special rates were rare.

Tilmanstone had been but one of many pits to suffer strike action as the mine owners initiated wage cuts following the end of Government control in April. Schneider had incorporated a British company, Downs Collieries Limited, in April but the outbreak of strike action throughout the British coal industry, coupled with a rapid fall in demand for coal as heavy industry went into recession, seems to have scared them off. Apart from paying some dead rents on various acquisitions of mineral rights, most notably from the Adisham Colliery Co. and the Ecclesiastical Commissioners, Downs Collieries remained largely inactive. Schneider sold out its interest in 1927 and Downs Collieries was wound up in 1930.

In the meantime the EKR had staved off any immediate danger of bankruptcy by taking a leaf from the Contract company's book and proposing a Scheme of Arrangement to its debenture holders under the Railway Companies Act 1867. A meeting of the debenture holders in January had agreed to such a scheme in principle but had requested that no final decision be taken for six months. By July the company's position had not improved and it was therefore proposed to the debenture holders that interest due on debentures to December 1921 should be paid in shares, and that in each of the next seven years 60 per cent of the company's net revenue should be devoted to payment of interest in cash with the balance, if any, to be paid in shares. By October a sufficient majority of debenture holders had given their agreement and the Scheme was then formally approved by the Court of Chancery.

1922

> DIRECTORS' REPORT: Although the tonnage of coal carried shows an increase on 1920, traffic was very much restricted for about 2 months owing to the flooding of Tilmanstone Colliery and, in consequence, the results are not so favourable as they would have been under ordinary circumstances. Every effort is being made to continue the line into Richborough Port in the hope that the company's traffic will be assisted.

In February 1922 the Contract company requested a further two years to repay its debts to the EKR. Since the former's finances showed little improvement the EKR Directors agreed to a deferment without too much heart searching. They did make the deferment conditional upon the Contract company paying interest on various loans, but there seems to have been little hope of it meeting its obligations in any substantial form unless the fortunes of the Allied Companies underwent a miraculous transformation. Salvation of a sort was in fact coming to the Allied Companies but not in a form that would revive the fortunes of the Contract company. Moreover the saviour of the Allied Companies was to prove to be no friend to the EKR.

The 'saviour' was a new company embodying the two main participants in the Channel Steel Company, the iron and steel enterprise of Dorman Long & Co. and the contractors S. Pearson & Son. These two firms had been working closely together for some time and much of the preparatory work for their grand design was carried out in the name of one or the other of the two companies even before their amalgamation. Their aim was to acquire as wide a holding of mineral rights throughout the known coalfield as possible and to develop coal and iron ore mines which would supply a major industrial complex at Richborough. The title of the new enterprise was Pearson & Dorman Long (PDL). It was incorporated in October 1922 and promptly set about acquiring the mineral rights of the Allied Companies to add to those which it had already acquired from the Channel Steel Company which included the proposed Betteshanger Colliery.

The Allied Companies must have been relieved to find a customer for their mineral rights at last. The essence of their agreement with PDL was that the lands over which the Allied companies held mineral rights would be divided into six areas: Wingham, Woodnesborough, Walmestone, Stodmarsh, Canterbury and Fleet. PDL would purchase each area just as soon as the various leases, rights and freeholds could be delivered, except that they would not be compelled to buy the less promising Canterbury and Walmestone areas until at least two other areas had been sold to them. Within two years of purchase PDL would sink at least two shafts in each area. A total purchase payment of £74,750 to the Allied Companies was anticipated together with super-royalties on coal raised. Although it took some time for the various purchases to be organised this agreement effectively marked the retirement of the Allied Companies from active development of the coalfield. Snowdown, their only working colliery, had already gone into receivership and separate negotiations were now begun to sell this pit to PDL.

The agreement with PDL certainly saved the day for those of the Allied Companies that had lands or mineral rights to sell but effectively sealed the fate of the Contract company. It had few mineral rights to sell and was most unlikely to be asked to carry out any work for PDL. The entry into receivership of Snowdown Colliery had already written off an unsecured debt of £30,442 and it was now just a matter of time before the Contract company went into liquidation. There was very little prospect of the latter meeting more than a fraction of its obligations to the EKR.

Obviously the creation of PDL was bound to have an influence on the fortunes of the EKR. As early as 22nd April, 1922 the Directors' Minutes refer to Stephens being authorised to negotiate with 'the Richborough Company and other companies concerned' in the matter of the extension of Lines 1 and 28 to Richborough. The response was disappointing. Pearson & Son, as they still were at that date, were reported in July as being prepared to purchase the railways company's shares at 3s. 6d. each provided that 75 per cent of the shareholders were willing to sell. Clearly Pearson's were only prepared to finance the railway by taking it over.

Initially the Directors seem to have been tempted by the prospect of selling out but not at Pearson's offered price. In August they insisted that nothing less than 6s. 8d. a share would be acceptable and in September actually agreed to an option with a Mr Sewill to sell him 300,000 shares at this price together with 150,000 debentures at 50 per cent discount. Unfortunately Mr Sewill never exercised his option and PDL was left as the only party with any apparent interest in the East Kent.

Meanwhile the railways company was tidying up the Wingham end of its line. The short mineral branch to the now derelict remains of Wingham Colliery appears to have had its last train in 1921 when staff recalled driver Jack Squires taking the locomotive *Northiam*, hired from the Kent & East Sussex, up to the colliery site. As the Wingham & Stour Valley Colliery Company were disposing of the colliery's surplus equipment at this time it may well have been in connection with this. The general view amongst staff who were questioned on this subject was that the branch to the colliery was lifted in 1922. There is unfortunately no documentary evidence on this question at all.

Considering the track-hungry state of the railway it is surprising that there is no mention of the fate of the rails and pointwork from the colliery branch. The branch had not been built under the railway's powers and must therefore have been laid under the general mineral rights of Kent Coal Concessions who might justifiably have looked on the track as its own property. There is no record of any dispute arising as to the disposal of the trackwork and it must be taken that all parties concerned were happy with whatever steps were taken. A similar situation later arose in respect of the ownership of various assets at Tilmanstone Colliery with less happy consequences.

1922 saw the future of another of the railway's colliery branches under threat. The Guilford & Waldershare Colliery Company suspended all work on the sinking of Guilford Colliery and the erection of a power station there. This was explained as being due to the depreciation of the franc but probably owed almost as much to the ailing state of the coal and steel industries. There is no suggestion in the company's reports that it was the difficulties with keeping water out of the pit that was to blame as has so often been suggested. The colliery had been making good progress with its power station, for which two extra boilers had been delivered earlier in the year, and had almost completed its pumping chamber for which two pumps had also been delivered. The colliery announced that it would continue to maintain its works in good order and was also bound by a contract with A. François to pay him £3,200 yearly for sinking the shafts. These payments continued until 1928 but no further sinking ever took place and the Guilford branch gradually fell into decay.

1923

DIRECTORS' REPORT: The tonnage of coal carried shows an increase on 1922 of 50,163 tons. The construction of the Line into Richborough Port has proceeded during the year under review and is being continued.

In January 1923 the resignation of Mr Richmond Powell from the Board was announced but the loss of this long-serving supporter of the line appeared to be balanced by the intervention of an entirely new party. This was Mr Philip Hill who had come forward with a novel means of restoring the company's fortunes. He proposed to set up a body to be known as The Freighters who would discharge the EKR's liabilities up to 21st December, 1922 by a payment of £25,500. They would additionally pay up to £175,000 to repair the existing lines and to construct and complete the extensions to Canterbury, Deal and Richborough as well as certain others of the lines that had been authorised. In return The Freighters would be entitled to act as common carriers over the EKR, for which they would '. . . provide and employ all proper and sufficient locomotive power, carriages and wagons, horses, vehicles, superintendence, labour, stores, materials and other requisites'. The EKR would keep the lines in good order and employ a Secretary, General Manager, station agents, gate keepers and other personnel. The Freighters would collect all receipts but would pay tolls to the EKR sufficient in the first five years to make up the difference between the company's net income and £3,000 pa which would be raised to £5,000 pa in succeeding years. Additionally The Freighters would pay the Directors' fees. The Directors seem to have had no difficulty in resolving to accept Mr Hill's proposals subject to negotiations.

Unfortunately, it was soon apparent that there was more to Mr Hill than met the eye. Loring, the EKR Chairman, had been the initial contact with Mr Hill but soon regretted introducing him and his associates to the railway:

> Meanwhile it is clear that they are working with Dorman Long if they do not actually represent them ; the idea being that Dorman Long shall have control of the coalfield by means of the railway thus enabling them to keep out rivals by refusing facilities. Dorman Long to make their profit out of the Railway, Hill & Co. to make their profit out of the increased value of shares and debentures.

The Freighters did have one sturdy advocate at the EKR. The company's solicitor, Mathews, obviously felt that the railway's position was so desperate that any straw should be clutched to keep the enterprise from bankruptcy. One immediate obstacle that he hoped Stephens might be able to circumvent was that the Light Railway Orders contained no provision for operation of the line by another company. Stephens did indeed have a solution and wrote to Matthews on the 8th January, 1923:

> We have had this agreement on the brain (and everything else) for the last 3 weeks. I suppose it will end in smoke.
> My scheme was to make application under the Railway Construction Facilities Act 1864 for some nominal alterations, thus giving an order in being.
> Having the Order, we could schedule any agreement we might think fit to it. There is a precedent ; the Van Railway Order in 1873, where an agreement between the promoters of the Van Company and the Owners of some lead mines respecting a guarantee of traffic etc. etc. was recited in the Order.
> The Van Railway Order is known as the Van Railway Certificate 1873.
> This Railway Construction Facilities Act has been very little used, I only know of 3 cases.
>   (1) The Van Railway Order
>   (2) Extension of the Wirral Railway
>   (3) The railway for conveying lunatics from Epsom Station to the 'lunatic magazine' at Epsom.

Mathews' reply to Stephens contained the hope that '. . . the precedent in respect to the lunatic railway will not be carried too far'. He obviously thought there was some merit in Stephens' proposal as he wrote to him again on the 11th January confirming that Hill was prepared to pay £25,500 to discharge the company's liabilities and up to £175,000 for repairs and extensions. He further asked, 'What should we apply for our certificate for - some sort of extension?' Obviously everyone in the company had got rather used to applying for extensions.

By the 23rd January Mr Hill's offer was beginning to look less generous. Matthews wrote to Loring that The Freighters were only actually agreeing to guarantee the Richborough Extension. Loring promptly instructed Matthews, 'Please do not negotiate with Mr Hill on behalf of the company any further'. In future Loring wished to handle any negotiations himself. This led Matthews to write to Loring on 26th January: 'I sincerely hope that you will come to terms with Mr Hill as with Dorman Long & Pearson working with us the future of the railway is assured but with people as powerful as Dorman Long and Pearsons working against us the future of the railway is a very different proposition'.

Mathews had little success in changing Loring's mind as by 29th January he was writing to Stephens in much the same terms that he had written to Loring, except that he added that Stephens' employment would be guaranteed in any agreement with PDL. Stephens was no more happy than Loring had been. On the 29th January he wrote to Mathews pointing out that Hill had revised his original proposals substantially. Amongst other points The Freighters were now proposing to maintain the line themselves which meant that they could abandon the agreement after 15 years leaving the line worn out. Whilst the company could then take them to court it would '. . . have no money to fight them with, and if it had, you can imagine a small company fighting a big coal Trust'. He concluded, 'It is not a question of Dorman Longs and Pearsons working with us, it is a question of Dorman Longs & Pearsons submerging us. If we are going to show the white feather in this business or in any other way we are not defending the trust placed in us by the present proprietors'.

Mathews was not to be dissuaded. He reminded Stephens that the company might owe a duty to the shareholders but also owed a prior duty to their creditors. Stephens was not to be swayed. On 31st January he wrote again to Mathews pointing out that The Freighters were offering too small a royalty for the carriage of coal over the line - three-eighths of a penny per ton compared with the railway's current profit of fourpence per ton. He continued with further arguments:

> I may tell you also that the last form of agreement, where the Contractors will work the line, including doing the station accounts, has not the faintest chance of getting through the Ministry of Transport or the Government on the grounds that competitive Traders would have their accounts examined by people who were in competition with them, and, as a very distinguished man said, only the day before yesterday 'this is against public policy'.
>
> You may take it from me that I shall get advice on all papers sent to me from people with far more experience in these matters than I have.
>
> We can get better terms than these people offer, from the Southern Group, if we want to commit suicide.
>
> The threat to run competitive lines and so starve us is bluff. The threat to buy shares and out vote us is also bluff. Rather than this should happen I would take the whole of my £7,000 for Fees owing to me in ordinary shares @ 2s. (which is about their present value). This would give me 70,000 votes.

Whilst this was probably not the end of the argument it is unfortunately the end of the surviving correspondence between Mathews and Stephens preserved in the Austen Collection in the Colonel Stephens Railway Museum Archives. A report in the *Railway Gazette* in April 1923 carries the story to its conclusion:

> Speaking at the Annual General Meeting of the East Kent Light Railways Company on 19th April Mr H.A. Loring, the Chairman, said that negotiations had been carried on up to the end of March with Dorman Long & Co. with the object of obtaining financial assistance towards the extension of the line to Richborough and in other directions. The interests of the debenture holders and the payment of Directors' fees were all nicely arranged but the results likely to be obtained for the ordinary shareholders were not attractive and consequently the negotiations were dropped. The Directors were, however, prepared to re-open the negotiations with Dorman Long & Co.

The negotiations were not re-opened and PDL adopted a policy of limiting the railway's role in the coalfield as far as was in its power.

Throughout the negotiations with Mr Hill the EKR was seeking alternative sources of finance. In March 1923 consideration was given to borrowing £4,500 from an insurance company to finance the Richborough Extension. This would probably have been the Excess Insurance Company with whom Stephens had had dealings on the Weston Clevedon & Portishead. An even more unlikely source of finance was a further approach by Invicta Coal & Iron in April with an offer of a loan of £5,000 to complete the Richborough Line. By July the Directors seem to have had enough of fending off unsuitable suitors. With two unspecified proposals to take over the line laid before them they decided to take action on neither and opted instead to strengthen the company's position by their own efforts as far as possible.

There were plenty of other matters to keep the Directors occupied in 1923. In February they had agreed to pay the fees still outstanding for Stephens' work in shares and 50,000 shares were subsequently allotted to him. This caused consternation amongst the shareholders. As a result Stephens returned the shares in April so that the Directors might re-allot them to him not as payment but as security for payment. This led Moens to lodge a serious objection on behalf of the shareholders at the Annual General Meeting as reported in the *Dover Express*: 'He wished to know whether it was a fact that 50,000 shares had been issued . . . without one single copper coming into the hands of the railway company. If the capital of the railway company was watered down in that way, and if those 50,000 shares were liable to be thrown on the market at any moment, the mere knowledge of that fact would send the shares to Jericho'. Loring explained that the shares were only being held as security and that Stephens had in any event agreed not to deal in the shares for three years. He added that, '. . . Mr Moens was speaking rather less as a shareholder than as the salvor of what remained of the Kent Coal Concessions and the allied companies, who were in an even less favourable position than this company'. Loring carried the day and the company's report and accounts were accepted by the meeting.

Despite the railway's financial difficulties funds were found to purchase two additional locomotives in 1923. The first of these, No. 5, was obtained in March 1923 and was a somewhat unlikely acquisition as it was an ex-London & South

Newly acquired 4-4-2T No. 5 lifting its safety valves in Shepherdswell yard.

Nos. 6 and 3 double-heading the 1.17 pm to Eastry out of Shepherdswell on 14th September, 1923. The train is about to descend to Golgotha tunnel and the crew of No. 3 will be bracing themselves for a double dose of smoke.   *Ken Nunn/LCGB Collection*

Western Railway (LSWR) 4-4-2T originally intended for fast suburban passenger services. A much more useful locomotive, No. 6, was obtained in May. This was an 0-6-0 tender locomotive originally built for the South Eastern Railway as one of their 'O' class. This was one of the most successful locomotives owned by the East Kent and was equally at home on the coal traffic from Tilmanstone as on the mixed trains to Wingham.

If PDL could masquerade as The Freighters it presumably seemed fair to the EKR that it should take on a disguise of its own. Thus an application was made in the Directors' names to the Ministry of Transport, who had taken over the functions of the Light Railway Commissioners, for authority to incorporate a Wingham & Adisham (Light) Railway Company. The function of the new company would be to build a line 2 miles 2 furlongs long linking Wingham Town on the East Kent with Adisham station on what was now the Southern Railway line from Canterbury to Dover.

The description of the proposed line in the draft Light Railway Order was as follows:

> The said railway 2 miles 2 furlongs 1 chain or thereabouts in length is wholly situate in the County of Kent commencing by a junction with the East Kent Light Ry Company's Eastry and Wingham Railway at a point 150 yards or thereabouts West of Wingham Town Station and running through the parishes of Wingham and Adisham terminates by a junction with the Canterbury and Dover Railway of the South Eastern and Chatham section of the Southern Railway at a point 400 yards or thereabouts north of Adisham Station.

The Application was made in the names of Arthur H. Loring, Lt Col H.F. Stephens and Lt Col C.E.G. Vesey and sought powers for local authorities to subscribe a total of £6,000 towards the enterprise.

The line could be leased to either the EKR or to the Southern. Although it would carry passengers and general freight its main purpose would be to carry coal from new collieries proposed in the Wingham district. The line was strongly opposed by the proprietors of the proposed collieries, PDL, who stated that they were perfectly capable of making their own arrangements for the transport of their coal and that the proposed line would place a prohibitive price on the carriage of coal in the district. As an alternative they were prepared to consider turning the coal into electricity at the pit and transmitting it as power to London. In the face of such strong opposition from the line's main potential customer the Minister of Transport had little choice but to refuse the application.

The application for the Wingham & Adisham Light Railway was only one of three applications made by the railway to the Ministry of Transport in 1923. The other two applications were not for additional lines but for extensions of time in respect of applications already authorised. The first, made in August, was for extensions of time for Lines 11, 12, 18, 19, 20, 22, 23, 24, 26 and 28 and the second, made in October, was for extensions of time for Lines 15 and 16. It will be noted that Line 13 from Guilford to Stonehall did not figure amongst the lines for which renewed powers were sought and that the company was still seriously contemplating Line 18 from Snowdown to Hammill, even though

Snowdown Colliery had been bought by Pearson & Dorman Long for £25,200 and was to be closed for refurbishment. The persistence with the powers for Line 23 from Coldred to Alkham may have been due to proposals then being made by Sir Percy Temple of the Southern Railway to build a Channel Tunnel. There certainly does not seem to have been any likelihood of collieries being sunk in the Alkham Valley at this date.

Both applications were strongly opposed by PDL and both were refused. The only consolation for the EKR was that the Minister of Transport was prepared to consider authorising an extension of time for the completion of Line 28 if extra time proved to be needed. The Minister also wished it to be known that his present decision would not preclude him from considering on their merits any further applications for extensions of time for works in progress that the EKR might make in the future. In the event a number of such extensions of time were granted.

Against this background of repeated setbacks the Directors obviously felt that economies should be made wherever possible. Since the railway was already being run with almost absolute economy only trifling savings were possible. Two such savings were the holding of the July Directors' meeting at Shepherdswell station, presumably in the office building, and the termination of Messrs Mathews' £150 pa secretarial contract in favour of the employment of a Mr W.H. Haslam at £75 pa. Neither experiment seems to have been particularly successful. Subsequent Directors' meetings were held at the Charing Cross Hotel and Mr Haslam only remained Secretary for seven months, a great relief for all students of the East Kent Light Railways who have attempted to decipher his handwriting.

At the meeting of the Directors on 16th August, 1923 Richmond Powell's vacant seat on the Board was filled by Mr Jeremiah MacVeagh who had long been associated with Stephens and was already a Director on the Shropshire & Montgomeryshire, the Kent & East Sussex and the Selsey Tramway. At the same meeting it was announced that the new address for the company's office was 15 Devonshire Square and hopes were expressed that the Richborough line might be completed by November. In the absence of any new source of finance it is not surprising that this somewhat optimistic aim was not fulfilled. The only new development in the remaining months of 1923 was hardly significant, the company's office moved again, this time to 81 Hamilton House, Bishopsgate.

The last months of 1923 must really be considered as the lowest point in the EKR's fortunes. PDL, now the dominant force in the coalfield, seemed determined to prevent any further development of the railway if it could not take it over. The Allied Companies, whose shareholdings in the EKR might have been expected to give them some incentive to help the railway out, had little interest in any sort of active role in the coalfield. Tilmanstone Colliery, the railway's main customer, was itself in financial difficulties. The Guilford & Waldershare Colliery Company, one of the few remaining friends of the railway, was marking time with work on the Guilford Colliery. Hopes of Schneider or any other new interest developing pits in the coalfield were becoming more and more remote. With both funds and powers running out the future of the EKR must have seemed bleak indeed.

Chapter Seven

On the Move Again -
1924-1927

If the years preceding 1924 had been years of desperation then those which followed saw the EKR achieving a degree of security. This security was achieved at the cost of much of the line's independence and, even more significantly, of much of its ambition. This is more evident in hindsight than would have appeared at the time. Given the financial circumstances of the country at large, and of the Kent coalfield in particular, it is a measure of this new realism that the EKR survived at all.

1924

> DIRECTORS' REPORT: The tonnage of coal carried shows a decrease on 1923 of 20,451 tons. This falling off is due to labour troubles at the colliery during July, and also to a breakdown of its machinery in November.

Despite the pessimistic note of the above extract the Directors were able to report that non-coal traffic was increasing and that real progress was being made with the Richborough line. Behind the scenes there was every prospect of financial salvation at last. The key to the changed fortunes of the EKR can be found in the Minutes of the first Directors' meeting of 1924 held on 17th January. Two items of business concerning the Southern Railway arose at this meeting. The first was an offer by the Southern to buy shares in the EKR. The Directors' reaction to this is not recorded although Stephens had previously expressed his opposition to such a move as being a form of 'suicide'. Caught between bankruptcy and the embrace of PDL it appears that the other Directors were less reluctant. Although there is no public record of the negotiations following the Southern's offer it is clear that discussions continued in earnest behind the scenes.

The second item was a report of the formal sealing of an agreement with the Southern for their consent to the bridge crossing the Deal to Minster branch at Richborough Castle and thus opening the way for the EKR to reach Stonar Wharf. Coupled with the fact that the EKR spent a considerable amount on the hiring of pile drivers during 1923 and 1924, it is clear that preparatory work on the construction of the bridges across the Southern and the River Stour can be dated to this period. Curiously we have been unable to trace any official record of the exact year of completion of these two bridges. From Richborough Castle Sidings to the level crossing on the Sandwich-Ramsgate Road was just over a mile yet from 1924 to 1928 the Annual Report to Shareholders regularly recited the statement: 'The construction of the line into Richborough Port has proceeded during the year under review, and is being continued'. Even on the EKR this must have been judged as slow progress!

February 1924 saw the appointment of a new Secretary, Mr H. Milner Willis. One of his first tasks was to record the agreement of the Directors to pay for the Application for the Wingham & Adisham Light Railway Order. This was a poor investment as May brought the decision of the Minister of Transport to reject the Application. Meanwhile the problem of the shares that Stephens had taken as security for payment of his fees continued to rumble on. In April it was provisionally agreed to pay Stephens £9,000 for his fees on condition that he return the 50,000 shares he was holding and then buy 25,000 shares for £5,000. Although this would have been a realistic price for the shares this agreement foundered on the fact that the company did not actually have £9,000 to pay Stephens.

Another long-standing issue to rear its head during the early months of 1924 was the question of the debts owed by the East Kent Contract & Financial Company and the wider question of untangling the last skeins of the relationship between the EKR and its erstwhile fellow companies of the Concessions Group. In March the Directors decided that the Contract company's debts could be ignored no longer and resolved to sue if these were not paid. In September the Contract company called a meeting of its creditors which Stephens attended on behalf of the Board. The way was being cleared for the liquidation of the Contract company.

In April it had also been resolved that the EKR should try to buy from Kent Coal Concessions '. . . the land at Eythorne on which the hut stands'. This presumably was one of the small station buildings at Eythorne and reflected the haphazard way in which different companies in the Concessions Group had acquired property on behalf of other companies in the Group. Since nothing further is heard of this matter it is to be presumed that this particular problem was resolved satisfactorily.

Less satisfactory was an attempt by the EKR to persuade St John's College, Cambridge, to accept a payment of compensation in debentures rather than cash. Mathews, as the railway's solicitor, reported the college's reply: 'They say that their clients are not disposed to accept Debenture Stock and their clients point out that the suggestion implied in the proposal appears to be that the Debenture Stock is of saleable value and if this be the case it would appear to be a simple course for the railway company to dispose of sufficient of the Stock to pay the balance due to the College'.

The final item of business formally recorded by the Directors in 1924, apart from the now customary payment of fees and income tax by the issue of shares, was the resignation of Henry Western Plumptre from the Board and the appointment of S.A. Parnwell in his place. This left Loring as the only survivor of the original Board convened by Arthur Burr. Parnwell had previously been Land Agent and Assistant to the General Manager of the Great Eastern Railway. He had originally trained as an auctioneer and valuer, skills that might have been seen as particularly appropriate to the EKR.

Meanwhile a number of significant developments had taken place in the locality. PDL had purchased Richborough Port but had exhausted much of its initial capital in doing so. There was still confident talk of steelworks, coal by-product plants and a host of other manufacturing projects; but the effective product of its enterprise at this date amounted to a wide range of mineral leases and freeholds, the colliery at Snowdown undergoing refurbishment, the colliery under construction at Betteshanger and an abandoned port with extensive but dilapidated facilities. Publicity material for the Port referred to export facilities, not only for coal from Chislet, Betteshanger and Tilmanstone but also for coal from Fleet and Woodnesborough. In a better economic atmosphere it is likely that these and other pits would have been sunk and that the steelworks would have been established but the prospects for heavy industry were far from promising at this time. Until Betteshanger and Snowdown began to provide a significant return on their investment it was imprudent to invest further.

At Tilmanstone Colliery progress was distinctly unpromising. The colliery was working but was handicapped by the makeshift equipment bequeathed to it by the Concessions Group. Government subsidies and compensation in the immediate post-war period had kept the colliery going and permitted some investment in new equipment, including what were claimed to be the first underground battery locomotives to be used in coal mining. Much more investment, however, was needed to bring the colliery up to a satisfactory standard. The colliery had increased its output in 1923 but the increase would have been greater if it had not struck a fault that took some months to negotiate. 1924 should have seen a further increase in output but a strike over pay closed the colliery during July and August and the eventual figures for the year were less than for 1923. Any decrease in coal production at Tilmanstone obviously reduced the revenue of the railway.

Perhaps the last word on the progress of the EKR in 1924 is to be found amongst the share price listings in *The Times* for 22nd October. EKR ordinary shares were being quoted at only 1s. 6d. but an asterisk alongside the quoted price indicated that in the paper's opinion this price represented '. . . an exceptional bargain'.

1925

DIRECTORS' REPORT: Your Directors have been engaged in negotiations during the past twelve months, in connection with the introduction of fresh Capital into the Undertaking. Up to the present however, the offers received have not been sufficiently attractive to warrant their submission to the Shareholders.

1925 began with a flurry of attention to the railway in the press. Similar articles appeared in the *Deal Mercury* and the *Kentish Observer* and at greater length in the *Iron & Coal Trades Review*. It would seem that various press releases by Stephens had initiated this attention which was very favourable to the railway. The articles are particularly interesting for the information that they give on the progress made on construction of the Richborough branch. The *Iron & Coal Trades Review* reported, 'Very little work remains to be done to make the connection between the present rail-head of the light railway and the port complete. The bridge over the River Stour has to be completed - not a very serious undertaking - and about half a mile of rails require to be ballasted on the Richborough side of the river; when this is done direct access will be established to the shipping wharves'. The version in the *Kentish Observer* stated that, '. . . rails are now laid to within a few yards of the Port lines' but added that the bridge still needed to be completed.

0-6-0 No. 6 waits at Shepherdswell with stock for the workmen's train to Tilmanstone.

0-6-0ST No. 2 still sporting its *Walton Park* nameplates ambles through the meadows on a generous right of way obviously purchased with double track in mind.

M. Lawson Finch Collection

These articles seem to have been intended to encourage greater support for the railway from PDL. The *Iron & Coal Trades Review* complained: 'It is difficult to understand why the East Kent Railway should meet with so much opposition from the present coal interests, for they cannot surely contemplate with any satisfaction such a restriction of its legitimate activities as would ultimately result in something like a monopoly of the coal traffic being secured by the Southern Railway'. PDL was unimpressed by these arguments which it preserved in a file of cuttings relating to the railway. This file also contained the following letter to the *Dover Express* on 23rd October, 1925:

Dear Sir,
I think the sooner the managers of the East Kent Railway discard their old engine, the 'Walton Park', and put on the line an engine that can do the journey and up to time, the better it will be for all concerned. A month ago it missed the connection with the main line at Shepherdswell and passengers to Dover had to wait an hour for the next train ; on the return journey, with a struggle, it crawled to Wingham an hour and a quarter late, and above all, passengers to Wingham were invited to walk from Staple as he could not keep up his steam. The climax came last Saturday night when the 'Walton Park' could not do the journey at all and the passengers home were conveyed by motor car. No blame is attached to the officials, who do all they can to run to time, and are very courteous.
A Supporter of the Local Line

The major event of 1925 was the official opening to passenger traffic of the section of Railway 1 from Eastry to Sandwich Road and of the section of Railway 2 from Wingham Colliery Halt to Wingham Canterbury Road. This followed an inspection of these two sections by Lt Col A.H.L. Mount whose report follows:

I have the honour to report for the information of the Minister of Transport that, in compliance with the instructions contained in the Minute of the 20th February, I made an inspection on the 3rd instant of portions of Railways Nos. 1 and 2 authorised by the East Kent Light Railways Order 1911, as follows:

Railway No. 1, length 2 m. 29.95 chs., running in a northerly direction from Eastry Junction to the Ash-Sandwich Road Level Crossing,
Railway No. 2, length 64.5 chs., running in a westerly direction, in extension of the section reported upon on 27.9.16.
The first named section has, I understand, been worked as a mineral line for nine or ten years (1) and a portion of the latter section for six or seven years (2). The ruling gradient is 1 in 40 and the sharpest curve has a radius of 15 chains.
2. The rails vary in weight but are not less than 60 lbs. per yard and are flat-footed. They are dog-spiked to sleepers measuring 9' x 9' x 4½". The ballast is colliery refuse, which has also been extensively used in the embankments (3). Up-keep in the past has been of a low standard and on certain portions of the sections inspected the permanent way was in bad order. This was particularly noticeable on Railway No. 2 in the neighbourhood of Tritton's Bank where straightening, lifting, packing, ballasting, and renewal of worn-out sleepers etc. are required. I understand that work here will be put in hand. Drainage, lifting and ballasting were in progress on Railway No. 1 and the works should be carried out to completion to include such sleeper renewals as may be necessary (4).
Neither section is at present fit for higher speed than 15 miles an hour and in respect of Tritton Bank, speed on this length and when approaching the bank should not exceed 10 miles an hour.

3. The line is fenced throughout with wire fencing [7 wires] with iron standards and oak straining posts. This or other suitable fencing is required at the level crossings on either side of Poison Cross Halt.

4. The only bridge (5) is one of three timber spans (centre span 18′ and side spans 12′) on the straight, carrying the line over a stream and diverted footpath at 5 m. 2 fur. point on Railway No. 2. Strutted double 12′ x 12′ rail bearers under each rail are supported upon four piers each comprised of two 12′ x 12′ uprights with cap and cill pieces. The transverse sleepers are secured to the rail bearers by 9′ spikes, a method suitable for a slow speed light railway, but it would have been preferable to have utilised screws instead of spikes. The bridge appeared to have sufficient strength under the test load of a six-coupled tender engine (9 ton axles) and passenger coach. The strut pieces of old sleepers require in some cases replacing and refitting. The hand-packed retaining walling on the Wingham side requires rebuilding as the bank here shows signs of slipping due to continual wet weather. Check rails should be provided with splayed ends and speed over the bridge limited to 10 miles an hour. It is approached from the Eastry direction upon a falling gradient of 1 in 40.

5. There are the following station halts at public road level crossings:

Railway No. 1
Poison Cross Halt (6), 6 m. 5.0 ch point. A platform 50′ x 6′ x 2′ 3″ high with a seat, name board, and two lamp-posts. The platform wall is of corrugated sheets and posts.

Woodnesborough Road Halt (7), 7 m. 22.50 ch. where similar facilities have been provided.

Ash Road Sandwich Halt (8), at the present terminus for passenger working, similar facilities with in addition a telephone for operating purposes.

Railway No. 2
Wingham Town Halt (9), platform 125′ x 6′ x 2′9″ high, the walling of brick, with a small shelter and booking office.

Wingham Station (10), at the present terminus for passenger working, a platform of 60′ x 6′ x 2′ 3″ high of corrugated sheets and posts.

A shelter and booking office with telephone have been provided.

An existing temporary platform [Wingham Colliery Halt (11)] at the commencement of the section under inspection requires slightly setting back at the Wingham end to provide adequate clearance.

6. The Company has extended the 'staff and ticket' system of working to the section between Eythorne and Eastry ; and proposes to work the two branches Eastry-Wingham, and Eastry-Sandwich under 'one engine, or two engines coupled together' system. I attach undertakings to this effect. (12).

7. Eastry Station, previously reported upon, has now been provided with a goods loop trapped at each end and equipped with home and starting signals for each direction relating to the main platform line. In addition a disc signal at the Sandwich end of the loop and a small semaphore at the Eythorne end are provided to control movements into the loop, the latter for running purposes, the intention if necessary being to admit goods trains from Eythorne direct into the loop.

The loop and junction points are fitted with economical facing point lock bars. The loop points and crossing at the Sandwich end require re-alignment. The lay-out of this lead is bad and the points require adjusting to gauge and line. The up home signals from the Wingham and Sandwich branches should be shifted 100 yards further out. A green spectacle is required in the latter. The down main and branch starting signals are carried on the same post but in the circumstances this arrangement may be accepted.

A ten-lever, second-hand ground frame has been installed at the Sandwich end of the station. It requires to be properly fixed on heavier timbers. The necessary locking in respect of the junction points has not been provided:

(a) No. 6 points reversed should lock No. 10 signal.
(b) No. 8 signal lever drawn should lock signal lever No. 2 and vice versa.
(c) The lock between No. 2 signal lever when drawn and No. 6 point lever is defective.
(d) Points and trap lever No. 5 drawn should lock No. 3 signal lever in the normal position.

A diagram showing lever numbers and the normal positions of the points should be provided in the cabin. The levers should be correctly lettered and the frame requires cleaning and oiling. Certain levers worked very stiffly.

8. The present terminals at Wingham and Sandwich are single line. Upon arrival trains will be drawn forward empty the engine being reversed at loops situated ahead in each case on sections open for goods traffic. (13)

In addition to the loop at Eastry the following single dead-end siding connections have been installed:

Railway No. 1:
Poison Cross goods yard, 6 m. 9 ch. The points are padlocked by key attached by chain to the Eastry-Sandwich staff.
Railway No. 2:
(a) Wingham Engineering Company's siding, 4 m. 6 fur. 1.5 ch.
(b) Wingham Station goods yard.

The points and traps of (a) and (b) are separately operated by hand levers controlled by the key on the staff. It would be preferable to fit the connection at Poison Cross in the same manner and to provide a staff for the Eastry-Sandwich section with relevant key fixed thereto.

9. Level Crossings

Railway No. 1. There are three public road crossings where cattle guards have been fitted. A fourth public road crossing No. 28, Ash Road Sandwich has been provided with double gates padlocked across the line, the key of which is attached to the train staff, the gates being operated by the guard (14). As I understand it has not been the practice to use the line after dark, red discs and lamps have not been provided. The former, however, should now be supplied to act as a warning to drivers during day time, and red lamps must be added to act as warning to rail and road traffic if and when the crossing is traversed after dark. There are also eleven occupation crossings, the gates of which are not capable of opening across the railway. One public footpath is provided with stiles.

Railway No. 2. There are three public road level crossings fitted with cattle guards, two private and one footway crossing.

The necessary warning boards upon the roads have been provided. Additional boards are desirable at Sessions House level crossing, Railway No. 2. Boards have also been erected to indicate the speed at which public road crossings should be approached and the restriction in this case should be 5 miles an hour. This speed should be indicated on the boards accordingly.

The cattle guards require extension and repair at Dam Bridge level crossing, Railway No. 2.

10. Subject to the speed restrictions mentioned, to the completion of the minor works referred to and the necessary permanent way signalling and interlocking alterations at Eastry, I recommend that approval be granted to the operation of these sections of single line light railway for passenger traffic on the methods of working indicated in the Undertakings attached.

Colonel Mount's report deserves comment on the points noted by bracketed numbers in the text as follows:

(1) This is one of the few official references to the Sandwich branch having been in use for goods traffic prior to 1925 and suggests that goods services had operated ever since the EKR had taken over the line in 1916. How much of the line had been available for traffic at first is open to question but the Railway Clearing House Map for 1920 certainly showed the line open as far as Sandwich Road. A note belatedly reporting the opening of the EKR in *Railway Gazette* in 1917 included Woodnesborough Road (the early name for Roman Road) and Sandwich Road amongst the Railway's stations which would indicate that both these stations had been open for goods traffic from the start.

(2) As has already been mentioned in Chapter 6 it is almost certain that passenger trains had been operating without authorisation to Wingham Town for some time.

(3) The use of colliery refuse as a construction material may have reduced costs but left the lines so constructed liable to catch fire from time to time.

(4) The poor track conditions attest to the fact that these sections had been open for some time. The fact that work was in progress at the time of Colonel Mount's visit suggests that the decision to open these sections to passenger traffic had been taken on the spur of the moment and that the inspection had not been expected to take place quite so quickly. There is no reference in the Directors' Minutes to any decision to seek approval to open these sections.

(5) This was the bridge by Dam Bridge level crossing and was subsequently replaced by a culvert surmounted by an embankment.

(6) Poison Cross Halt had previously been known as Eastry (Goods).

(7) Woodnesborough Road Halt does not actually seem to have carried this name and was instead opened as Roman Road Halt to avoid confusion with Woodnesborough Halt.

(8) Ash Road Sandwich Halt was actually opened as Sandwich Road even though it was located on Ash Road. Railways always seem to have had trouble knowing how to name stations that were not actually anywhere at all. A more accurate title would have been North Poulders (For Sandwich). A further cause for confusion was the fact that the highway named Ash Road was also known as Roman Road!

(9) Wingham Town Halt is credited with a shelter and booking office. The booking office was subsequently removed to Wingham Canterbury Road and a basic shelter put up in its place. There is no reference in the Report to the loop which had previously existed here, but this is not conclusive as there is no reference to the loop at Poison Cross which certainly did exist at this time and probably had done so since 1916.

(10) Wingham station subsequently became Wingham Canterbury Road.

(11) It is strange that Colonel Mount should refer to Wingham Colliery Halt as being a temporary platform. Wingham Colliery Halt remained open until passenger services ceased even though work on the colliery had stopped two years before the halt was opened! It should be added that the Colliery buildings were still extant in 1925 and there were hopes that the Colliery would be re-opened by PDL.

(12) Even with staff and ticket extended to Eastry there was still a short section beyond Eastry before the Wingham and Sandwich branches diverged. It is not clear from Colonel Mount's description whether it was intended that only one engine should be allowed to proceed anywhere beyond Eastry or whether it was intended that there could be one engine on the Wingham Branch and another on the Sandwich Branch. The Colonel's words suggest the latter. Common sense would suggest the former.

(13) At Sandwich Road there was a loop on the northern side of the level crossing but there is no evidence that a loop ever existed at Wingham Canterbury Road. Did somebody tell Colonel Mount that there was a loop which he failed to inspect and how did the locomotive on Colonel Mount's train reverse round its train without revealing the lack of a loop? We shall probably never know.

(14) The level crossing at Sandwich Road was the only one on the East Kent ever to be equipped with gates. Ironically the road signs on either side warned LEVEL CROSSING - NO GATES.

Services to Sandwich Road made their first appearance in the May 1925 edition of *Bradshaw*. It was a minimal service consisting of one Saturdays-only return trip by which the 3.10 pm train from Shepherdswell arriving at Eastry at 3.32 was extended to stop at Roman Road at 3.40 and terminated at Sandwich Road at 3.50. In the return direction it left Sandwich Road at 3.54, called at Roman Road at 4.04 and arrived back at Shepherdswell at 4.34. Trains were also advertised to stop at Poison Cross in both directions but no times were given. In July a Saturdays-only morning return trip was added to the timetable arriving at Sandwich Road at 10.25 am and departing at 10.28. At a later date trains also ran to Sandwich Road on Wednesdays. It might be questioned why the railway ever bothered to open the section to passenger traffic at all. The answer appears to be that the deposits that had been lodged as a guarantee that the line would be built could only be released by opening the line or abandoning it. Since it was still hoped to reach Richborough the line could hardly be abandoned and by opening this part at least it was possible to recover part of the deposit.

With two further sections of the EKR officially open the company now began to make up for lost time in respect of the other lines for which they had obtained powers. This took the form of the resumption of land purchases on the routes of the Stodmarsh (Railway 15) and Mongeham (Railway 11) Extensions. This may have been made possible by the appearance of a new investor in the affairs of the EKR, a Mr Edmund de Quincey, who purchased £10,000 debentures in February for £4,500. As the EKR only actually had 9,948 debentures available Stephens saved the day by lending the Railway 52 debentures of his own. Quincey's interest was presumably speculative rather than philanthropic and nothing further is heard of him but his cash must have been a welcome sight at this time.

Equally encouraging to the EKR were the results of a meeting attended by Stephens and Parnwell with Directors from PDL and the Chislet Colliery Company in July 1925. At this meeting it was agreed that PDL would withdraw its opposition to the construction of Line 11 and that the Chislet Colliery Company would withdraw its opposition to the construction of Line 15. In return the EKR would deviate both lines to the satisfaction of the other parties, would withdraw any claims to rights of support from them, would undertake to make no claims for compensation for damage against them and would agree '. . . not to interfere with the proposed private line of the Chislet Colliery Ltd from the Stodmarsh site to the Southern Railway'.

There had been plans to sink a colliery at Stodmarsh from the days of the Concessions Group and the Chislet Company had acquired the mineral rights here from PDL. However, it planned to transport the coal from this pit by a short branch of its own to the Southern rather than by the very roundabout route of the EKR. Despite the opposition of the Chislet Company, Stephens did not abandon hope of serving the Stodmarsh Colliery:

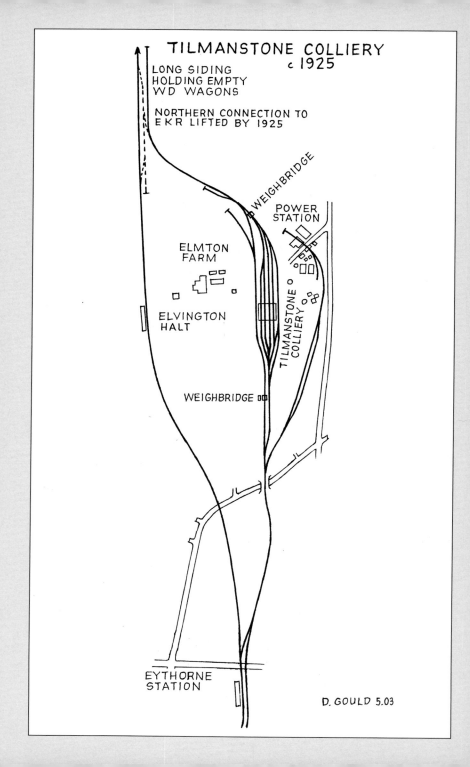

TILMANSTONE COLLIERY
c 1925

LONG SIDING
HOLDING EMPTY
WD WAGONS

NORTHERN CONNECTION TO
E KR LIFTED BY 1925

WEIGHBRIDGE

POWER
STATION

ELMTON
FARM

TILMANSTONE
COLLIERY

ELVINGTON
HALT

WEIGHBRIDGE

EYTHORNE
STATION

D. GOULD 5.03

With regard to Railway No. 15 previously proposed, Colonel Stephens pointed out that construction work had been carried already to a point within half a mile of the proposed colliery site, and he stated that he assumed that, if the new line met with the approval of the Chislet Company, they would raise no objection to his continuing the old No. 15 Line so as to afford a connection to the colliery, to be used by them or not as they desire. The Chislet Company expressed no objection to this proposal.

It is true that quite a lot of land had been purchased and fenced off along the route of Railway 15 and some minor earthworks had been carried out, but to say that construction work had reached to within half a mile of the colliery site was a considerable exaggeration.

The meeting concluded with agreement, as a basis for discussion, on proposed rates for the carriage of coal for PDL on the EKR. Although each party at the meeting could only agree in principle, and subject to the subsequent approval of their respective Boards, it is evident that relations between the railway and two of its more influential neighbours were improving. It is likely that this improvement was prompted by knowledge of the Southern Railway's interest in the East Kent but another explanation is possible. This was that events at Tilmanstone had led to the emergence of a new force in the Kent coalfield. With the status quo under threat erstwhile rivals might have felt that it was time to bury past differences and find common cause against the newcomer.

The 'newcomer' was no stranger to the coalfield, being none other than Mr Richard Tilden Smith. He had been one of the leading lights in the last years of the Dover Colliery, had been a Director and major shareholder in the Channel Steel Company, the predecessor of PDL, and had attempted to take over the East Kent Colliery Company as early as 1914. He had ceased to play an active part in the Kent coalfield during World War I and had transferred his attentions to South Wales and Burma instead. However, he had retained control over £30,000 in East Kent Colliery Company debentures and in February 1925 had used these debentures to have the colliery company placed into receivership. He had then formed the Tilmanstone (Kent) Collieries Limited which was now in the process of buying out the colliery from the Receiver.

Neither PDL nor the Chislet Company can have relished the prospect of a vigorous new competitor in the coalfield and it was popularly supposed that PDL had expected Tilmanstone to fall into its own hands eventually. For the EKR there was reason to believe that Tilden Smith would prove a far less compliant customer than the East Kent Colliery Company had been. For some time relations between Tilmanstone and Shepherdswell had been uneasy. The colliery had long complained that it was being over-charged for its coal traffic and that the railway company had defaulted on its hire purchase instalments for locomotive No. 4. For its part the railway had claimed that the colliery had defaulted on payments for the carriage of coal and had not met promised levels of traffic. There were also disputes between the two concerns over the ownership of land at Tilmanstone. The colliery's weak financial condition and the railway's dependence on the colliery for the bulk of its traffic had prevented these simmering disputes from ever reaching boiling point. This was now likely to change.

The appearance of a new player in the coalfield was matched by the first clear signs of the withdrawal of an old hand. In October 1925 the railway's Directors heard that East Kent Contract & Financial Limited was to go into liquidation. It remained to be seen what portion of its debts it would be able to pay as the Contract company had its own claims to make against Kent Coal Concessions, South Eastern Coalfield Extensions and the Extended Extension Limited.

In light of the above it was appropriate that 1925 should see the tangled history of the Kent coalfield receiving detailed attention with the publication of the East Kent Regional Planning Scheme Survey. This was a report by Patrick Abercrombie and John Archibald on the economic prospects for East Kent. The report had been commissioned by a joint committee of the various local authorities in East Kent to determine their town planning needs for the future. The survey began with a detailed account of the geography, geology and agriculture of the region. It then recounted the long story of the development of the Kent coalfield and its associated ironstone reserves. The coalfield was estimated as extending for 150 square miles on land with a further 50 square miles below the sea. It was considered that the coalfield contained 9,600,000,000 tons of coal.

Nine pitheads had been established in the coalfield: Dover, Tilmanstone, Guilford, Stonehall, Snowdown, Wingham, Chislet, Hammill and Betteshanger. Wingham and Hammill were dismissed as merely surface workings but it was felt that viable pits were either already open or could be developed at the other sites including Dover and Stonehall. In addition to these sites a further nine pits should be sunk to ensure proper exploitation of the coalfield. Adisham, Deal and Ripple were suggested as sites worthy of consideration.

Turning to transport facilities within the area the Survey briefly summarised the development of the EKR. Curiously the Survey reported that the East Kent had recently completed its link to Richborough. It is possible that Abercrombie and Archibald had confused the opening of the line as far as Sandwich Road with the actual completion of the whole line. It was to be some years yet before services to Richborough could commence.

The Survey also investigated the question of harbour facilities. These were considered to be of particular importance for the importation of Spanish iron ore for any steelworks that might be developed in the area. Despite the proven existence of iron ore in East Kent it was now expected that the cheaper and better quality Spanish ore would be used instead. Harbour sites existed at Reculver, Richborough, Deal and Dover. Reculver (Birchington) would require a deep water channel to be dredged. Richborough was only considered suitable for barge traffic, bigger ships would need to be loaded or off-loaded at sea. Deal would require a completely new port to be constructed and there was a risk of damage to its recreation value. Abercrombie and Archibald unreservedly recommended Dover as the best site for development. This must have disappointed both the EKR and PDL.

The conclusion of the Survey was that a population increase of 278,000 could be expected. Some of these would find homes in the existing towns and villages of the area but it was anticipated that some eight new towns or villages should be established. By careful zoning these could be located as advantageously as possible for access to the new pits and other industrial developments. The location of these new settlements should take account of existing road and rail facilities, including the EKR, although it was also suggested that an entirely new rail network could be developed in place of the East Kent!

How much attention the EKR paid to the Survey is uncertain. There is no reference to it in any of the company's reports or in the Directors' Minutes. Perhaps it was more sensible to see whether the various new pits and villages came to anything before making any definite plans. The existence of the Survey did, however, show that further development of the coalfield was still confidently expected. It was not just the EKR that had high hopes for the future.

There is evidence that the railway was making positive progress with the Richborough extension in 1925. PDL had purchased the strip of land across which the EKR was building an embankment linking its intended bridges over the Southern's Deal & Minster line and the River Stour. The embankment had encroached on PDL land and a long correspondence began in late 1925 between Stephens and Colonel Cobb, PDL's Estate Agent, over this issue. Stephens and Cobb appear to have got on well and the correspondence is spiced with such invitations as 'P.S. What about a chop and chat at the R.A.C. 1.40 Friday?'

Before concluding this account of the events of 1925 mention must be made of one curious event. An Extraordinary General Meeting, held after the Annual General Meeting of 4th August, gave the Directors power to renew the application for the East Kent Light Railways (Extensions) Order 1914. This was the application for the Birchington Extension which the railway had asked to be suspended on the outbreak of the war. It had continued to be mentioned from time to time as a possible alternative to Richborough, but it is strange to find it being given serious consideration at a time when the connection to Richborough seemed at last to be in sight. As the Directors did not actually renew the Birchington application we do not know what sort of case they might have made for it. Quite possibly the Regional Survey's dismissal of Reculver as a potential harbour ended the railway's interest in Birchington.

1926

DIRECTORS' REPORT: The large decrease in the net receipts is due to the General and Coal Strikes, in consequence of which, Tilmanstone Colliery was shut down from May 1st to November 15th 1926.

The first event of note in what was to prove to be an eventful year was the delivery of an additional locomotive. This was No. 7, an ex-LSWR 0-6-0ST, which had been purchased from the Southern Railway in 1925 but which had required overhaul before delivery. 1926 also saw the acquisition of two additional carriages, ex-LCDR six-wheeled vehicles.

These additional items of stock do not appear in the Minutes of the Directors' Meetings. The first Meeting of 1926 took place in February and started with the appointment of Mr Alex Parkes of Moorgate Station Chambers as the railway's Secretary; he was to remain with the railway until Nationalisation.

The Directors' main pre-occupation in the early months of 1926 was to receive and consider the terms now offered by the Southern Railway for making a

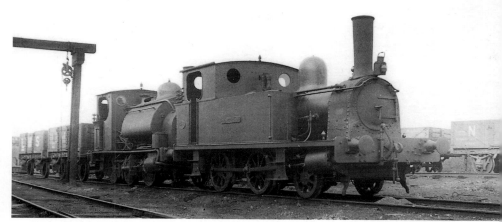

Kent & East Sussex Railway No. 2 *Northiam* and EKR 0-6-0ST No. 1 sidelined at Shepherdswell on 14th May, 1927.

H.C. Casserley

0-6-0ST No. 7 takes water at Woodnesborough. The water tank and its attendant ladder appear to have been constructed 'in house'.

major investment in the EKR. At their Meeting on 26th March the Directors heard from Loring that the company's debts amounted to £49,176 which could only be discharged by coming to an agreement with the Southern. The Southern was offering to take up 220,000 shares at 4s. each, an investment of £44,000, in return for which it would expect to appoint three of the company's five Directors. Holman Stephens had already announced his willingness to step down from the Board and Loring invited the two most recently appointed Directors, MacVeagh and Parnwell, to surrender their seats in the interests of the company. To soften this blow the Southern was offering an *ex gratia* payment of £320 to each of the retiring Directors. As a token of their serious intention the Southern was prepared to invest £20,000 immediately by taking up 100,000 shares at 4s. each. The Directors had no hesitation in agreeing to issue the necessary number of shares.

Certain incidental matters remained to be settled. The Southern insisted that the 100,000 shares that they were to buy should include the 50,000 shares held as security by Stephens. Stephens agreed to surrender these shares as soon as the company discharged its debts to him. These debts then stood at £14,385. Stephens was prepared to accept 8,800 debentures in settlement of £6,600 with the remaining £7,785 in cash. Similarly Mathews would accept 1,666 debentures to discharge £1,250 owed to him for legal services. The Southern was not prepared to be quite so generous as it required 14,009 debentures in settlement of a £7,004 debt owed to it by the company. Finally the Directors hoped that Stephens, MacVeagh and Parnwell should not have to surrender their seats on the Board until 1927 and that Parnwell should be appointed as Surveyor for the company in any future works.

The eventual details of the agreement with the Southern worked out somewhat differently. The eventual shareholding of the Southern Railway was 190,000 shares purchased at 5s. each. The reason for the higher price was that under its Light Railway Orders the EKR was only able to issue debentures in the proportion of one debenture for every two shares sold. Since most EKR shares had been sold at a considerable discount the question had arisen as to whether shares sold for less than their face value could be counted for the purpose of enabling the railway to issue debentures. For some time legal advice on this point was divided between those advising that shares sold for at least 5s. could be counted for this purpose and those advising that shares sold for less than 6s. 8d. did not qualify. Although the question was eventually decided in favour of 5s. this division of opinion meant that the company could not safely issue further debentures until the matter was resolved. The result was that there were insufficient debentures to satisfy the various settlements that had been agreed. Once again Holman Stephens came to the rescue. Not only did he defer his own claim for 8,800 debentures but he also lent the company the 1,666 debentures needed to meet Mathews' account and a further 3,906 debentures to make up the 14,009 debentures due to the Southern Railway. Stephens did at least get his payment of £7,785 in cash. Another consolation for Stephens was that the Southern investment enabled the EKR to pay off its debts to two of his other railways: £148 to the Hundred of Manhood & Selsey Tramway and £2,666 to the Kent & East Sussex Railway.

One disappointment of the final arrangements with the Southern was that it was not prepared to allow Stephens, MacVeagh and Parnwell to remain as Directors until the end of the year. Accordingly these three resigned as from the 19th August, 1926 and their places were taken by Sir Francis Dent, Sir George Loyd Courthope and Major Gilbert Savil Szlumper. The three new Directors had much to offer. Courthope was a Director of the Southern Railway and was also to become a Director of the Kent & East Sussex Railway. Dent had been General Manager of the South Eastern & Chatham Railway, had served on the Railway Executive Committee (REC) during World War I and was now also a Director of the Southern Railway. Szlumper, a personal friend of Stephens, had also served on the REC and, having led the London & South Western Railway's Docks & Marine Department, had taken a similar role with the Southern Railway and had subsequently taken on the role of Assistant General Manager of the Southern Railway. Quite how much time these three ever had to devote to the affairs of the East Kent is debatable but their status certainly added to the prestige of the EKR and gave it some influence with its larger neighbour. In practice the running of the railway remained very much in the hands of Holman Stephens who retained his position as General Manager and Locomotive Superintendent despite losing his seat as a Director. The two remaining Directors, Loring, who remained Chairman, and Vesey, were used to working with Stephens and there seems to have been no serious attempt to interfere in his management of the line.

A typical example of Stephens' particular methods of running his railways was the employment of internal combustion passenger railmotors. During 1926 Stephens seems to have intended to procure a Ford back-to-back unit for the

Ford railmotor on the Derwent Valley Light Railway which Stephens hoped to buy for the EKR.

EKR as he entered into correspondence with the Derwent Valley Light Railway at York which was proposing to sell its Ford railmotor set. His enquiries came too late as negotiations were already in hand to sell this set to the County Donegal Railway. Whilst the acquisition of this set would undoubtedly have cut the costs of providing a passenger service to Wingham, it would also probably have accelerated the decline in EKR passenger figures. The units operating on his other lines were renowned for their noise, vibrations and fumes.

The EKR was not alone in obtaining a substantial injection of capital in 1926. In February PDL obtained a Treasury guarantee of £2,000,000 under the Trade Facilities Acts 1921-25. These Acts had been passed to relieve unemployment by guaranteeing loans raised by industrial firms for capital investment using British manufactured goods. PDL would issue debentures to the value of £2,000,000 on which the Treasury would guarantee repayment of both capital and interest should PDL default on payment. The money would be used to complete Snowdown and Betteshanger Collieries, to equip Richborough Port for the export of coal and to build a power station and repair workshops there, to provide subsidised housing for miners, to buy wagons and to build coke ovens and a coal by-products plant.

As a result of fierce criticism in Parliament the agreement between the Treasury and PDL was amended in March. The revised agreement required PDL '. . . to employ suitable miners who have been thrown out of work through other pits closing down'. Although many of the skilled miners in the Kent coalfield had come there from other mining areas the bulk of the unskilled labour force had been recruited locally. The terms of the Treasury guarantee now created work in Kent for unemployed mine workers from all over the country and gave the Kent collieries a uniquely cosmopolitan character. Although the agreement only applied to the PDL collieries it was followed by the Mining Industry Act 1926 which restricted the engagement of adult mine workers to men who were employed in the industry prior to April 1926. This brought Chislet and Tilmanstone under the same rules as Snowdown and Betteshanger.

Amongst all these developments it is surprising to find no reference amongst the Directors' Minutes to the major historical event of 1926, the outbreak of the General Strike and the very much longer Coal Strike. Union membership had always been strongly discouraged on Holman Stephens' railways and there is no record of strike action taking place on the EKR but Tilmanstone, along with the rest of the British coal industry, was very seriously affected. The General Strike itself began on 4th May and was called off on 12th May. Tilmanstone was already on strike on 1st May and remained on strike until November. Tilden Smith made a virtue of necessity and used this period to carry out a programme of refurbishment at the colliery, as well as extending the miner's village at Elvington and improving the miners' hostel accommodation at Elvington Court. Tilden Smith seems to have intended to maintain better relations with his employees than were generally to be found in the coal industry, a policy Arthur Burr would have approved. This may explain why the Tilmanstone miners allowed safety work to continue throughout the Strike, including the mining of sufficient coal to keep the pumps going.

Locomotive sidings and shed at Shepherdswell c. 1926.

For the miners at Tilmanstone and the other Kent pits there was perhaps less extreme hardship during the Strike than in the other coalfields. Eastry Rural District Council made work available for 50 of the Tilmanstone men for some weeks and there seems to have been a certain amount of work available in agriculture and elsewhere to mitigate the poverty of this period. Life for the miners during the Strike was far from comfortable, but in absolute terms the wretched conditions found in the Midlands, South Wales and the North East were avoided.

The Strike led to a substantial decrease in EKR traffic. The railway carried 130,055 tons less in 1926 than in 1925 and its net receipts were only £318 1s. 1d. compared with £2,824 3s. 9d. for the previous year. This setback does not, however, seem to have dented the railway's new confidence. An Extraordinary General Meeting, held on 8th August, approved an application to the Ministry of Transport for the East Kent Light Railways (Extensions & General Powers) Order 1926. Since this application was not actually made until 1927 we shall consider its details and progress later.

An important step towards realising the powers previously granted to the railway was taken in October when the company purchased Sholden Lodge on the course of Railway 19. It may be recalled that the original approval of Railways 18-28 had been delayed by the Light Railway Commissioners' insistence that Railway 19 cut directly through the village of Sholden rather than interfering with the amenities of Hull Place. This direct route not only cut through the village but also through the grounds of Sholden Lodge. Mr Elgar, the owner of Sholden Lodge, had objected to the railway passing so close to his property and his objections could only be met by purchasing the whole of his estate amounting to six acres, five cottages and the Lodge itself. The price paid was £4,000. Since the railway only needed two acres of this land they intended to sell off the remaining land for building and to sell or let the Lodge and the cottages.

The re-opening of Tilmanstone Colliery on 15th November was almost immediately followed by a development which threatened to take much of the colliery's traffic away from the railway. On the 19th November a statutory advertisement was published announcing the intention of Tilmanstone (Kent) Collieries to apply for authority to construct an aerial ropeway to carry coal directly from Tilmanstone to Dover. Tilden Smith intended that a substantial part of Tilmanstone's output should go for export. This was a highly competitive market in which Kent coal had been disadvantaged by the low prices charged by collieries in the North East. These were able to offer small coal cheaply because of the higher prices they were able to charge on the home market for their large coals. The friable nature of Kent coal meant that small coal made up a much larger proportion of its production and could not therefore be sold at a similar discount. Shorter transport distances enabled Kent coal to remain competitive in much of South East England, notably to the paper and cement industries. However, for the very short distance between Tilmanstone and Dover the colliery had to pay what it considered to be an unreasonably high minimum rate to both the EKR and the Southern. This prevented it from matching the low export prices that the North East could afford to charge. Tilden Smith hoped to solve this problem by building the ropeway.

The chimney of Woodnesborough Colliery is felled to make way for the new Hammill Brickworks. No sinking had ever taken place at this 'colliery'.   *G.V. Parker*

The Hammill Brickworks, under construction, promises traffic for the long unused track of Railway No. 14.   *G.V. Parker*

The ropeway was discussed by the Dover Rural District Council on 14th October. A report in the *Dover & County Chronicle* for 16th October gave details of the proposed route and the Council Surveyor's description of the ropeway itself:

> The aerial ropeway will consist of two lines of wires carried by means of a series of standards approximately 120 yards apart. The standards will consist of a plane pole of ferro-concrete, or steel, and it is proposed to train vines or other plants to be grown up the standards with a view to making the standards an attraction to the countryside. The sizes of these standards is not stated, but I assume they will require to be substantial . . . The bucket, or carrier, will, I understand hold about 10 cwt., and will be covered, and when the system is in full working order it will be capable of transporting 200 tons of coal per hour. The ropeway will be worked by motor. No definite reply could be given to my question whether the ropeway would be worked on Sundays. As regards overhead clearance, the height shown on the plan is 18 feet, which I think the Council will consider is sufficient.

Such a ropeway would pose a considerable threat to the livelihood of the EKR. Although the railway still hoped for further collieries to be opened along its length and for sinking to be resumed at Guilford there was no escaping the fact that the bulk of its revenue came from Tilmanstone and was likely to do so for some time to come. The prospect of up to 200 tons an hour travelling along the ropeway instead of by train could not be accepted lightly and the company began to prepare its case for opposing construction of the ropeway. The hearings did not, however, take place until 1927 and will be considered later.

Mention has been made of hopes for further collieries. Despite the Coal Strike, Pearson & Dorman Long made at least one significant purchase of land for this purpose in 1926. Where Railway 2 should originally have joined Railway 1 by a connection facing Richborough it had been built with a Shepherdswell-facing connection joining Line 1 just outside the station at Eastry. The railway had bought the land for the Richborough-facing connection and pegged out the route for this only to find that PDL had purchased the triangle of land contained by this unbuilt section and the tracks of Railways 1 and 2 as laid. They had purchased a large site to the north of this triangle where they intended to build a new Woodnesborough Colliery, but until work began on this they were concerned that their tenants whose lands would be enclosed by the triangular junction should be able to get to their land by a level crossing. The correspondence between Stephens and Cobb begun in 1925 was now augmented by discussion of where the level crossing should be located. The railway began earthworks for the Richborough-facing connection in 1926 but these were never completed and the new Woodnesborough Colliery was never built. The site was eventually inherited by the National Coal Board and sold by them for agricultural use in about 1951. Coincidentally, the site at Hammill where the original Woodnesborough Colliery had been located promised to provide traffic of quite a different sort for the railway in 1926. The site and the colliery buildings had been purchased by the Hammill Brick Company, who not only developed their brickworks in the colliery buildings at the end of Line 14 but also laid a short narrow gauge railway across the fields to their claypits. The brickworks, which actually opened in June

1927, hardly generated the volume of traffic that a colliery would have provided but did require coal to be delivered regularly. Staff recollect three or four 10 ton trucks of coal being delivered each week, usually by *Walton Park*. Some loads of bricks also left the works by rail but in general the brickworks distributed its products by road directly to its customers' building sites.

1927

BRIEF FOR ROPEWAY PUBLIC HEARINGS: The Railway Co. have constantly run special trips to oblige the Colliery Co. at the nominal price of 42s. per trip so that the Colliery Co. should not be kept waiting for wagons, in fact during the whole time the Railway Co. has been opened the Colliery Co. have never been kept waiting for any reason which the Railway Co. could prevent.

On 20th January, 1927 the Directors heard that the railway was to receive a first dividend of £5,250 from the liquidation of East Kent Contract & Financial. This represented a payment of 1s. for every £1 of the £105,000 that the railway was owed. At the same meeting the Directors agreed to invest £17,000 of the Southern Railway's share purchase in 4½ per cent Treasury Bonds. Presumably the Directors intended this as a temporary measure while they sought authority to renew their existing powers and obtained powers for additional extensions. It must certainly have been a novel experience to have money to invest. It should be noted that these capital funds could not be used to discharge the railway's obligations to its debenture holders. The Scheme of Arrangement continued by which the debenture holders' interest payments were to be paid partly out of revenue and partly in shares. In 1927 the 5 per cent interest was paid as 1 per cent in cash and 4 per cent in shares.

A major pre-occupation for the Directors in the early part of 1927 was the application by Tilden Smith to build the ropeway from Tilmanstone to Dover. The main justification argued for the ropeway was the high cost of rail transport for which it was alleged the EKR was charging 1s. 1d. per ton. The railway's reply was that 2d. of this was not for carriage at all but for '. . . internal services provided by the Railway Co. for the Colliery Co.', that they were in fact entitled to charge 2s. per ton, and that they would be only too happy to carry coal at 9d. per ton if only the colliery would guarantee 1,000 tons of export traffic per week with bigger discounts for larger quantities.

Tilden Smith further claimed that the railway was incapable of carrying coal in the quantities that he anticipated the colliery would be producing. The railway replied that until Guilford Colliery started to produce coal the 2½ mile Guilford branch could be used to accommodate as many empty wagons as Tilmanstone was ever likely to need. The existing junction with the Southern at Shepherdswell was admitted to be incapable of handling any serious increase in coal traffic but the earthworks for Railway 10 were complete and could provide a much higher capacity junction with the Southern as well as extensive marshalling facilities. A signal box had been installed by the Southern to control this junction and it would prove a straightforward matter to lay the necessary tracks.

The railway had other objections. The ropeway would cross its projected Railway 11. The EKR already owned the land at this point and had fenced it in preparation for laying the line. Powers for Railway 11 did not expire until 1928 and the railway was currently in the process of renewing the powers for the onward extension to Deal by way of Railway 19. Whilst the EKR was entitled to object to the ropeway crossing its land the nature of its objection is unclear. Equally debatable was its claim that Dover was an unsuitable port for coal exports on account of the '. . . strong south-westerly winds'. The EKR considered that Richborough would prove a much better port for this traffic.

The Railway & Canal Commission did in fact reject Tilden Smith's application to build the ropeway on 8th April but not on the grounds put forward by the railway. The Commission agreed that the ropeway was feasible and might even be desirable but Tilden Smith's plans were incomplete and his estimates were '. . . inaccurate and illusory'. Tilden Smith was ordered to pay the costs of the EKR, the Southern Railway and the various other objectors, including the Channel Steel Company of which he had once been a Director. Undaunted, Tilden Smith put in a new and more complete application on 26th July. On 20th October the Commission granted his application. An appeal was lodged against the Commission's decision but on 15th December the Court of Appeal found in favour of Tilden Smith. By the end of the year construction of the ropeway had begun.

October 1927 may have seen the railway defeated on the matter of the ropeway but this did little to dampen its general ambitions. The same month saw the appearance of the statutory advertisements for an application for the East Kent Light Railways (Extensions and General Powers) Order. This was a wide-ranging proposal which began with the renewal of the railway's powers for compulsory purchase and completion of works on Railways 1, 2, 4, 8, 9, 10, 19 and 20 and for parts of Railways 11, 15, 22 and 28. Authority was sought to abandon those parts of these latter lines for which no renewal of powers was sought. Authority was also sought to abandon the opening bridge over the Stour at Richborough and to replace it by a fixed bridge. A miscellaneous collection of provisions was then proposed: the railway should be allowed to run 'motor vehicles' on its lines; the railway should be granted powers to run omnibus services 'between any points in the County of Kent'; funds deposited to guarantee various lines should now be released; the railway's capital and borrowing powers should be increased; and the Southern Railway should be specifically authorised to invest in the railway. Finally eight new Lines were proposed as follows:

Railway No. 33 (2 miles 2 furlongs 2 chains) from Wingham to Wickhambreux.

Railway No. 34 (5 furlongs 2 chains) from Railway 1 between Roman Road and Sandwich Road Halts to a southward-facing junction with the Southern's Deal and Minster Branch.

Railway No. 35 (2 furlongs 0.5 chains) a northward-facing junction between Railway 34 and the Southern's Deal and Minster Branch.

Railway No. 36 (2 miles 0 furlongs 2.5 chains) from Railway 15 near Stodmarsh to a westward-facing junction with the Southern's Canterbury to Ramsgate Branch.

Deviation *Railway No. 37* (3 miles 6 furlongs 1 chain) replacing much of Railway 11 between Eythorne and Mongeham.

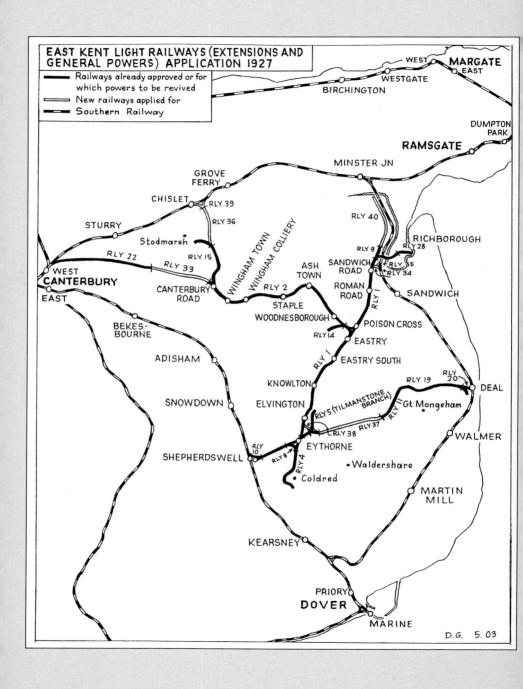

EAST KENT LIGHT RAILWAYS (EXTENSIONS AND GENERAL POWERS) APPLICATION 1927

Railways already approved or for which powers to be revived
New railways applied for
Southern Railway

D.G. 5.03

Railway No. 38 (3 furlongs 3.25 chains) a short line to create a northward-facing junction between Railway 37 and Railway 1 at Eythorne.

Railway No. 39 (2 furlongs 6 chains) a short line to create an eastward-facing junction between Railway 36 and the Southern's Canterbury to Ramsgate Branch.

Railway No. 40 (1 mile 5 furlongs 7 chains) an extension of Railway 9 running parallel to the Southern's Deal and Minster Branch to terminate on the bank of the River Stour.

The public hearings for the Application were not held until 1928 and final approval for a much modified version of the scheme was not granted until 1931 but some comment on the proposals seems appropriate at this stage.

The outstanding feature of the proposals was the abandonment of the railway's previous policy of attempting to guess where collieries might be sunk or to provide branches to sites that already had railway connections. No powers were sought to renew Railway 12 to Maydensole, Railway 13 to Stonehall, Railway 16 to Ripple, Railway 18 to Snowdown, Railways 23 and 24 to serve the Alkham Valley nor of Railway 26 to Telegraph Farm Brickworks which had long since closed. In place of these there was a return to the basic principles of the original Application of 1910. Railway 1 together with the completion of Railways 10 and 28 would provide a South-North axis from Shepherdswell to Stonar. Railways 34 and 35 would provide a substantial connection from Railway 1 to the Southern's Minster-Deal branch near Sandwich while Railway 40 would form an alternative access from Railway 1 to the banks of the Stour for barge-borne traffic.

Going East from Railway 1 at Eythorne Railway 37 would replace most of Railway 11 to provide an undulating but more direct alignment to Great Mongeham whence the renewal of powers for Railways 19 and 20 would ensure the connection to Deal. At Eythorne it was proposed to renew the powers for Railway 8, the Shepherdswell-facing connection from Railway 4 from Guilford to Railway 1, and to construct Railway 38 as an Eastry-facing connection to Railway 1 from Railway 37. Going West, the Richborough-facing connection to Railway 1 from Railway 2 at Eastry would be completed. Just beyond Wingham, Railway 33 would resume the course originally proposed for Railway 2 in 1910 and, with an end-on connection to Railway 22 at Wickhambreux, would complete a direct link to Canterbury. Railway 15 would be cut short at the chosen site for Stodmarsh Colliery and Railways 36 and 39 would provide links from Railway 15 to the Southern's Canterbury-Ramsgate branch. In the absence of a Stodmarsh-facing connection, traffic from the colliery would have to reverse on Railway 15 to make use of these.

If all these proposals had been approved and built the EKR would have neatly divided the main coalfield area with a network of lines to which any future colliery could easily be connected, together with a wide range of alternative connections to the Southern Railway and to the Stour for water-borne traffic. More insidiously, it would be difficult for any new colliery not to make use of the EKR, a point which was immediately apparent to many concerned with the coalfield.

Despite the General Strike and the impending construction of the Tilmanstone Ropeway, it can be seen that the railway had found a new confidence and expected to play an important and profitable role in a reinvigorated coalfield. These hopes would continue for some years to come.

The ropeway from Tilmanstone Colliery terminated on the quayside at Dover.

Colonel Stephens Railway Museum

Chapter Eight

Richborough at Last -
1928-1931

The period from 1928 to 1931 saw the expansion of the EKR to its greatest extent and the granting of powers for further extensions. The railway suffered some reverses during these years but the overall picture was one of victories achieved and further successes to come.

1928

DIRECTORS' REPORT: The construction of the line into Richborough Port has proceeded during the year under review and is being continued.

The railway was still confident that it was only a matter of time before further collieries were sunk. Proof that it was not only the railway that continued to believe this can be found in the publication of the final version of the East Kent Regional Survey. This largely confirmed its findings of 1925. It was now estimated that it would take 30 years to develop the coalfield fully and that 12 pits could satisfactorily achieve this. The erection by PDL of a 'new town' of 402 houses at Aylsham was reported on favourably as showing how best the influx of industries and their employees should be accommodated with least damage to the existing environment. The housing developments at Elvington by Tilden Smith earned some disapproval for the use of imported bricks and tiles. Railway enthusiasts are likely to disapprove in their turn of the description of the Tilmanstone Ropeway: '. . . not a thing of beauty (but for that matter, no railway can really be classed as such)'!

For the railway the main concern of 1928 was the progress of its Light Railway Order. Even before the Public Hearing there were lengthy negotiations with the Ministry of Transport. At first these concerned the vexed question of the railway's capital and borrowing powers for which the Ministry obtained counsel's opinion. The advice given to the Ministry was that shares could not be issued at a greater discount than 75 per cent but that any shares issued for at least 5s. would count as legitimately issued shares for the purpose of borrowing. As matters stood this meant that the railway could issue a £1 debenture for every two shares sold for at least 5s. But to complicate matters the railway was now seeking permission to issue one debenture for every share instead of for every two shares as previously authorised. The Ministry seem to have been somewhat doubtful of the legal advice they had received and had considerable reservations about the railway's debenture proposals. Apart from a general reluctance to authorise even more borrowing by a concern that was already unable to meet interest payments in actual cash, there was concern that considerable quantities of shares had been issued under Light Railway Orders for lines either not built or which had been abandoned completely. A compromise was eventually found but for some time the question of finance

A rare sighting of a potential passenger at Sandwich Road.   *A.W. Croughton*

The bridge over the Southern Railway and adjoining road to Richborough Castle under construction. The section over the railway has had its brick piers installed, but the section over the road still stands on temporary wooden trestles.   *M. Lawson Finch Collection*

posed very real questions as to whether any part of the Order might be granted at all.

The Ministry then had to determine how much of the work authorised by previous Orders had been completed. It was quickly established that nothing had been done, nor was any further authority sought, on Railways 12, 13, 16, 23, 24 or 26. Railway 14 had been partly completed to what was now the Hammill Brickworks and no authority was sought to complete the remainder. The powers for Railway 18 from Snowdown to Hammill had been renewed by the Minister until 30th June, 1928 but it was not now proposed to build this line. This was one of the lines for which renewal of powers had been turned down in 1923 but for which the Minister had subsequently granted an extension of time.

Varying degrees of success had been achieved with Railways 1, 2, 4, 5, 8, 9 and 10. Most of Railway 1 had been built and was in public operation between Shepherdswell and Sandwich Road. At Shepherdswell the junction with the Southern differed from that originally authorised but was within the limits of deviation. Beyond Sandwich Road the line was in use for goods and construction traffic as far as Richborough Castle. There is no reference to the bridge across the Stour although it is clear that some work had been done on Railway 1 from the further bank of the Stour to its junction with Line 28. This may mean that the bridge existed in at least temporary form. It was not intended to complete the final 2½ furlongs of Railway 1 as originally authorised in 1911 but the railway did not seek to abandon its powers for this section. This puzzled the Ministry. The railway's reason for not abandoning this section appears to have been that until PDL agreed to allow the railway access to the Stonar Wharf it would be unwise to give up the original planned terminus altogether.

Railway 2 was considered to be complete except for the Richborough-facing connection at Eastry for which an extension of time for completion was now sought. A closer examination of the original Light Railway Order would have shown that the end of the line at Wingham Canterbury Road actually fell short of its authorised length which should have continued to the junction with Railway 15 at the Wingham Parish Boundary. Railway 4 to Guilford Colliery was also complete if only for mineral traffic. Stephens admitted that it still required to be made into a permanent line but added that it '. . . would be finished in the process of development'. Quite what this was intended to mean is unclear. Had the Ministry actually inspected the line they would have found it to be practically derelict. Little if any traffic had passed over it since 1921 and much of the formation was overgrown or waterlogged by this date. Guilford Colliery had not yet been officially abandoned, however, and it was possible that the line might yet be needed.

Railway 5 to Tilmanstone Colliery had also been completed. The Ministry felt that it had gone considerably outside its limits of deviation but since it had done so to serve the colliery's needs and had aroused no opposition there was no need to take this matter up. Although not mentioned in the Ministry's files it seems that by this date the northern connection of Railway 5 to Railway 1 had been taken out. Access to Tilmanstone Colliery could now only be made from the junction at Eythorne.

Railway 8, the Shepherdswell-facing junction from Railway 4 to Railway 1, was reported to the Ministry by Stephens as '. . . rapidly approaching completion'. This would appear to have been Stephens' way of saying that some earthworks had been completed. There is evidence that some work was done on this junction line during the 1920s but it cannot have amounted to much. Stephens was quite safe in adding that Railway 8 would be opened when Railway 4 was '. . . open for passenger traffic'.

Stephens reported that Railway 9, originally authorised as a junction between the East Kent and the Deal-Minster branch at Richborough Castle, had been opened but only as a siding. The fact that the line petered out at the top of an embankment looking down on the Southern's lines seems to have escaped the Ministry's attention. It would have taken considerable excavation to bring Railway 9 down to the level of the Southern and would have created a sharply curved line on a stiff gradient. There is no evidence that a junction here had been seriously contemplated since 1917.

Railway 10, the high capacity junction to the Southern at Shepherdswell, could actually have had track laid on it without requiring too much additional work. It is believed that at least a single line of track was laid throughout its length at one time but had never been connected to the Southern's sidings. If this was so then much of this track must have been lifted subsequently, leaving only a long siding where spare goods wagons could be stored out of the way of traffic movements in the cramped environs of Shepherdswell Yard.

Progress on the remaining authorised lines for which powers were still sought was even more varied. Some parcels of land amounting to 1½ miles had been bought for Railway 11 (Eythorne to Great Mongeham) of which half a mile had been fenced but this land was mostly on a section that it was now proposed to abandon. On Railway 15 (Wingham to Wickhambreux via Stodmarsh) some 1¾ miles had been purchased. Most of this had been fenced and about 1½ miles of preliminary earthworks had been constructed. On Railway 19 (Great Mongeham to Deal) it appears that the only land purchased had been that at Sholden Lodge and nothing had been done towards acquiring land for Railway 20, the connection to the Southern. No land appears to have been purchased for Railway 22 (Wickhambreux to Canterbury) although it was subsequently claimed by Stephens that a site had been obtained for a station at Wickhambreux. Finally, Railway 28, the connection to the Stonar Wharf, still depended upon an agreement being reached with PDL.

As regards the new lines proposed the Ministry had little to say about Railway 33 (Wingham-Wickhambreux direct), Railways 34 and 35 (connections from Railway 1 to the Southern near Sandwich) or Railways 36 and 39 (connections from Railway 15 to the Southern near Chislet). Railway 37, the new alignment between Eythorne and Mongeham, was recognised as being more direct but would require embankments up to 28 feet high, cuttings 42 feet deep and a tunnel 88 yards long. Railway 38, the Richborough-facing connection to Railway 1 from Railway 37, would cross Railway 5 on the level and two roads by bridges. The Ministry considered that Stephens had under-estimated the cost of earthworks for this line at £199 12s. 0d. It would require 42,678 cubic yards of soil of which only 26,000 could be expected to be obtained from the excavations for Railway 37. Stephens probably intended the balance to be made up with mine spoil from Tilmanstone.

Railway 40 clearly perplexed the Ministry. Allegedly this was intended to extend Railway 9, with or without a connection to the Southern at Richborough Castle, alongside the Southern to the banks of the Stour. Correspondence between Stephens and Sir Herbert Walker of the Southern reveals that Stephens' intention was to prevent any colliery built to the west of Railway 40 from building its own connection to the Southern. The Directors' Minutes record that Walker advised against proceeding with Railway 40 and it was deleted from the Application.

A number of other objections had also been received. The War Department had let part of their cavalry training grounds at Fordwich on the course of Railway 22 to a golf club and wished to be indemnified against any claims the club might make against them. Canterbury City Council was now firmly opposed to any revival of Railway 22 and the interference it would occasion to their roads. Eastry Rural District Council felt that no further railways should be authorised in the area until the sites for new collieries had been fixed. Even then they doubted that the East Kent had the resources to serve such collieries: 'At the present time the proposed railways are entirely unnecessary for the needs of the district for passenger traffic or for the carriage of agricultural produce, minerals and merchandise. Provision for mineral traffic will be more satisfactorily provided by the colliery undertakings concerned'. The same point of view was expressed by PDL: 'Nothing more should be done to establish in the locality a concern which is financially unstable and is never likely to prove a real public facility'.

A considerable number of objections were received to granting the railway powers to run road omnibus services. These were led by the East Kent Roadcar Company in which the Southern had an interest. The railway accordingly withdrew this part of the Application. This relieved the Ministry from having to decide whether it was within the powers of the Light Railway Acts to grant such powers anyway. The East Kent Roadcar Company also strenuously objected to any new level crossings in the district and urged that all roads should be crossed by bridges. Many similar objections were received from local authorities in the area, the most strenuous appropriately coming from Bridge Rural District Council. The Ministry of Transport was generally reluctant to permit level crossings by this date and the following note of caution was expressed: 'Where the railway is now planned to traverse fields the future may see densely populated settlements whose residents will be gravely inconvenienced by the level crossings which today appear innocuous'.

It was against this background that the Public Enquiry into the Application opened on 19th April, 1928 at the County Hotel, Canterbury. Once again the circumstances in which the railway had originally been promoted were recited. This time the railway distanced itself from the memory of Arthur Burr and the other companies with which he had been associated. Instead much play was made of the investment made by the Southern Railway in the EKR and the majority role of the Southern on the railway's Board of Directors. With such backing it could not, '. . . be seriously urged that if these powers were granted the Light Railways Co. would not be in a position to implement the powers of raising the necessary capital and construct the proposed lines'. In case any doubts remained as to the interest of the Southern in the East Kent a letter from the Southern's General Manager, Sir Herbert Walker, was read out.

Having established the company's new financial strength it was also necessary to explain the failure of the railway to build the previously authorised lines. The argument put forward makes an excellent summary of the railway's troubled past:

> It would no doubt be urged against them by some of their opponents that since 1911 they had made but little headway. Nineteen and a half miles - something like one third - of the total mileage authorised: and that more rapid progress should have been made. In order to deal with that argument he asked them to think back over the events which had happened since 1911. Trade and commerce had been beset with extraordinary difficulties. Since abandoning their original Orders the country had been subjected to two railway strikes, four years of war, a General Strike, and two prolonged coal strikes, one of which lasted some seven months. In 1916 - in the middle of the War - the Co. succeeded in opening a very considerable mileage of the line for passenger traffic. It was a very considerable effort to have succeeded, in the middle of the War, to purchase railway stock when the Government were requisitioning it and securing the necessary labour to finish a very considerable mileage. It was a testimony to the Engineer and General Manager that he was able to do this at a time when other lines in other parts were being torn up and stock transported abroad.

Having heard evidence from various farmers in support of the Application, the rest of the day was spent hearing a variety of objections mostly on the subject of road crossings. Where level crossings were proposed the objectors wanted bridges built and where bridges were proposed the objectors wanted them built to more generous dimensions, lest the costs of future road widening fall upon the ratepayers. Stephens answered these objections as best he could but inevitably a degree of confusion overtook the proceedings as to which crossing was currently under consideration. Eastry Rural District Council avoided such confusion by accepting level crossings in general but asked that every level crossing in their area should be fitted with gates and served by a gatekeeper.

One potential topic for objection seems to have been avoided. A number of owners of mineral rights had lodged objections to the Application on the grounds that they would have to give rights of support [to avoid subsidence] to the railway and this would prevent them from exploiting their mineral rights. A flurry of agreements were made during April by which the railway agreed to waive its rights to support from these objectors. Not only did this avoid such objections but it also enabled Stephens to claim that these mineral owners clearly intended to develop collieries along the railway.

A good example of this sort of objection was that lodged by the Ecclesiastical Commissioners against Railway 33. This led to a substantial file of correspondence from which it appears that preliminary negotiations between the Commissioners and the railway had been proceeding since 1925. The Commissioners had been anxious to avoid the situation that had arisen with Railway 15 where the land purchased by the railway before the war had lain derelict since work ceased in 1914. They had therefore agreed in principle to allowing Railway 33 through their lands at Ickham provided that opening of the line through to Canterbury would proceed forthwith. However, upon receiving notice of the Application for the Light Railway Order they had been advised by their solicitors that this might prejudice the mineral rights which had been leased to Downs Collieries in 1922. There were also some objections to interference with a hop garden and a tar tank and a novel concern about one particular level crossing: 'The drainage of the public road will have to be watched when the Level Crossing is made as at present the Tenants stack their manure on the side of the road and there is a considerable quantity of foul water from this'.

The Ecclesiastical Commissioners therefore submitted a formal objection to the Minister of Transport. Their objection recited the problems the proposed railways would pose for their mineral rights and hop garden and suggested that Canterbury could be reached satisfactorily by Railway 15 and the proposed Railway 36 without having to build Railways 33 and 22. Even then they feared that the railway could not be relied upon to build the proposed lines.

Upon receiving these objections the railway entered into negotiations with the Commissioners. The end result was an agreement signed on 28th April, 1928 by which the railway gave up its rights to support under the Mines Facilities Act, agreed not to purchase any of the Commissioners' land until they could satisfy the Commissioners that they were in a position to construct Railways 33 and 22 and to open these simultaneously, agreed that if Railways 22 and 33 were not open within 3½ years of the granting of the Order they would abandon their powers to purchase the Commissioners' land and would make no further Application to the Minister to construct these or other lines on the Commissioners' lands without the Commissioners' prior consent. The Commissioners struck a hard bargain but at least their objections were withdrawn.

One potentially serious objection was averted with very much less difficulty. No objections were lodged against the River Stour being crossed by a fixed bridge rather than an opening bridge. Agreement to this had already been obtained from the Board of Trade, Sandwich Corporation and the East Kent River Commissioners. The matter does not seem to have been mentioned at the Public Enquiry at all.

The day drew to a close without having heard the objections of PDL so that it was necessary to adjourn the Enquiry. It resumed at the offices of the Ministry of Transport on 29th June, 1928. However, the railway had met with PDL in the interim and their differences had been resolved. It was the Southern's backing of the EKR that was the crucial factor in PDL's change of mind. No general objections would be lodged against the Application and the specific issue of access to the Stonar Wharf had finally been agreed. In theory it only remained for the Minister to authorise the EKR to lay its rails across the Sandwich to Ramsgate main road and the railway could finally reach its goal on the banks of the Stour. In practice the EKR had anticipated that such approval would be forthcoming and had already laid the crossing with rails borrowed from PDL. Fortunately the railway's optimism was justified and the crossing was allowed to remain. It is not

0-6-0ST No. 7 in the loop just beyond the Sandwich Road level crossing on 22nd September, 1928 with the ex-LSWR and Midland Railway six-wheelers.

0-6-0 No. 8 at Sandwich Road with the Pickering carriage No. 1. This view is dated 1932, but passenger services had ceased in 1928. Was this Lt Col Gore Vesey's annual inspection train perhaps?

clear how long it took to complete the remainder of Railway 28 but the first clear record of traffic going through to the Wharf does not occur until 1929.

The absence of objections from PDL did not mean that the adjourned hearing was without business. Some further discussion of level crossings took place. A bridge was being asked for at Wickhambreux, but Stephens argued that the land they had bought for a station there would be useless if they had to put the line up on an embankment to cross the road by a bridge. Whilst on the matter of land purchases Stephens reported that 80 per cent of the land for Railway 37 had now been bought. Although the Line had not yet been authorised they had made these purchases under the powers granted for Railway 11, which permitted the railway to go beyond the limits of deviation if the landowners agreed.

The matter of Stephens' estimates for constructing the new and revived lines was also raised. It was pointed out that his estimates were double those that had been authorised in the 1920 Order. Stephens replied that the estimates approved in 1920 had originally been made in 1913 and that this explained the discrepancy. One is forced to wonder what would have happened if the railway had attempted to build these lines in 1920 at 1913 prices? Stephens was also asked to explain why there had been no reduction in his estimates even though Railway 40 had been dropped from the Application. He answered that the saving that might have been made had been swallowed up by the cost of additional bridges to which the railway had agreed.

The final issue investigated was the vexed question of the capital powers sought by the railway. Stephens explained that they would need these powers on the basis that they only expected to get 5s. for each £1 share and only £80 for every £100 of debentures!

The net result of these deliberations was that the Ministry was prepared to revive the purchase and completion powers for the remaining portions of Railways 11, 15 and 22 and for Railways 19 and 20. If any extension of powers was needed for Railway 28 this would also be authorised. The period for completion for Railways 2, 4, 8, 9 and 10 would also be extended, the construction of the fixed bridge over the Stour would be confirmed and Railways 33 to 39 would be authorised. However, the Ministry insisted that eight proposed level crossings be replaced by bridges in addition to those to which the railway had already agreed. Additionally the Ministry reserved the right to require bridges to be built in place of level crossings if increased road traffic made this necessary in the future. The Ministry would also require further discussions with the railway over the means by which all of these works were to be financed. These requirements brought the progress of the Application to a standstill. The additional bridges would increase the cost of the new lines by £45,194 and this led the East Kent to a lengthy re-examination of their need for these lines. The discussions on finance were to occupy the railway and the Ministry for several years to come. It was not until 1931 that a much-modified Order was eventually granted. In the meantime the railway had to struggle on with its existing powers.

Even though the 1927 Application was obviously not going to be approved in 1928 it was clear to the railway that the Ministry believed that powers still existed for the completion of the extension to Richborough Port. Under these circumstances it is strange that the EKR should now choose to abandon the limited passenger service from Eastry to Sandwich Road. This ceased on 1st November, 1928 although, as the following account by A.P. Miall in *Railways* in February 1945 indicates, it had not always run even before that date:

> I made a journey over this line in October 1928, the train service then consisting of two trains only on Thursday and Saturday only. Apparently the train did not usually run beyond Eastry but I insisted on the booked journey being made. At the end of the month the train service was finally withdrawn though the stations were shown in *Bradshaw* up to 1939. The state of things on this branch was such that the train was propelled from Eastry to Sandwich Road of course without any 'pull and push' arrangement.

It would appear that the service to Sandwich Road was not so much abandoned as suspended. This would explain the continued appearance of the stations in *Bradshaw*. Despite the shortage of passengers on the branch it is clear that the railway originally intended to run passenger services all the way through to Richborough as they had constructed a passenger platform there. Stephens had written to Colonel Cobb on 23rd January, 1928 in connection with this, '. . . it seems to me that it might be useful to have a central Passenger Station at Richborough for future use, if the place develops'. Despite building this platform it seems that by October the railway saw no point in shuttling occasional empty carriages between Eastry and Sandwich Road until such time as Richborough developed.

The only other event of note in 1928 was the acquisition of a further 'O' class locomotive from the Southern. This locomotive, No. 8, arrived at Shepherdswell in September and seems to have been acquired as a result of the increasingly decrepit state of the existing locomotive fleet, rather than in preparation for any extension of the East Kent's mileage.

1929

> DIRECTORS' REPORT: The construction of the line into Richborough Port was completed and opened for traffic in the past year.

A formal agreement with PDL for the EKR to run trains through to the Stonar Wharf was signed on 29th December, 1928 and arrangements were subsequently made to convey the necessary lands to the railway. A new feature of this agreement was that the EKR would build its own entirely independent line to the wharf rather than simply connecting up to the existing lines laid by the War Department. After so many years of effort, not to mention so many years of paying rent for a wharf to which the railway had no access, this achievement was to prove to be an anti-climax. On the 18th April, 1929 it was reported to the Directors that freight traffic was now being carried into Richborough and on the 18th July it was reported that the first trainloads of coal from Snowdown Colliery were being carried to Richborough. By comparing the 1928 and 1929 figures for coal traffic onto the EKR, as opposed to that originating at Tilmanstone, it is possible to estimate that this Snowdown traffic amounted to about 17,000 tons in 1929. This would be a welcome addition to the line's revenue but hardly compares with the 294,447 tons from Tilmanstone. The Snowdown to Richborough traffic continued until 1931, diminished considerably in 1932, flourished at over 30,000 tons in 1933 and then seems to have petered out. In the opposite direction there were occasional loads of pit props for Tilmanstone and possibly also for Snowdown.

If it had not been for PDL's interest in both Snowdown Colliery and Richborough Port it is doubtful whether any serious traffic of any sort would have developed at this time. The railway had reached Richborough too late. With work progressing on the ropeway to Dover there was little prospect of Tilmanstone wanting to export its coal through Richborough. At Guilford Colliery, the other potential source of traffic for Richborough, the French management finally conceded defeat in 1929 by selling the colliery to Mr Tilden Smith, the proprietor of Tilmanstone Colliery. This at least enabled them to cancel the £3,200 pa contract for pit sinking with A. François which they had kept up since sinking ceased in 1921. Included in the purchase was Guilford's 3000 kw generator which was transferred to Tilmanstone. It is believed that large quantities of iron tubbing originally acquired from Wingham Colliery also went to Tilmanstone at this time. This was originally delivered to Wingham over the EKR, had been brought from Wingham to Guilford by the EKR and made its final journey to Tilmanstone by the same means. Some refurbishment must have been necessary on the Guilford branch to enable this traffic to be carried. It is clear that Tilden Smith had no immediate plans to resume sinking at Guilford.

This was not the only example of unusual traffic to occur in 1929. On 29th June the railway ran a number of special trains in connection with a Garden Fete held in the grounds of Eythorne Court. Special trains were advertised from Shepherdswell at 1.10, 1.30, 1.45 and at 2.30 if required with return journeys being run at 8.40, 8.55, 10.35 and 10.50. Similar special trains may have been run on other occasions but this is the only example that we have discovered in the local press.

The railway had received less welcome press attention in the preceding month. On 31st May the *Dover Express* had carried the following item:

SERIOUS ACCIDENT ON EAST KENT RAILWAY - A serious accident occurred on the East Kent Railway at Shepherdswell on Friday morning last week. George Rogers, aged 62, a married man living at Tilmanstone, who is employed by the railway company as a foreman platelayer, was crossing the line about 7 am when he was knocked down by the mineral train, and the engine and 21 trucks passed over his left leg, his body being in the four-foot way. His leg was practically severed below the knee, and after the damaged portion had been cut away by Doctor Bellamy, he was removed to the Dover Hospital in the Tilmanstone Colliery Ambulance. His leg was amputated and he is reported to be going on satisfactorily.

The railway caught the attention of the *Dover Express* again on the 5th July when the trial was reported of three youths caught trespassing on the line at Woodnesborough on 19th June. It may be suspected that the allotment holder who alerted the police to this criminal outrage was more concerned with the security of his allotment produce than with that of the railway. The youths were bound over for 12 months but a fourth who did not present himself for trial was fined five shillings. This was quite a rare example of a prosecution under the bye-laws of any of the Stephens' railways.

A fortnight later the same paper reported that Tilmanstone (Kent) Collieries were applying to the Railway and Canal Commission for an extension of time for the completion of the ropeway. By this date much of the work had been completed but delays had been experienced in cutting the tunnels through the cliffs at Dover. The extension of time was granted on 29th July.

1929 saw a revival of the question of the railway's debts to Stephens. After a complicated series of calculations by Alex Parkes, the Secretary, and Mr E.F. Marsh, the Accountant, it was believed that sufficient debentures could now be issued to Stephens to cover all the railway's debts to him. As a result £12,849 in debentures was issued to Stephens in July. No sooner had this been done than a mistake was discovered in the calculations and it became apparent that the railway had exceeded its borrowing powers and the issue had to be cancelled. Stephens seems to have accepted this reverse philosophically but it must have come as a disappointment at a time when he was helping out several of his other lines from his own pocket. Stephens had almost decided in June to give up the idea of payment in debentures if he had to pay income tax on them.

The East Kent attracted attention at the 1929 Annual General Meeting of the Southern Railway. A circular had been put out by one of the Southern's shareholders, Mr Gough, attacking Sir Herbert Walker and the Southern management for driving Tilmanstone Colliery into building its ropeway. Mr Gough claimed that mismanagement had lost the Southern 1½ million tons of coal traffic. The Southern was compared unfavourably with business enterprises like Harrods and Selfridges. Walker's reply was that the Southern could not charge less than 2s. a ton including payments to the East Kent and that the colliery had never managed to produce more than 300,000 tons a year anyway.

1929 also saw the expiration of the current scheme of Arrangement with the railway's debenture holders. A new scheme was proposed and approved by which the whole of the railway's net revenue each year would be applied to the payment of debenture interest with the remaining balance to be paid in ordinary shares. This Scheme was to run from January 1929 to December 1933. It can hardly be a coincidence that it was at this point that the railway began to set aside much larger sums for the renewal of rolling stock and permanent way each year. Not only did this substantially reduce the railway's net revenue but, since the sums set aside comfortably exceeded the actual expenditure on renewals, they also provided a source of funds to invest. Moreover the Income Tax payable on the railway's earnings set aside for these renewals was also charged against revenue. The amount of cash liable to be paid out as debenture interest was therefore significantly reduced.

Betteshanger Colliery finally entered production in 1929. Although this brought no traffic to the EKR it did show that there was still life in the Kent coalfield. It may also have prompted Tilden Smith to engage in proposals for amalgamating the collieries in the Kent coalfield. He had recently begun to buy heavily into gas companies in Kent and was developing a scheme to bring Chislet, Snowdown and Betteshanger together with Tilmanstone in an undertaking that would dominate coal and gas production in South East England. Not surprisingly PDL and the Chislet management had no time for these proposals. As a result Tilden Smith began an energetic campaign of lobbying at Westminster and it was while he was so engaged that he collapsed and died at the House of Commons in December. His was the first of a series of deaths that were to have a profound effect on the fortunes of the Kent coalfield and the railway.

1930

DIRECTORS' REPORT: The tonnage of coal carried shows a decrease of 42,676 tons and a reduction in earnings of £1,461. The Merchandise and Mineral Traffic shows an increase of 12,870 tons and an expansion in earnings of £883. The number of passengers carried has decreased by 25,181, and the earnings therefrom by £534.

Tilden Smith's death did not immediately alter the situation at Tilmanstone as the Court of Chancery permitted money from his estate, which had been placed in trust for his family, to be spent on developing Tilmanstone for a further seven years. The ropeway was officially opened on 7th February, 1930 and the first ship to be loaded was the *Corminster* which sailed the same day with 2,500 tons. The ropeway carried 65,000 tons in its first year of operation, somewhat less than its potential capacity of 1,000 tons a day.

The remaining mineral leases belonging to the Guilford and Waldershare Colliery were acquired by the Tilmanstone management in 1930 but more with a view to exploitation from Tilmanstone than with any apparent aim of resuming work on Guilford Colliery. The Depression was now in full flood and it was lucky for Tilmanstone that Tilden Smith's money was available to finance progress during this difficult period. Lucky too for the EKR; despite the opening of the ropeway some 247,762 tons of coal still left Tilmanstone by rail in 1930. An indication of the risks involved in the coal industry may be seen in the fact that the French proprietors of Guilford Colliery only got back 4½d. for every £1 they had invested.

One change in the railway's traffic in 1930 that cannot be blamed on the ropeway was the ending of workmen's services. These had hitherto been subsidised by Tilmanstone to the tune of £1 a day and despite the increasing availability of bus services in the area there had been no significant decrease in passengers, 22,473 workmen's tickets being issued in 1929. With the end of the workmen's trains much of the railway's passenger stock became redundant, but in the tradition of all of Stephens' railways no attempt was made to dispose of the surplus carriages which were simply left to vegetate at Shepherdswell.

One curious event of 1930 was a report to the Directors in July on the progress of the railway's claim against the Receiver of the East Kent Colliery Company, the previous proprietors of Tilmanstone. While this claim continued the East Kent Colliery Company could not be wound up, despite the fact that the colliery itself now belonged to the Tilmanstone (Kent) Colliery Company founded by Tilden Smith. This may not have seemed so curious in 1930 but was very peculiar indeed by 1945 when the company was finally liquidated.

0-6-0 No. 8 returning to Shepherdswell with a workmen's train. These trains were discontinued in 1930.

2-4-0T *Northiam* had been on hire from the Kent & East Sussex Railway since 1921. Here it is being given a thorough overhaul in 1930 before returning to its home line.

The EKR Directors would have been more concerned by two reports made to them at their October meeting. Driver Reuben Griffin had apparently driven a locomotive through the back of the engine shed on 6th August causing considerable damage, while a head-on collision between locomotives 7 and 8 at Shepherdswell two days later was blamed on fireman Merrick. In Stephens' absence his deputy, W.H. Austen, was instructed to warn both Griffin and Merrick that they would be discharged if there were any repetition of such conduct. The same meeting also accepted with regret the resignation of the Chairman, Arthur Loring, the last survivor of the original Board. Lt Col Gore Vesey was elected as the new Chairman. The meeting also closed the connection between the railway and the East Kent Contract & Financial Company. A final dividend of 3*d*. in the £1 was paid out by the Contract company which could now decently be laid to rest. The railway's share of this dividend came to £1,312 10*s*. 0*d*.

Stephens had recently been absent from a number of meetings. He had suffered a stroke early in 1930 which had left him slightly paralysed. A marked change can be seen in his signature on a letter dated 19th February and another dated 28th February. In a letter dated 10th March he explained the substitution of a rubber stamp for his signature: 'I have had a severe attack of neuritus, and cannot use my hand'. The subject of these letters was once again the debentures owed to him. Correspondence continued on this subject throughout the year but by September it had become clear that the issue of sufficient debentures could only be achieved by obtaining approval of the Light Railway Order applied for in 1927. This had in turn been delayed by Stephens' own poor health.

He suffered a second stroke in late Spring and in June was reported as, '. . . not being well enough to be consulted'. He spent six weeks in a London nursing home before discharging himself and going to Hastings to convalesce. During the Autumn he returned to his rooms at the Lord Warden Hotel at Dover but required virtually constant nursing as he was no longer able to feed or clothe himself. He had also lost the power of speech but despite these handicaps he made occasional visits to the EKR when employees would take him by car.

With little immediate prospect of new collieries being established it was agreed with the Southern in December to drop Railways 34 and 35 (the junctions with the Southern near Sandwich), Railways 36 and 39 (the junctions with the Southern near Chislet) and Railway 38 (the Eastry-facing connection between Lines 37 and 1 at Eythorne). Railways 33 (Wingham to Wickhambreux) and 37 (Eythorne to Mongeham) were still to be sought as were extensions of time for Railways 11 (the short portion of this at Mongeham), 15 (Wingham to Stodmarsh), 19 (Mongeham to Deal), 20 (junction with the Southern at Deal) and 22 (Wickhambreux to Canterbury). Since the junctions near Sandwich were to be dropped Stephens intended to complete Railway 9 as a junction with the Southern at Richborough Castle but did not include this in his revised estimate of costs. His revised estimate came to £242,868 compared with an original estimated cost of £298,125. In a letter to the Southern he anticipated that borrowing powers of £332,402 would be needed but, apparently on Southern advice, increased this to £340,000 in subsequent correspondence with the Ministry of Transport. The year closed with the revised Application awaiting the Ministry's decision.

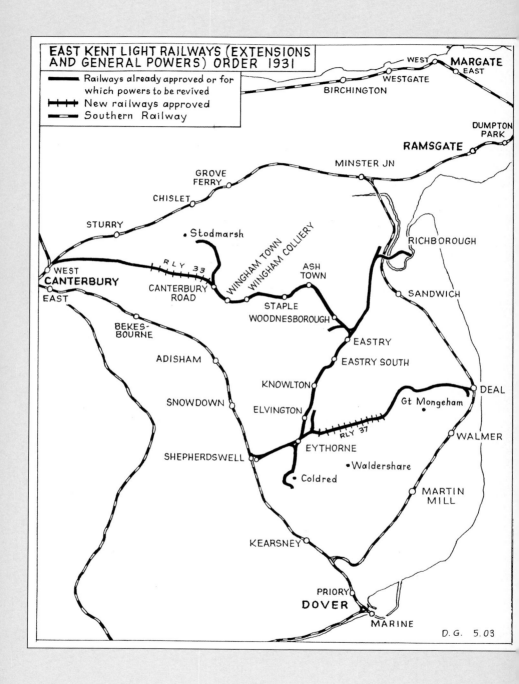

1931

DIRECTORS' REPORT: Economies have been effected in the working expenses totalling £1,950.

The year began with a further sign of Stephens' deteriorating health. Power of attorney to handle Stephens' financial affairs was granted on 17th January to J.A. Iggulden, another of Stephens' aides at Tonbridge. This seems to have occasioned some bad feeling between Austen and Iggulden as to who should do what during Stephens' illness. This was presumably the cause of the Directors recording their view, during their meeting on 26th February, that a power of attorney was insufficient to transfer responsibility for Stephens' duties on the railway.

The February meeting had two other consequences. The Directors authorised the expenditure of £2,050 on renewal of permanent way. This is the first such specific authorisation recorded. It should not be imagined that no such renewals had taken place before but it marked a more active policy of management on the part of the Directors who seem previously to have left all such matters to Stephens' discretion. The other significant matter for discussion was whether to discontinue the passenger traffic completely due to the 'great falling off' in 1930. Even allowing for the disappearance of the workmen's trains in 1929 ordinary passenger figures had dropped from 6,083 in 1929 to 3,375 in 1930. No immediate decision was made at the February meeting but it is clear that something would have to be done.

On 27th March the East Kent Light Railways (Extensions & General Powers) Order was finally granted. The extensions of time for Railways 11, 15, 19, 20 and 22 were agreed and new Railways 33 and 37 were approved. The fixed bridge over the Stour was sanctioned. New features in the Order were the omission of any mention of Railway 28, already open to freight traffic, and the formal abandonment of Railway 1 beyond its junction with Railway 28. Of greatest significance, however, were the financial powers contained in the Order. Instead of creating new powers specific to the Order the Ministry of Transport had simply set a ceiling of £250,000 to all new borrowing by the railway. This had the advantage of freeing the railway's borrowing powers from dependence on the number of shares sold. Moreover, the £250,000 was an actual cash ceiling rather than the face value of debentures that could be issued and so avoided the problem of guessing what actual price debentures might fetch. It was a practical solution for both the Ministry and the railway, though it might be doubted that it represented a sufficient sum to pay for the works proposed. There was, however, no immediate move on the part of the railway to make use of its newly authorised powers.

The granting of the Order did resolve one problem. Stephens could now be issued with debentures to the value of the railway's debt to him. As the following extract from a memorandum by E.F. Marsh, the railway's Accountant, shows, there seems to have been some urgency in this matter: 'In view of the state of Lt Col Stephens' health, and to avoid the possibility of the company having to pay, in certain eventualities, the above debt in hard cash, it appears desirable that a settlement of the debt due to him in respect of his Engineering Fees and Expenses, &c., in connection with Capital Works, &c., &c.,

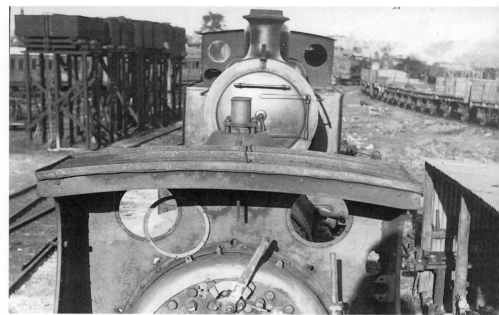

A view from the tender of locomotive No. 3, retired in Shepherdswell yard. Locomotive No. 4
isn't actually as tall as the view suggests but has been jacked up for repairs.

M. Lawson Finch Collection

A full view of No. 3 taken on the same day as the above. The original LSWR number, 394, is
showing through what remains of the paintwork.   *M. Lawson Finch Collection*

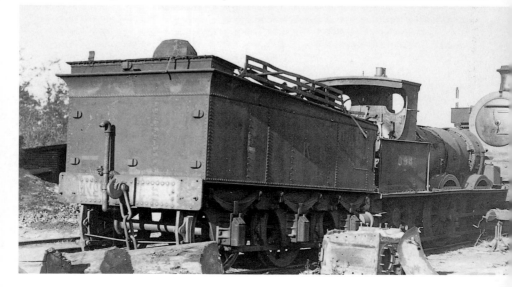

should be effected by the issue to him of the equivalent amount in Debenture Stock at an early date'. Having first satisfied themselves that Iggulden's power of attorney was in order, the Directors set about ascertaining the exact number of debentures to be issued.

In the meantime Gore Vesey, the Chairman, had instituted an annual inspection of the line on 17th March and at the 16th April Meeting of the Directors he professed himself satisfied with the railway's condition. It was a busy meeting. It was resolved to fit a new pump at Shepherdswell and to erect a wind pump at Woodnesborough. Although the reference is clearly to 'Woodnesborough', and was repeated in July when the completion of the work was announced, there is good reason to think that the actual location was Staple as neither of the authors have come across any evidence of a wind pump ever being erected at Woodnesborough. Austen was appointed Acting Manager and Engineer. The death of Arthur Loring, the recently retired Chairman, was also recorded and it was resolved that the Directors' condolences be sent but that his place on the Board should remain vacant. Finally, the passenger service would be retained but the morning train would be discontinued from 1st May.

The 16th July Meeting recorded a decrease in receipts of £1,622 16s. 0d. due to the loss of tonnage from Tilmanstone but £1,850 had been raised by the sale of Sholden Lodge, originally bought to meet its owner's objections to Railway 19; the adjoining cottages and 'useful land' were to be retained. More importantly agreement had been reached with Iggulden to settle Stephens' debts by the issue of £14,372 debentures. This was finally done in September but Stephens had little time to relish his long awaited payment. On Friday 23rd October the Lord Warden Hotel night porter brought Stephens his morning papers only to discover that he had suffered a fatal heart attack in the night.

It might be thought that Stephens' death effected a profound change in the affairs of the railway. It would be more true to say that the change had already taken place. With Loring's death earlier in the year the East Kent was already more tightly within the grip of the Southern. Tilden Smith's death had opened the way towards a better relationship between Tilmanstone Colliery and the railway. Even PDL had lost some of its impetus with the death of Sir Arthur Dorman in 1930. Above all it was the onset of the Depression in the wake of the financial crashes of 1929 which effectively put a stop to further development in the Kent coalfield. No new collieries would open. Richborough would acquire some light industries but would not see the steelworks and by-products plants for which it had been acquired. Reasonable but not massive quantities of coal would travel over the ropeway from Tilmanstone to Dover. Quantities of coal leaving Tilmanstone by rail would remain fairly stable until the outbreak of war, but the railway's existing facilities would prove perfectly capable of handling these. Not only would no further extensions be built but even those lines on which work had already been started would never be completed. No connection would be put in at Richborough Castle on Railway 9, the triangular junctions at Eythorne and Eastry would remain incomplete, the surface works on Railway 15 towards Stodmarsh would become more derelict and the embankment and cutting for the new junction line at Shepherdswell would never see more than a single siding holding empty wagons.

Although Stephens' death did not cause this end to expansion it did at least deprive the railway of the only means by which expansion might have been achieved. The contribution that Stephens' energy, ingenuity, influence, negotiating skills and indomitable resistance to defeat made to keeping the hopes of the railway alive for so long cannot be denied. The Directors for whom he worked over the years and amongst whom he had briefly held a place were by no means without ability or determination themselves. But it is clear that the building and running of the railway, the planning and presentation of the numerous extension schemes and even the financing of the railway in the post-Burr period were largely left to Stephens. As a young man Stephens had written to his parents, '. . . it is absolutely essential to have a policy and stick to it, if it fails try some other way, I am sure that this is the only way to get on'. This might almost have been the motto of the EKR, throughout the years that it was in the charge of Holman Fred Stephens.

The final Directors' meeting of 1931 took place on 15th October, eight days before Stephens' death. It was not a busy meeting and the only decision of significance was strangely prophetic. The Directors agreed to dispose of locomotive No. 3 for scrap if no other purchaser could be found. This was the first locomotive to be disposed of by the EKR and the first of the 'Ilfracombes' on any of his lines to be officially withdrawn. The old order was passing and it was perhaps fitting that Stephens passed with it.

Locomotives Nos. 2, 7, 5 and 8 lined up at Shepherdswell on 24th October, 1931, emphasising the variety of locomotives to be found on the East Kent in the 1930s.

H.C. Casserley

Chapter Nine

Austen Takes Over -
1932-1939

Stephens' position on the EKR, and on most of the other 'Stephens' railways, was filled by his longtime assistant W.H. Austen. Austen had more than 40 years of experience of working for Holman Stephens and was therefore familiar with the practices and problems of all these railways. Probably no other single individual could have succeeded in salvaging as much from the rapidly foundering assortment of lines as he did. Some of the lines were already beyond salvage, notably the Selsey Tramway and the Welsh Highland Railway, but Austen proved able to keep the remaining lines going provided that no major loss of custom occurred. If Tilmanstone had sent all its coal along the ropeway it is likely that the East Kent would have suffered the same fate as the Weston Clevedon & Portishead Railway did when the quarries along its route turned to road transport.

However, it should not be imagined that Austen ran the lines which he took over as Stephens would have done. Where imaginative improvisation and the enlisting of persons of wealth and influence to the support of his lines had enabled Stephens to work wonders, Austen substituted a healthy mixture of realism and, wherever possible, efficiency. There was a drastic sweeping away of worn-out rolling stock accompanied by a general tidying up of what was considered to be worth keeping. Services and those who provided them were pruned to contain losses but efforts were made to improve the services that survived. There was no more talk of extensions but locomotives and carriages began to appear in smart standardised liveries.

It may have been less fun to travel or work on these lines, and there were no more generous tips or free cigars to reward individuals, but losses were contained. Wherever bankruptcy was staved off there were still trains to travel in or send goods by and employment to be had at a time when it was scarce. None of this is to denigrate the work of Stephens but rather reflects the changed circumstances of the early 1930s when economic depression and growing road competition were leading to branch line closures throughout the nation.

1932

ANNUAL REPORT: 'The reduction in Working Expenses of £845 is due to economies.'

Austen's appointment as General Manager at £350 pa was confirmed at the Directors' meeting on 21st January, 1932. This was a landmark meeting in many respects. Receipts for the previous year had decreased by £2,499 due in part to the loss of traffic to the ropeway but Austen estimated that he had been able to reduce working expenses by £1,500 so that the railway's situation was a great deal less perilous than it might have been. Further reductions in engine mileage during 1932 would continue to safeguard the railway's viability. In 1931 the revenue from railway working had only exceeded its costs by £51 but by the end of 1932 the difference had increased healthily to £643.

At the same meeting Austen reported to the Directors that Guilford Colliery was being dismantled by Tilmanstone Collieries Ltd and added that the Guilford branch had not been used for some three or four years past. A figure of 10 years might have been more accurate but Austen had obviously learnt from Stephens that it was not always wise to over-inform Directors.

One item of very welcome news was that the management at Tilmanstone Colliery was now prepared to settle the long dispute between the colliery and the EKR. The terms proposed by the colliery were that if the railway cancelled all debts owed by the colliery for coal traffic then the colliery would cancel the debts owed by the railway for the hire purchase of locomotive No. 4, for refunds on coal traffic and for coal supplied to the EKR. New traffic rates were also proposed: all coal traffic from Tilmanstone to Shepherdswell should be charged at 7½d. a ton while internal shunting at Tilmanstone should be charged at 3d. a ton. In return the EKR was asked to agree to obtain all its coal from Tilmanstone and to pay 18s. a ton. These terms were to be for five years and met with agreement from the Directors except for two counter proposals: the first was to pay 16s. a ton for Tilmanstone coal and the second was to receive one ton of coal free for every 300 tons consigned. The colliery stuck to its price of 18s. but was prepared to concede the free coal up to a limit of 1,000 tons a year.

Alongside this welcome news of a settlement with an existing customer came news of the appearance of a new customer. The Hampshire Chip Basket Company had leased land at Staple station to erect a store and had undertaken to dispatch its traffic by rail. It is not clear when the store, 100 feet by 19 feet, was actually built nor how long it remained in the hands of the Hampshire Chip Basket Company as most photographs show the name C.W. Darley Limited clearly emblazoned across its end wall.

Two items of locomotive business were also dealt with at the January meeting. Austen reported that he had received an offer of £50 for locomotive No. 3 but was instructed to try for £60. The second item concerned a 'Terrier' boiler which was reported as surplus to the railway's requirements and which had cost £218 in 1926. Austen was instructed to try to sell this boiler.

Unfortunately this is the first mention in the East Kent records that the railway ever owned a 'Terrier' boiler and there is no explanation of why such a boiler should have been purchased. The 'Terriers' were a class of small but energetic tank locomotives built for the London, Brighton & South Coast Railway (LBSCR) in the 1870s. Stephens had purchased 'Terriers' for several of the lines which he managed but not for the East Kent. It has been suggested that the boiler may have been obtained with the intention of fitting it to one of the smaller locomotives on the line, possibly 0-6-0ST No. 1 or the hired Kent & East Sussex 2-4-0T *Northiam* which the East Kent had extensively overhauled before returning her to Rolvenden in 1930 or 1931. Peter Cooper, who has studied the careers of the Brighton 'Terriers' in detail, has been able to identify the boiler concerned as Stroudley boiler No. 62, originally fitted to London Brighton & South Coast Railway 'Terrier' No. 60 in 1875 and subsequently fitted to No. 642 from 1903 until 1925. The boiler had then been put into store until, as its surviving record card relates, it was 'Sent to Shepherd's Well, East Kent Railway 8/27'. We need not worry too much about the discrepancy of dates as it may well have been purchased in 1926 but not delivered until 1927. Despite its lack of use on the East Kent hitherto this boiler was to prove a good investment in the months to come.

A Directors' meeting held on 29th February, 1932 only dealt with one significant item. It was reported that the Hammill Brick Company was in financial difficulties. This not only threatened the loss of some £504 owing for traffic carried, but obviously posed the possibility of the ending of traffic to and from the brickworks altogether.

When the Directors met again on 21st April, 1932 it was to hear that the settlement with Tilmanstone Colliery had now been confirmed, with the additional good news that the Southern would credit the East Kent with 10d. a ton for Tilmanstone coal traffic forwarded onto their line. Other news, good or bad, seems to have been in short supply but Austen gave his opinion that traffic to Richborough would improve during the year. This seems to reflect the fact that there had been a substantial drop in coal consigned by PDL from Snowdown to Richborough so far that year.

The Directors did not meet again until 21st July. Austen was now able to report that the Southern had agreed to accept the 'Terrier' boiler as part payment for an 'O1' boiler to be fitted to locomotive No. 6, which had gone to Ashford for overhaul on 18th August. The 'Terrier' boiler was not required by the Southern until July 1934 when it was sent to Eastleigh. Here it was fitted to 'Terrier' No. B653 in July 1935. By a strange stroke of coincidence this locomotive was subsequently purchased by Austen in February 1937 for use on the Weston Clevedon & Portishead Railway (WCPR) where it became No. 4. On the closure of the WCPR in 1940 it was taken into Great Western Railway stock as No. 6 and survived in this guise until 1948.

The commissioning of the overhaul of No. 6 at Ashford ensured that this locomotive would be back in traffic much more quickly than if the East Kent had attempted this task itself. This would be all the more important as the July meeting also received news that locomotive No. 4, at long last fully the property of the EKR as a result of the settlement with Tilmanstone Colliery, was in need of a new firebox and tyres. With No. 6 away and No. 4 in poor condition there must have been some concern that the remaining locomotives might not be able to maintain the coal traffic. This may explain an entry of £18 16s. 8d. in the Accounts for 1932 under the heading of 'Engine Hire'.

The last Directors' meeting of 1932 took place on 20th October. Cheered perhaps by the news that the Hammill Brick Company had been able to pay off £205 of its debt to the railway, the Directors authorised the purchase of a new copper firebox and new tyres for No. 4 which the Southern would fit. On 26th October No. 6 returned to Shepherdswell and on 7th December No. 4 went off to Ashford to be fitted with a Hunslet firebox and new tyres. The immediate locomotive crisis was therefore well on its way to a conclusion at the year's end.

Unreported in the Directors' Minutes during 1932 was the fact that staff wages were reduced by 2½ per cent during the year. Under the prevailing conditions of widespread unemployment there was little that the staff could

Although neither of these locomotives ever ran on the East Kent, the boiler fitted to them was EKR property from 1926 to 1932. LBSCR No. 642 working as Battersea Shed pilot in the top photograph carried the boiler from 1903 to 1925. Weston, Clevedon & Portishead Railway No. 4 (*below*) carried it from 1935 to 1948, initially as a Southern Railway locomotive and at the end as a Great Western Railway locomotive. Curiously nobody ever seems to have reported the boiler's presence at Shepherdswell. *(Lower) Ron Jarvis Collection/Midland Railway Trust*

have done about this, but it is probably no coincidence that it was around this period that individuals in the railway's employment began to join the National Union of Railwaymen. This would have been to invite instant dismissal in Stephens' time and it is far from clear that Austen was at first aware that this was happening. However, it must have been safer for staff on the East Kent, surrounded by union members at the various Kent collieries, to have contemplated such a step than on any of the other lines under Austen's control. The strong Southern Railway presence on the Board of Directors must also have given them some encouragement. This is not to say that Southern Railway Directors were any more enthusiastic about the benefits of a union presence, but they would certainly have been reconciled to the existence of trade unions as a fact of life.

It should be added that the reduction of wages on the East Kent followed a reduction of wages at Tilmanstone Colliery. Here the management had obtained the agreement of the unions by giving them full access to the company's books. The unions agreed to this pay cut subject to their wages being restored at such time as the colliery was able to resume paying dividends to its shareholders. This led to a curious situation in 1946 when the colliery made a record net profit of £65,610. This would have enabled the colliery to pay its first dividend to shareholders but the colliery refrained from doing so on the grounds that this would have triggered a wage rise for the miners. Of all the Kent collieries only Chislet ever paid a dividend to its shareholders.

1933

DIRECTORS' REPORT: The increased Receipts are mainly due to additional coal traffic, viz £1,543, and receipts from Collection and Delivery, viz £112. The additional expenditure is made up of £870 for heavy locomotive repairs and £186 for the provision of Collection and Delivery facilities at Staple Station less economies in Working Expenses totalling £264.

1933 began with two welcome reports to a meeting held on 19th January. The Southern Railway was to lend a lorry to the East Kent for a trial road collection and delivery service. Hitherto the railway had depended on local carriers to handle deliveries and such a service of its own should serve to cut outgoings and might even bring in a surplus. Equally useful was a further payment of £150 by the Hammill Brick Company.

On 13th April it was heard that the 'motor lorry traffic' was proving very satisfactory. The railway's accounts for 1933 include a sum of £186 for '. . . the provision of collection & delivery facilities at Staple Station' and it is to be presumed that this covered the purchase of the railway's Chevrolet lorry. The receipts from the delivery service only amounted to £112 in 1933 but in succeeding years the service always covered its costs.

At the same meeting the Directors also decided to make use of the land owned by the railway on Golgotha Hill to build four bungalows at an estimated cost of £310 each. These would be let to the railway's staff at 10s. a week and would enable them to avoid the inconvenience of travelling to work from

No. 2 *Walton Park* ready to depart from Shepherdswell with carriage No. 10 and a respectable
tail end of freight in June 1934.   *H.C. Casserley*

Shepherdswell locomotive shed in July 1936. The first new section has been completed and the
remnants of the old shed are about to be demolished and replaced in the same style as the new
section. 0-6-0ST No. 2 is under overhaul.   *H.C. Casserley*

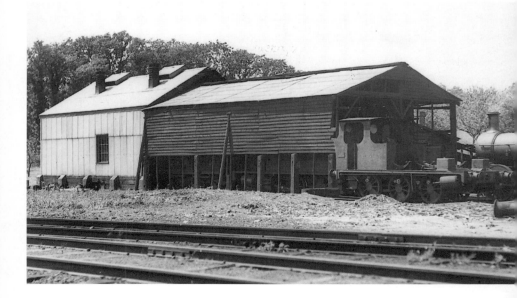

Dover. A meeting held on 20th July heard that a tender to build the bungalows had been accepted from Mr Castle of Shepherdswell at £265 apiece. Less satisfactory was the news that locomotive No. 4 was still at Ashford.

At a meeting held on 19th October it was reported that No. 4 had at last returned to Shepherdswell in a new green livery. The first bungalow had been completed and the frames for the 'remaining two' had been erected. From this it would appear that only three bungalows were now to be built.

1934

RAILWAY OBSERVER March 1934: EAST KENT RAILWAY - At the present time the locomotives of this line present a somewhat woe-begone appearance, with the sole exception of No. 4, recently repaired and repainted at Ashford Works with the initials E.K.R. and the number on the side tanks and in the same colour and position as adopted for SR tank locos. Most of the work appears to be shared by No. 4, and the two 0-6-0s, Nos. 6 and 8. The 'Ilfracombe Goods', No. 3 which has been in a dismantled state at Shepherdswell for some time has now disappeared, while the 0-6-0ST No. 1 and the 4-4-2T No. 5 are both in a derelict condition and appear to be awaiting either thorough overhaul or scrapping. The other two 0-6-0ST, Nos. 2 and 7, are in good repair but apparently out of service.

The first Directors' meeting of 1934, held on 17th January, formally recognised that the East Kent was as complete as it would ever be by resolving to allow the unused land purchase powers for Lines 11, 15, 19, 20, 22, 33 and 37 to lapse. From now on the railway's main interest in land would be to realise the best possible prices for those plots which it had already acquired and for which it now had no further use.

The existing Scheme of Arrangement with the debenture holders had now expired and it was necessary to return to the Court of Chancery in February for approval of a new Scheme. This was to run for a further five years and differed from previous Schemes. Hitherto interest had been paid as far as possible by the distribution of the entire net revenue with any remaining balance paid in shares. Under the 1934 Scheme the Debenture holders agreed that if the entire net revenue was used to pay off interest then any remaining balance of unpaid interest would be extinguished or cancelled. On this basis the 5 per cent Debenture holders received a payment of 2 per cent in 1934. All further renewals of the Scheme of Arrangement were on the same basis and very few shares were issued after this date.

The Directors met again on 21st March, 1934 when they learnt that all three bungalows on Golgotha Hill were now occupied. They also received a request from PDL to lease the mineral rights of the land owned by the EKR at Sholden Lodge on the course of the ill-fated Deal Extension. In 1933 the Directors had turned down a request from the same source to buy these rights but were now disposed to consider the matter favourably. A 99 year lease was formally authorised at their next meeting on 18th July at which it was also reported that a plot of land opposite Sholden Lodge had been sold. The Fairlight Cottages adjoining Sholden Lodge remained the property of the railway and generated a

0-6-0T No. 4 in its new livery of Southern green with yellow lettering at Shepherdswell in 1935.

The completed locomotive shed presents a much more respectable look to Shepherdswell yard in this 1939 view.

small income from rents. In fact receipts from rents for houses and land amounted to £239 10s. 0d. in 1934, which compared very favourably with the company's total net revenue of £2,401 1s. 9d. Another small source of income was dealt with at the same meeting when it was resolved to let the advertising rights along the line to Partington's Kent Billposting Company.

The final business of 1934, discussed at a meeting on 17th December, was the Directors' growing concern over the condition of the wharf at Richborough. Alex Parkes, the Secretary, was instructed to discover who was responsible for repairs.

One item of information unrecorded in the Directors' Minutes was the fact that locomotive No. 3, withdrawn in 1931, had eventually been sold for scrap in 1934.

1935

RAILWAY OBSERVER May 1935: EAST KENT RAILWAY - The shed at Shepherdswell is being rebuilt, as is also Adams 4-4-2T No. 5. On the occasion of a visit (31/3/35) the only locos noted in a workable condition were the two 0-6-0s 6 and 8 (SEC) and the Kerr Stuart 0-6-0T No. 4. The three 0-6-0 tanks Nos. 1, 2 and 7 (ex-GWR, WC&P, and LSWR) were in a deplorable condition. A Weston, Clevedon and Portishead Railway time-table is prominently displayed in the waiting room at Shepherdswell station.

The Directors still had Richborough Wharf on their minds when they met again on 16th January, 1935. Parkes was instructed to write to PDL saying that the Wharf was in such a bad state that the railway wished to discontinue its rental. In subsequent negotiations PDL offered to accept the trackbed of the extension from Richborough Port station to the Wharf in lieu of rental. This was to be another long-running dispute which eventually petered out without any obvious conclusion, and for that reason we do not propose to chronicle its progress which took the usual form of intermittent correspondence and occasional action. The dispute is more significant for the changed tone of the proceedings than for their eventual resolution. Gone was the outraged rhetoric that Burr or Stephens would have employed and equally apparent for its absence was any hostile reaction on the part of PDL; the days of high drama in the Kent coalfield had passed.

The January 1935 meeting was not solely concerned with the Richborough Wharf. The 2½ per cent cut in pay that had taken place in 1932 was to be restored now that the worst of the economic depression appeared to be over. Thought was also given to the locomotive fleet with Austen receiving authorisation to dispose of locomotive No. 1 if a new boiler could be found for locomotive No. 8.

The remainder of the year's new business was concentrated in a meeting held on 17th July. Austen was able to report that he had completed the construction of a reservoir at Shepherdswell. This was built alongside the embankment of the uncompleted connection to the Southern and was fed with the aid of an oil pump from a spring on the railway's own land. This enabled the EKR to dispense with the ramshackle row of cisterns that had previously stood outside the locomotive shed. Austen was also able to report that work had begun on rebuilding the locomotive shed. In keeping with the planned improvements in accommodation it had been decided not to proceed with the scheme to reboiler locomotive No. 8 but to purchase a new locomotive for £850. The 'new' locomotive was 'O1' 0-6-0 No. 100 which was delivered on the 23rd June, 1935. Locomotives Nos.1 and 8 were reported as having been sold for scrap to Cohens for £95.

Otherwise the Directors' discussions were concerned with various sales of surplus plots of land and further episodes in the continuing dispute over Richborough Wharf. This may explain a note attached to the railway's accounts recording that no coal was sent from Snowdown to Richborough during 1935 although some 2,234 tons had been carried in 1934.

One new source of traffic to which the Directors' attention does not seem to have been attracted was the carriage of 336 pigs in 1935. These were the first items of livestock to have been carried since 1921.

1936

ACCOUNT WITH SOUTHERN RAILWAY 6th November, 1936: To repairing Locomotive No. 6 (September 1936) £1 18s. 11d.

It will by now have become apparent that the actual business of running a railway entailed far less 'excitement' than the promotion of extensions or fighting off imminent bankruptcy. 1936 is the shining example of this as almost nothing of note or newsworthiness occurred during that year. The most positive event of the year appears to have been a suggestion by Austen that the railway might contemplate inaugurating a programme of permanent way repairs. By now the track was in a truly appalling state with many sleepers so rotten that the spikes holding down the flat bottom rails could be lifted out by the passing of a train. If too many spikes broke free on any single length of rail then the rail was likely to turn on its side and the train would derail. Had there been any significant number of passengers still travelling on the East Kent this would have occasioned considerable inconvenience, but it was becoming increasingly rare to find more than a handful of passengers on either of the two daily mixed trains to Wingham.

1936 saw a further 353 pigs being carried but these were to prove to be the last items of livestock to be included in the railway's returns. There may possibly have been further carriage of livestock during World War II but the statistical returns during the two World Wars were required to omit such information.

The only other events of interest in 1936 were the overhaul and repainting of locomotives 5 and 7. These were painted in the railway's new standard livery of green with yellow lettering and lining which had first appeared on locomotive No. 4. There is no clue in the railway's records as to what sort of repairs to No. 6 were able to be obtained from the Southern Railway for £1 18s. 11d.

1937

RAILWAY MAGAZINE March 1937: Perhaps no concern illustrates better than the East Kent Light Railways Company the utility of the Light Railway Acts in facilitating the development for agricultural and industrial purposes of otherwise inaccessible areas.

1937 provided quite a contrast with the inactivity of 1936. At a meeting held on 20th January the Directors learned that the rebuilding of the locomotive shed had been completed and that all the railway's locomotives could now be kept under cover. At the same meeting the Directors also received a request for compensation for loss of office from Mr J.H. Ashworth. 'Jimmy' Ashworth was one of the Salford Terrace staff and had served Holman Stephens almost as long as Austen. His main occupation had been to assist Stephens with the surveys, plans and applications for Light Railway Orders but in the absence of any further work of this sort he had been dismissed by Austen. The Directors asked Alex Parkes to write to Mr Ashworth confirming his dismissal and regretting that '. . . the Directors were unable to accede to his application'.

On 24th February, 1937 the Directors heard that a set of 'old bridge girders' stored at Shepherdswell had been sold to the Kent & East Sussex Railway (KESR) for £8. It was also reported that the Secretary had written to Tilmanstone (Kent) Collieries asking whether it was probable that the Guilford branch would be required for their use in the future. A reply was received at the Directors' next meeting on 24th March. There was very little possibility of Guilford Colliery being opened for some years and the railway was at liberty to do as they wished with regard to the track, although Tilmanstone might purchase half a mile of track materials for their own use. The logical consequence of this was a formal decision on 14th July to dispose of the track on the Guilford branch. It was also agreed to dispose of one of the coaches and six wagons.

On 20th October the Directors congratulated Gilbert Szlumper on his new appointment as General Manager of the Southern Railway. There can have been few independent light railways to have had such an influential post represented on their own board of Directors. The same meeting heard that Tilmanstone (Kent) Collieries had undergone a further change of ownership. It will be recalled that Tilden Smith had left money in trust to keep the colliery going for seven years after his death. The trustees had discharged their duties well and had overcome much of the distrust with which Tilmanstone had been regarded under its previous owners but the period of trusteeship had ended. The new owners were the Harley Drayton Group who intended to deepen the colliery's shafts to open up new seams of hard household coal.

By now all but 650 yards of the Guilford branch had been lifted. It was intended to keep the remaining section as a siding. Some 163 tons of rails had been pulled up of which 100 tons had already been sold at £6 a ton. On paper this represented a profit since they had originally been purchased at £5 14s. 6d. a ton. However, it was pointed out by the Accountant that the capital cost of the branch had been £1,900. Even if £1,000 could be recouped by the sale of materials this would leave a capital loss of £900. There had already been a capital loss of £400 on the sale of surplus fang bolts for scrap, and the scrapping of the coach and wagons had written off a further £200. In all there appeared to be a capital write off of £1,500.

The abandoned buildings of Guilford Colliery in July 1935.   *Dr J.R. Hollick*

Distorted trackwork on the Guilford branch in the 1930s.   *M. Lawson Finch Collection*

Consideration was also now given to closing the Richborough branch, initially on a temporary basis. Some figures were given for the receipts and expenditure for the branch:

Year	Receipts	Expenditure
1935	£56	£127
1936	£115	£128
1937 to date	£46	£108

These figures were solely for traffic originating on the branch and it was shown that the branch also accounted for traffic coming over the line from Shepherdswell that would not otherwise have done so. Presumably the bulk of this was coal travelling through from Snowdown to Richborough. The receipts for this traffic were:

1935	1936	1937 to date
£189	£383	£153

On the basis of these figures it was decided to keep the branch open.

Just as 1934 had seen the East Kent abandoning its plans for further extensions so had 1937 seen the first major closure, albeit of the Guilford branch which had rarely carried any significant traffic. The railway was covering its operating costs and steadily restoring its locomotive stock. The debenture holders were continuing to receive interest of a sort on their investments. The East Kent Railway of 1937 may have been a far cry from the original hopes of 1911 but amongst the lines operated from Salford Terrace it was a model of prosperity.

1938

RAILWAY MAGAZINE January 1938: Mr R. Dyson started a journey over the East Kent Railway at Shepherdswell on the 4.45 pm train, drawn by No. 6, an ex-SE&C 0-6-0 with a train of freight vehicles and a six-wheeled passenger coach. The guard, who also officiates as porter, shunter and booking-clerk, having obtained our correspondent's ticket from his house, the train started. Much shunting took place at intermediate stations, in which the passengers were involuntary participants as their coach was shunted about with the wagons. At Eastry the train ran up the Sandwich Road line, apparently in error, and had to be backed onto its proper line again ; the next incident was a stop in a field, where the engine secured a couple of wagons from an adjacent brickworks and a grateful passenger who lives in the locality - which has no station - boarded the train. At Canterbury Road terminus the engine uncoupled and ran into a siding, after which the coach ran by gravity into the platform and the engine was attached to its opposite end ; arrival here was 40 min. late. The return journey to Shepherdswell was, however, made punctually.

The first part of 1938 was uneventful. Further plots of land were sold off and negotiations were begun to let portions of the Guilford branch trackbed to Lord Guilford for grazing. On 13th July the Chairman reported that he had made his annual inspection trip over the line on 13th May and added, somewhat plaintively, that, '. . . it would be a satisfaction to the General Manager if next year some of the Directors would inspect the line'. There is no evidence that they ever did so.

On the same date the Directors considered the question of extending the special traffic rates agreement with the colliery and resolved to extend the agreement for three years from January 1939, provided that the colliery undertook to send any additional tonnage by rail rather than by road or over the ropeway. The 'additional tonnage' appears to have been a reference to the anticipated increase in coal production arising from the deepening of the Tilmanstone shafts.

This may be a convenient point to consider the effect of the ropeway on the traffic of the East Kent. According to Dr W. Johnson the total figures given by Tilmanstone (Kent) Collieries for coal carried by the ropeway and adjusted to calendar years (these figures were originally September to September from 1930 to 1934) were as follows:

Year	Tonnage	Year	Tonnage
1930	65,000	1935	40,000
1931	93,000	1936	50,000
1932	95,000	1937	55,000
1933	65,000	1938	70,000
1934	29,000	1939	84,354

Although, apart from 1934, these were substantial figures it must be remembered that the ropeway had an estimated capacity to carry 365,000 tons a year. In order to compare these figures with the tonnages carried on the East Kent, it is possible to refer to an entry amongst the papers relating to the valuation of the East Kent at Nationalisation which gave the three main destinations of Tilmanstone traffic between 1936 and 1939:

Year	To Shepherdswell	By Ropeway	To Landsales Wharf	Total
1936	218,000	50,000	36,000	304,000
1937	213,000	55,000	41,000	309,000
1938	204,000	70,000	59,000	333,000
1939	233,000	89,000	29,000	351,000
Total	868,000	264,000	185,000	1,297,000

Although the amount of coal travelling over the ropeway increased during this period it cannot really be said to have had any significant effect on the quantity of coal dispatched by rail. If Tilden Smith had hoped to make himself independent of the railway by building the ropeway it is not evident from the figures that his successors ever felt this to be a feasible or necessary step.

At their next meeting on 26th October it became apparent that there was unlikely to be any problem over additional tonnage. Lloyds Paper Mills at Sittingbourne, one of Tilmanstone's main customers, had cut its orders for Tilmanstone coal as a result of installing electrical machinery. Moreover, as a result of the 'political situation', the new owners of Tilmanstone had not proceeded with their intended share issue to deepen the workings at Tilmanstone. As so many times before, the railway's heavy dependence on the Tilmanstone coal traffic cast a shadow over the viability of the whole line. Nor was any comfort to be drawn from the condition of the railway's merchandise traffic which was reported to have decreased as a result of road transport competition.

1939

RAILWAY OBSERVER August 1939: EAST KENT RAILWAY - On 3/7/39 the 4.45 pm train from Shepherdswell to Wingham consisted of one old SR coach and three wagons hauled by 0-6-0T No. 2. Although there were no passengers the train stopped at all stations so that the stationmaster at Shepherdswell, who also acts as Shunter and Guard on the train, might affix new timetables to notice boards. Water was taken in both directions at Woodnesboro. At Staple which seems to have a fair amount of goods traffic a considerable amount of shunting and general re-arranging of the contents of the goods yard took place, with coach coupled all the while ; the train was twenty minutes late reaching Wingham. The coach did not proceed beyond the goods yard. On the return journey the train with a few wagons and a fruit van left at 6.18 pm and proceeded non-stop to Staple where more shunting took place ; on the downhill stretch to Eastry about 25 m.p.h. was maintained for about two miles ; more fruit was picked up at Eythorne and Shepherdswell was reached a few minutes late, just after 7 pm.

All locos were in working order except No. 4, the wheels of which were at Ashford being re-tyred. Two loco turns are in operation a day - one passenger and one goods. Coal traffic is about 800/1000 tons per week and is expected to increase when a new deep shaft at Tilmanstone Colliery is completed.

Although cheap tickets are only advertised as being issued on Wednesday, Thursday and Saturdays, the writer was issued with one on Monday although it was dated 1938! A good head of steam has to be maintained for the prolonged use of the whistle at the many ungated level crossings.

The line runs through quite pleasant rural scenery with distant views over Sandwich Bay to Ramsgate.

The Richboro' Branch is used periodically to convey pit props to Tilmanstone which have arrived by boat. - (K. Bates)

On 8th March, 1939 the Directors received confirmation of a further reduction in Tilmanstone's output and of two further setbacks. The Hammill Brick Company had gone into liquidation owing the EKR £64 18s. 6d., though some consolation was gained from the fact that 24 tons of the brick company's coal was being held by the railway against payment of the brick company's debt. At Staple the tenancy of the store built by the Hampshire Chip Basket Company, and subsequently occupied by fruit and vegetable wholesalers C.W. Darley Limited, had been relinquished and the railway had to consider whether to purchase the store or to require it to be removed. Subsequent letters to C.W. Darley went unanswered and the store remained in place with no apparent record of payment ever being made for it.

On a brighter note it was reported that there was the possibility of a lime works being established at Tilmanstone which it was hoped would bring a great deal of traffic. On the permanent way front the Directors were at last persuaded to authorise the complete renewal of the line between Shepherdswell and Eythorne at an estimated cost of £2,736.

Against a background of increasing international tension the railway seems to have got on with its work as normal. On 12th July the Directors heard that the Southern Railway was prepared to continue its 2½d. a ton subsidy for Tilmanstone traffic until the end of the year, pending a longer term agreement with the colliery. The task of relaying the line from Shepherdswell to Eythorne proceeded at a leisurely rate with work confined to Sundays to avoid interfering with the railway's regular traffic.

Locomotive No. 100 running into Eythorne with a loaded coal train from Tilmanstone in August 1939.   *M. Lawson Finch Collection*

Newly overhauled No. 6 midway through repainting at Shepherdswell in April 1939.
                                                                                Jim Jarvis

On Sunday 3rd September war was declared against Germany and the railway's independent existence ended with the onset of Government control. Austen's careful stewardship of the line was to continue throughout the war and afterwards but he was now answerable to higher authorities than the East Kent Board of Directors. Fortunately, with one notable exception, there was to be little friction between Austen and his new masters and the East Kent was to survive the war largely unscathed.

A standard East Kent trespass notice. It was not considered necessary to replace these when W.H. Austen took over from Stephens.   *M. Lawson Finch Collection*

Chapter Ten

Third Return, Canterbury Road!

The outbreak of war in 1939 marked a significant change in the life of the EKR so we shall abandon the strict business of history and accompany an early enthusiast on a trip over the line.

A train journey from Shepherdswell to Canterbury Road, Wingham, was rather a solitary affair and the traveller seldom had cause to worry about the possibility of finding a seat. Two might be company and three a crowd in the outside world but on the East Kent either figure represented a good trainload. In spite of all this it should not be imagined that anyone, the few regulars definitely included, ever took the trip without some misgiving. So many and so curious were the tales told by those who had gone before that an entirely uneventful trip left the passenger with the distinct feeling of not having had their full money's worth.

To cross the forecourt of the main line station and crunch around the black cinder path to the railway's Shepherdswell terminus was almost to cross an unseen barrier into a realm where reality softened and everyday things became just a little fey. This illusion was helped by the fact that most of my visits were made in early summer when the unaccustomed heat gave an additional touch of pleasure without having had time to parch the fields.

On the occasion of the visit described here the warmth of the sun helped considerably to alleviate the burst of apprehension on finding the platform deserted and no train in sight. Had it gone? Had the timetable been read correctly? Was the train still running? All fears were allayed when it proved possible to purchase a ticket from the cream wooden office some way behind the platform. This was an unusual event in itself as tickets for subsequent journeys were invariably bought from the guard on the train. On this occasion I and a fellow enthusiast settled down to wait on the little plank seat on the platform. On later visits, secure in the knowledge that the train would indeed run and would not leave us behind, more enterprising occupations could be found. These might include an inspection of the mouldering timetables, way bills and correspondence littering the curious circular corrugated iron hut behind the platform, or a trek across the tracks to visit the engine shed and carriage sidings.

For those travelling for the pleasure of it alone the likely choice would be a morning trip and, had such a journey been undertaken prior to 1925, the only train going further than Eastry, which left at 7.00 am, would have officially taken us no further than Wingham Colliery, even assuming that we had climbed out of our beds early enough to have caught it. Even after the extension to Canterbury Road had been opened there was still only one morning train, except that in 1927 a second one was put on at five minutes past midday. Two years later this was brought forward to 11.45 am, arriving at Canterbury Road at 12.28 pm. It left there at 1.10 pm and arrived back at Shepherdswell, barring anything untoward, at 2.00 pm. From 1932 the midday train vanished altogether and the line settled down to two trains a day on weekdays. The first left Shepherdswell at 7.30 am and the second at 4.45 pm and thus it was on this later train that the greater number of pilgrimages were made.

As we sat on the platform we were able to enjoy the general air of calm and tranquility, relieved only by a gentle movement in the trees behind the station and by a tantalising metallic clinking sound carried on the still air from within the engine shed. Intermittently, the noise of a main line train intruded rudely into the place whence, we had begun to believe, all noise had been banished long ago. Here perhaps only the drowsy hum of the duty coal engine's safety valves was truly in keeping.

Suddenly the melodious cry of a locomotive whistle rang out over the trees, loud and clear. As its calls echoed around the woods an engine bustled into view propelling a single six-wheeled carriage of antique appearance. It ran down the incline from the level crossing, curved round towards the station and ground to a halt at the platform with a violent shudder. The guard was out in an instant followed immediately by the fireman and driver and all three vanished into the office. All was once again as quiet as before with only the presence of the train as evidence of the activity of the few previous minutes. It was subsequently explained to us that there had been a mishap up the line in which a boy had sustained a broken arm and that the train had been dispatched on some unspecified mission of mercy.

The locomotive on this occasion was No. 7 and very smart she looked in her new green livery with black and white lining but oddly transformed by the loss of her stovepipe chimney. The carriage, No. 11, was also in fair condition in Southern green with white wheel tyres; at least we assumed they had been white for they were now an oily yellow. The guard politely held open the carriage door and in we all climbed, ourselves and two ladies who had apparently divined the exact moment to arrive. The guard closed the door, glanced at his watch and, expertly swinging it back into his waistcoat pocket on the end of its chain, simultaneously gave the 'Right Away'. With a blast of the whistle and dead on time we were off. Leaving the platform the train passed the engine shed and stock sidings on the left and an ancient wooden signal on the right. The adventure had begun.

Our progress was accompanied by further loud and prolonged whistling as we climbed towards the main road. Speed, it was noticed, slackened considerably but it was not clear whether this was a result of the caution of the driver or the age and condition of his engine. We clanked over the level crossing, accelerated into the cutting and literally flashed into Golgotha tunnel. Perhaps flashed is an exaggeration for although the carriage lights came on, to the oft expressed surprise of regular travellers, they were never overly bright and tended to wax and wane. Before we came out into the sunlight again we were able to glimpse the massive squared-off blocks of chalk lining the right hand side of the tunnel. The gradient continues to fall beyond the tunnel and our train picked up more speed as it ran parallel to the road between Shepherdswell and Eythorne. For the last stretch of this section we were paced and finally overtaken by a large open tourer without windows but possessing a high fabric roof which was torn and flapping. This contained a party of young men who appeared to be in the highest of spirits. We were to see them again.

0-6-0ST No. 7 and LCDR six-wheel carriage No. 11 at Shepherdswell.

M. Lawson Finch Collection

Wagons stored on the remaining stretch of the Guilford branch as described in the text.

M. Lawson Finch Collection

We ran smoothly into the station at Eythorne and found ourselves in what appeared to be the most densely inhabited location served by the line with houses visible in both directions. Most of the stations, apart from Shepherdswell, were so located as to face onto expanses of fields and trees or to be shielded from sight of human habitation by grassy cutting sides. One or two spectators had gathered at the level crossing at the end of the platform and over and behind them loomed the unmistakable winding stocks of Tilmanstone Colliery. We could see the branch to the colliery climbing up and away from the crossing to the right, and by craning our heads out of the windows and looking backwards we could see the Guilford Colliery branch. This was being used to house a string of empty open wagons curving back into the trees.

The platform was on the left and although no actual passengers entered or left the train a certain amount of activity was generated by the handing out and taking on of parcels. The activity about the level crossing and the brick-built station building coupled with the physical presence of the village combined to create a busy atmosphere. With a wave from the porter-cum-station master-cum-parcels agent we were off again. As we passed over the level crossing we caught sight of a rival attraction. There was the tourer again but its occupants had dismounted and were busily engaged with a policeman in what must have been a very one-sided argument.

It was at this point that we realised that the guard had chosen to travel with us in the carriage rather than in his brake compartment. We took it that perhaps he had an eye for the ladies but on reflection recognised that this was just another example of the general sociability of the East Kent. In the event there did not appear to be any duties which he could not discharge just as easily from within the main body of the carriage as from the isolation of the brake compartment.

Beyond Eythorne the track began to climb and for some distance ran on a chalky embankment. Whistling loudly, our train crossed the road from Lower Eythorne to Tilmanstone attracting the concentrated stares of a crocodile of hikers. On the far side of the road the climb continued and, with speed decreasing, we puffed past the colliery with its great heaps of shale on our right. We passed the brick-faced platform of Elvington Halt without stopping but, at the speed we were now travelling, this would hardly have been necessary. We spent some time gazing at the colliery buildings and in consequence completely failed to look out for the end of the colliery siding where it ran back in alongside our track. We had read at the time that the siding was used for stabling the disused French rolling stock converted, unsatisfactorily it seems, for special use by the colliery. But to our everlasting regret we forgot, both on this occasion and on the return journey, to look out for them. We did, however, notice that the track ran in a much more open strip of land than it did in later years when trees and scrub encroached on the left and huge mountains of shale crept over the siding tracks on the right.

Still climbing, we ran around the eastern face of a hill which afforded expansive views of cornfields and farmland towards Betteshanger before abruptly running into a cutting and pulling up at Knowlton Halt. Here a large box was put off the train for an old gentleman who seemed to have appeared

The site of the northern connection to the Tilmanstone branch. The colliery lines now end in a siding with the East Kent 'main line' in the background.　　　　*M. Lawson Finch Collection*

No. 7 running into Staple *en route* to Wingham.　　　　*M. Lawson Finch Collection*

from nowhere with a horse and cart to collect it. Whistling as never before we bumped over the level crossing, caught a glimpse of a fine string of fir trees, and rumbled into a long deep chalk cutting. The noise of our progress was thrown back at us in such deafening waves that we were forced to close the window and sit down for the first time.

The guard, with whom we had struck up quite a friendship, told us that one of the lady passengers was to alight at Eastry South. We did not know the locality too well at the time and when we arrived we thought it an odd place to be leaving the train. We were soon to discover that there were odder places to come.

On we went, the whistle blowing most of the time, now passing through arable fields with another grand view to the south-east. We were just admiring this when we spotted the signal posts heralding the presence of Eastry Junction dead ahead. Here we were to swing off the main line from Shepherdswell to Richborough and take the branch to Wingham. At least, this was the way these two lines were intended to be regarded but their roles had long since been reversed.

Our locomotive, running bunker first and which had hardly ceased to whistle since leaving Shepherdswell, came to a gentle halt at the platform and our friendly guard, who had by now realised that we were no ordinary passengers and possibly not even ordinary humans given our inexplicable interest in the railway, informed us that there was 'a bit of shunting to do'. He suggested we might like to stretch our legs 'but don't get into trouble mind', whatever that meant. Since we had only been in the train for just over 20 minutes we had little need for exercise but the opportunity to look around was too good to be missed and, along with the remaining lady passenger who had reached her destination, we alighted. For the remainder of the trip we were the only passengers.

It was immediately apparent that the signals, more in evidence here than at any other point on the line, were not in use on this occasion. The ones which should have controlled our entry to the station were off long before we arrived and remained so for the rest of the day. We inspected the corrugated iron hut containing the 10-lever ground frame, made an unsuccessful attempt at pulling off a signal some way down the Richborough branch, and nosed around in general. We were told that the original hut had been burnt down some time earlier. We worried a little about the lack of effective signalling as well we might for on at least two occasions trains are known to have set off down the Richborough branch in error. We were to have no such luck ourselves but when we eventually did get going again we were two wagons up and 16 minutes down.

Our train clanged loudly on the metal plates of the bridge over the Selson Road and we began to gather speed. The curve at this point appeared to be formed from a number of short lengths of straight rail and as a result we proceeded in a series of sickening jerks. In so doing we caught a glimpse of the Richborough branch signal which looked for all the world as though it stood in the middle of an orchard.

As we ran around the village of Selson our direction altered through a good right angle and we now headed north-west through more orchards and large fields. We saw the overgrown siding to Hammill Brickworks go over the hill on the left and straight into the sun and then whistled our way into the Prince of Wales Cutting. We emerged, with whistle still going full blast, and ran over the level crossing and through Woodnesborough Halt without so much as a by your leave!

Our guard was chatting freely by now and told us the following tale concerning a certain Mr Fagg which had occurred some years previously. Mr Fagg was a well respected and religious member of Wingham Parish Council and as such had occasionally to attend the Eastry Council Meeting by train. On the day in question his train home drew into Woodnesborough Station and stopped. After half an hour had passed Mr Fagg, thinking to himself that this was a long delay even by East Kent standards, looked out to see what was amiss. He was surprised to see the fireman hurrying up the lane from the village. He was even more surprised to observe him mount the footplate, place a few shovelfuls of coal on the fire, and then climb down and proceed as rapidly back down the lane as he had come. Mr Fagg, his curiosity by now very much aroused, left the train and hurried after the fireman sufficiently speedily to see him disappear into the local tavern.

Mr Fagg, solicitous of his own reputation, was reluctant to enter such an establishment and contented himself by putting his head around the door and politely enquiring as to when they might be proceeding. The crew, he noted, were engrossed in a game of darts but the driver, just then throwing, replied, 'Just a minute Guv'nor, it's horse an' horse and we're just settling who's to pay for the wallop'. As can be imagined, further and more acrimonious words followed before the journey was resumed.

We fully accepted this story at the time but I have come across several variations upon it since. In one the passenger is not named but as a result of his subsequent complaints the entire train crew is dismissed. In another version the passenger is none other than Colonel Stephens himself but instead of the delinquent crew losing their jobs the Colonel pays for the round of drinks to get the train on its way again, an extremely unlikely act of benevolence! There must be some truth at the root of these stories but successive tellings appear to have embellished the original tale to the point where the exact truth is unlikely ever to be discovered.

On this occasion it would appear that neither our locomotive nor our train crew were sufficiently thirsty to warrant a stop at Woodnesborough and we were soon running into more rolling countryside than previously. Our route wound through piggeries, paddocks and orchards, past Moat Farm Siding and through the trees to Ash Town. This was the part of the line known in the early days as the 'Overland Route' and, judging by the bumps and dips we encountered, overland it appeared to have remained. Ash Town, Elvington and Eastry were the only stopping places on the line without level crossings in their immediate vicinity but it was only Ash Town that appeared to be totally remote from any road at all. Instead a grassy path ran mysteriously across the meadows towards the spire of Ash Church on our right. On this sunny afternoon it appeared almost to be more inviting than our railway.

By now our guard was reminiscing even more profoundly than before and it began to appear that he could supply a couple or so stories about each station and a greater number about every man who had ever worked on the line. His current tale concerned the amorous adventures of one of the line's guards. His lady friend was a resident of Ash where she would often catch the train. After it had left the Halt she would lean out of her compartment window and signal to her beau that she was alone. The guard would then desert his brake compartment and clamber along the outside of the carriage to join her. One day the couple were signalling to each other shortly after leaving Woodnesborough when the lady was startled to see the love of her life fall clean off the train and disappear rapidly into the distance.

The lady, in some distress, now directed her attentions to the front of the train and eventually succeeded in getting the driver to bring the train to a halt. Explanations having been made with due embarrassment, the driver began to reverse the train back to Woodnesborough but had not gone far before the red-faced guard came into sight running to catch up with his train. He naturally took a fair amount of ribbing over the affair and our informant assured us that his ardour showed a marked decline following this incident.

As for ourselves, we had left Ash Town behind and were following a sinuous path through rank after rank of hop poles, past Poulton Farm Siding on which stood a forlorn and possibly abandoned wagon, past the culverts of Frying Pan Spring and, whistling fit to empty the boiler, crawled over the road from Guilton to Staple and into Staple station. Despite its isolated location this was obviously one of the busiest stations on the line. Its sidings showed clear evidence of considerable activity earlier in the day, with a number of loaded wagons and vans standing in the sidings behind the platform and a rake of coal trucks in the process of unloading in the coal bay. A lorry was parked at the far end of the platform and a horse and cart stood in the road at the yard entrance.

The place had simmered all day in brilliant sunshine and this now shone through the dusty windows on our left and onto the backs of our seats which gave off a musty and unforgettable aroma. There was not a breath of wind anywhere and the vanes of the station wind pump stood motionless at the top of their steel tower.

The station agent had a short conversation with our guard just outside the compartment window during which he passed a remark or two in our direction which, as was no doubt intended, we were unable to catch. The engine, our coach and a wagon were uncoupled from the rest of the train, drew forward and deposited the wagon in the sidings. The guard had told us something about it being easier to collect from Staple on the outward journey than it was when returning because of the lie of the sidings. Nevertheless we made our pick up on the return journey, perhaps our wagons were not yet quite ready. The train was soon coupled up again and with a wave from the station agent we were on our way again.

The distance between Staple and Wingham Colliery Halt was about two miles and an exhilarating stretch it proved to be. On both outward and return journeys we reached quite respectable speeds, easily the fastest we had travelled so far. The track began to climb and we reached its highest point some distance before Wingham Colliery Halt into which we descended. We slowed for the inevitable level crossing and again for two others by the Wingham Engineering Company premises and Wingham Town Halt but stopped at none

No. 7 stands at Canterbury Road with the LSWR and Midland Railway six-wheelers. No. 7 carries its original smokebox and chimney.

The modest facilities at Canterbury Road did not even extend to a buffer stop though in this 1926 view the usual sleeper chained across the rails has been supplemented by an abandoned cart.

of these. Topping the final bank before Wingham Canterbury Road we had a clear view of the Wingham Well Windmill and the green spire of Wingham Church. Our carriage gave a sickening lurch causing the guard to remark mysteriously, 'She's taken a turn for the worse'. We never discovered whether he meant the carriage, the track or the embankment. Shortly after this we came to a full stop half way along the embankment. Our engine uncoupled and ran forward into the single siding. Our guard then released the train brakes and we rolled gently down to the goods platform. This was the closest we got to the station proper which stood on the far side of the road. The engine came back onto the running line, picked up the remaining wagon and deposited it in the siding. It then returned for the coach and since there were no wagons to be taken back from Wingham the one coach train was ready for its return journey.

Due to one thing and another we had arrived at the end of our journey some time after we should have left. The journey which should have taken 42 minutes had taken over an hour but nobody had been seriously inconvenienced and we were assured that it did not happen very often. Subsequent accounts by other travellers led us to doubt this.

Of the return journey there is not a lot to record. Our speed was generally faster than it had been on the outward trip which is what might be expected. It was the last train of the day. The sun was going down behind us and the early evening was still and warm. As we trundled through the unspoilt Kentish countryside little could we have known what the next few years were to bring, nor did it then seem possible that one day in the none too distant future it would become impossible ever to make the journey again. The whistle sounded more mellow than earlier in the day and the hitherto deserted countryside was now populated with occasional knots of locals taking the evening air. They gathered here and there to watch us pass and now and again to wave.

We stopped at Staple to collect two vans and hurried on to Eastry where three more joined us. By now we had a sizeable train and up the bank to Golgotha old No. 7 caught her breath more than once. By now we too were tired and no longer stirred from our seats.

We stopped near the North Bank at Shepherdswell and the engine came off and ran down into the sidings. The guard released his brake and we free-wheeled to a nicely judged stop at the platform after which the engine returned to collect the wagons while we stood and watched. We had put up for the night at Shepherdswell so had time on our hands for taking a few photographs but there was not really enough light and the results proved poor. The vans were left in the loop, the engine ran back to the shed and all was silent. We sat on the seat for a while but there was not a lot of talking and as evening slowly slipped toward night the railway gradually faded from view. When it had gone we began to wonder . . . had it all perhaps just been a dream?

Dean Goods No. 70197 at Kinnerley in 1947. It had previously carried pannier tanks for condensing purposes. This locomotive managed to serve on three 'Colonel Stephens' railways during World War II - the Kent & East Sussex Railway, the East Kent and the Shropshire & Montgomeryshire.   *H.C. Casserley*

No. 6 stands on the embankment leading to Wingham Canterbury Road in 1931. This was one of the embankments that broke blackout regulations during the war by intermittently bursting into flames.   *Dr Ian C. Allen*

Chapter Eleven

At War Again - 1939-1945

With the outbreak of World War II we lose a number of the sources of information upon which we have hitherto relied. The Annual Reports give only the barest details of the railway's operations and there are few contemporary accounts from visiting enthusiasts. If it had not been for the prompt action of Alex Parkes, the railway's Secretary, we would also have lost the Directors' Minute Books for the whole of the railway's history. The charred bindings testify to the effects of a bomb attack on the Secretary's office at Moorgate and serve as a reminder that it was not just Kent that was in the 'front line' during this war.

It is, however, true that the EKR was a great deal closer to the 'front line' in the 1939-45 War than it had been in World War I. The railway played a number of important roles during the war but probably none so important as its continued role in carrying coal from Tilmanstone. The connection to Richborough which could have been so important in the first war played little or no part in the second.

1939

Annual Report to Shareholders: By an Order made under the Defence Regulations 1939 the East Kent Light Railway was placed under Government Control as from 1st September, 1939.

The outbreak of war had little immediate visible effect on the railway, even the submission to Government Control was more a matter of additional paperwork than direct intervention. The railway continued to be managed by Austen from Tonbridge but was subject to various provisions for pooling revenue with the rest of the country's railways and for compensation for damage occasioned by the war. One immediate effect of the outbreak of war was the closure of the Tilmanstone ropeway. There are references to the ropeway being damaged by anti-aircraft fire but it is not clear whether this damage led to the closure or was suffered afterwards.

Trains appear to have continued to make intermittent use of the Richborough branch in late 1939 but there was no immediate move to re-establish a military presence at Richborough Port. Some months before the outbreak of war the remaining residential accommodation at the Port had been acquired by the Home Office to house refugees, but this seems to have been the only significant Government use of the Port during the early part of the war. The train ferry equipment had long been dismantled and the usefulness of much of the waterfront had been reduced by a steady accumulation of silt.

Some of the railway's younger employees left to join the services or to work in the collieries. Air raid precautions were introduced and gas masks accompanied the remaining regular passengers on the twice daily trains. Otherwise little changed in these first quiet months of the war.

1940

Annual Report to Shareholders: The amount of the guaranteed minimum net revenue of this company - the average of 1936, 1937 and 1938 - is £3,283, with a maximum - calculated in ratio to that of the main line railways - of £4,596 per annum.

The calculation of the guaranteed minimum net revenue for the EKR generated a massive correspondence between the various parties concerned. Not the least interesting feature of this correspondence was the fact that, in the interests of economy, much of it was conducted on the backs of Southern Railway timetables and other paperwork. Unfortunately the surviving correspondence is too fragmentary to be able to identify the exact issues that were in dispute. There were certainly aspects of the railway's book-keeping and capital accounts which came in for scrutiny. What does not seem to have been questioned was the fact that revenue from railway operation in the three years under review constituted only an average of 53 per cent of the railway's total net revenue. The remaining 47 per cent was derived partly from rents but mainly from interest on investments. In 1938 the EKR had actually earned more, £1,566, from investments than it had from running trains, £1,398. The money invested was mainly derived from the Southern's purchase of EKR shares and from the money set aside for permanent way renewal.

A Directors' Meeting on 3rd April, 1940 heard that the Richborough bridge over the Stour was in need of repair or replacement. Given the limited traffic to Richborough it is not surprising that the Directors were only prepared to authorise minor repairs. They were, however, pleased to hear that the relaying of the main line as far as Golgotha tunnel could be resumed now that the necessary materials had been made available.

The following month saw the first instance of specifically wartime traffic. It was described by W.H. Austen in *Railways in War Time*, an unpublished account of the work of the railways under his management:

In May 1940 a squadron of the Royal Air Force entered upon the railway and took over complete control of Staple station, for all intents and purposes that station being closed to the general public. Both the inwards and outwards traffic formerly dealt with at Staple station had to be diverted to either the company's Wingham or Woodnesborough station, and the company's clerical and other staff attached to the station had to be temporarily transferred to Woodnesborough station. The company's trains were only permitted to pass direct through the station except in cases where goods were consigned for or to be dispatched by the RAF, and that procedure continued until August 1940 when the squadron was transferred elsewhere, after which Staple station and premises were handed back to the company.

Austen's account does not give the reason for the presence of the RAF at Staple which was to service an emergency stockpile of bombs. The departure of the RAF, given in the Directors' Minutes as 18th July rather than Austen's later date, ties in with the outbreak of the Battle of Britain that month. With the intense aerial activity over East Kent, Staple was no longer a suitable rural backwater in which to locate large quantities of high explosive.

Austen's account also omits the fact that the railway charged the War Department £100 for damage done by the RAF to the Staple 'bungalow'. This was either the grounded carriage body installed at Staple in 1926 at a cost of £87 9s. 5d. or the wooden bungalow previously occupied by Mr Carnell, the station agent. The RAF itself paid a further £43 for other unspecified damage here.

The damage was reported to the Directors when they next met on 13th August, 1940. They also heard that the well supplying Fairlight Cottages, purchased along with Sholden Lodge for the construction of the Deal branch, had been condemned and that it would be necessary to lay on a supply from the water company at a cost of £17 10s. 0d. Even in the midst of war the railway was to be reminded of the days when it still had hopes of building its various extensions.

September brought a completely new dimension to life on the railway. Austen's description of these developments introduces them well:

> On the 8th September, 1940 three super heavy batteries of Artillery entered on the railway with their 0-6-0 six-wheeled tender engines together with heavy guns, which were mounted on six-wheeled bogie undercarriages, each of which weighed approximately 82 tons. These guns, together with the locomotives, were stabled in the company's sidings at Shepherdswell, Eythorne and Staple stations, also at Poulton sidings. At frequent intervals exercises took place at certain points on the railway, the guns with their gun crews for such exercises being hauled by WD locomotives. Firing practice took place on several occasions with live shells, the sidings in which the guns were stabled being specially equipped with anchorage for securing the gun carriages when firing took place. On the occasion of such practices a good deal of damage was done to the company's buildings by gun fire concussion, doors and windows blown out, portions of roofs being lifted etc. When firing practices were to take place it was necessary to cease all traffic movements within a certain area and to withdraw the staff from the sheds and shops. On the first occasion of such practices it was considered unnecessary to remove the coaching stock from the station and as a result of not doing so some of the drop and quarter lights were blown out of some coaches which were stabled about 100 yards from the guns. It was then decided to remove such stock during the period of the practices to other sidings as a precautionary measure.

The guns located on the EKR were only a small part of a large number of rail-mounted guns deployed in Kent to hinder German shipping in the Channel and, particularly in the Autumn of 1940, to resist invasion. The biggest of the mobile guns were four 13.5 in. super-charged guns intended for cross-Channel shelling. Although they were far too heavy to have been used on the EKR one of their bases was located on the site of the abortive Stonehall Colliery and occupied the area at which Railways 13 and 24 would have joined the SECR main line if they had been built.

The first guns to arrive on the EKR were two 12 in. howitzers in the charge of the 5th Super Heavy Battery and named 'Sheba' and 'Cleo'. 'Cleo' was based at Shepherdswell where the carriage siding was relaid with stronger materials. 'Sheba' occupied a new siding laid in at the back of Eythorne station alongside the coal siding. These guns were subsequently joined by guns of the 8th and 12th Super Heavy Batteries. The 8th Super Heavy Battery brought two further 12 in. howitzers and took up position at Eythorne, which allowed 'Sheba' to return to Shepherdswell where an additional gun siding was laid in the Southern Railway goods yard. The 8th took over Eythorne Court and erected wooden huts in the grounds there as accommodation. The 12th also brought two 12 in. howitzers and in November 1940 these were based separately at Staple and Poulton siding. In both cases new sidings were laid to accommodate the guns. The Staple gun was moved to Poulton siding in 1941. The guns were occasionally moved along the line although it is doubtful, given the state of the EKR track, that this was done with any regularity and may only have been evacuation practice. There appears to be no official record of the EKR guns ever being fired except for practice or calibration purposes but local legend claims that they were used to shell the *Scharnhorst* as it made its way through the English Channel.

The locomotives used on the EKR by the War Department were 0-6-0 Dean Goods tender engines purchased from the Great Western Railway. Some of these were equipped with pannier tanks to condense their steam and thus render them less visible to German observers. It has proved difficult to identify particular locomotives allocated to the EKR as they seem to have come and gone fairly freely. A number are known to have been described as located in East Kent, but this does not necessarily mean they were on the EKR as other guns were to be found at Adisham, Bishopsbourne, Grove Ferry and Canterbury East.

The regular base for the WD locomotives was the remaining length of the Guilford branch previously used for wagon storage. Austen records that WD locomotives ran 10,349 miles over the EKR between September 1940 and January 1945. Much of this movement must have been connected with the delivery of stores and movement of personnel but other exercises may have been carried out. A mysterious feature of the War Department's presence on the EKR was the laying of a 150 yard extension of the track beyond the platform at Wingham Canterbury Road in 95 lb. bullhead steel rail. As the rail-mounted guns never came this far up the line the purpose of this extension is unknown. In addition to their locomotives the War Department also brought a variety of other rolling stock onto the EKR including French and German Ferry vans. The presence of additional stock seems to have strained the railway's siding accommodation and this, together with the somewhat free and easy operation of the line, led to some potentially disastrous incidents. Fortunately no loss of life was occasioned.

September 1940 was marked by two other war-related incidents. On 15th September a particularly intense episode of the Battle of Britain was taking place over the EKR when senior apprentice Alan Onions saw a Hurricane hit by German fire and descending rapidly on what appeared to be a direct course for Shepherdswell locomotive shed. Fortunately locomotive No. 5 was standing in the yard and he was able to take shelter beneath it. Even more fortunately, the crippled Hurricane actually crashed beyond the Southern main line. Leaving the shelter of No. 5 Mr Onions saw that the pilot had parachuted from his plane and was drifting down towards the Golgotha tunnel entrance so he set off on foot to give such assistance as might be needed. In the event the parachute was caught by a breeze and the pilot landed close to Eythorne. By the time Mr Onions reached him he was already being attended by the local Anti-Aircraft crew.

Shepherdswell Shed may have had a lucky escape but the Richborough branch was less fortunate when a high explosive bomb fell on it on 19th September. A 14 ft 0 in. length of track was destroyed and a crater was created 8 ft 0 in. deep by 12 ft 6 in. in diameter. Austen records that the crater was filled in and the tracks replaced within 12 hours of the incident. He does not record the exact location although he refers to it as being 'on an embankment'. As most of the Richborough branch ran on a low embankment this is not particularly helpful. It is unlikely that it was either of the high embankments leading to the Richborough bridges as it would have taken somewhat longer to repair these. This was the only direct hit sustained by the railway during the war. On a number of occasions telephone wires were brought down and train crews recall being 'buzzed' by enemy aircraft but without being hit. Considering its location the EKR escaped remarkably well.

The Directors met again on 22nd October, 1940. Gilbert Szlumper had resigned to become Railway Control Officer to the Ministry of Transport. His place on the Board was taken by Mr Eustace Missenden, OBE, who had also succeeded Szlumper as General Manager of the Southern Railway. Austen reported that the railway had suffered no major damage yet as a result of enemy action. Discussion then turned to the condition of the bridge at Richborough, mistakenly given in the Minutes as 'Queenborough' and not for the first time. The Directors agreed to dismantle the bridge provided that it could be reinstated at the end of hostilities.

After the excitements of September the remainder of 1940 passed relatively quietly apart from practice firings of the newly installed howitzers. The daily dog-fights of the Battle of Britain gave way to bombing raids on London and the other major cities. During one of these the railway Secretary's offices at Moorgate were destroyed by fire on 29th December. Alex Parkes was able to save the Minute Books but it is not known what other records of the East Kent went up in flames that night.

The threat of invasion disappeared during the winter of 1940. In its place came a state of siege. Coal supplies were a vital element in Britain's survival at this time and it is significant that the East Kent carried a record 330,684 tons of coal during 1940.

1941

Annual Report to Shareholders: The fixed annual sum receivable by the company under the revised arrangements is £3,578, as compared with the previous minimum amount of £3,283, the increase being in the same ratio to the increase in the aggregate of the fixed annual sums agreed for the Main Line Companies and the London Transport Board.

The extract from the Annual Report reflects a change in Government thinking which replaced maximum and minimum shares of a pool of receipts by a fixed annual sum. The intention behind this was to stabilise transport charges and to avoid the complications of adjusting fares and rates to meet variations in working costs. War damage, which had previously been intended to be compensated out of the pool of receipts, was now to be paid on an entirely

The bridge over the Southern at Richborough Castle with track removed as a wartime precaution. Despite repeated announcements that the bridge would be dismantled it was still intact when British Railways took over in 1948. *David Kevan*

The adjoining bridge over the River Stour also survived the war though this was considered to be something of a miracle by the EKR staff. *David Kevan*

separate basis to avoid it becoming a charge on net revenue and further inflating transport costs. For a concern like the EKR, which had only been recovering its minimum share of the pool of receipts and which had not yet suffered major war damage, the new arrangements must have been very welcome.

Less welcome was the news of the destruction of the Secretary's offices which was reported to the Directors at their meeting on 12th February, 1941, though the Directors, pleased to learn that the Minute Books had been saved, were prepared to authorise their rebinding if necessary. As their current condition testifies it was presumably not considered necessary. The only other substantial business of the Meeting was to renew the traffic rates agreement with Tilmanstone Colliery until 31st December, 1941.

The Directors met again in March, August and November. Their main concern was the extent of damage being done to the railway by the military traffic. Compensation was received in March for damage at Richborough and Staple. In August it was reported that damage done to stations by the military was being repaired but there was concern that military trains had already run between 3,000 and 4,000 miles over the line which was causing excessive wear and tear. In November it was announced that an engineer from the War Office was to inspect the damage to the line caused by the military traffic.

The November Meeting also heard that Tilmanstone Colliery wished to increase its price for coal used by the railway. The Directors considered that any such increase would require an increase in the railway's charges for shunting at Tilmanstone. If Tilmanstone could come to an amicable agreement they would be prepared to renew the traffic rates agreement with the colliery until 31st December, 1942.

On 1st December, 1941 a War Department train, equipped with the train staff for the section, collided with a number of wagons that had been left overnight in the cutting leading to Golgotha tunnel. Not only had driver Griffin and guard Buttifint left these wagons on the line without securing the train staff but they had also failed to leave lamps fixed to the wagons. Austen dismissed Griffin and Buttifint immediately. Other staff considered Griffin and Buttifint to have been unlucky as it had been the practice for some time to leave wagons here to collect chalk that had fallen in the cutting, and the absence of lamps was attributed not to oversight but to a chronic shortage of these articles.

Griffin and Buttifint were not prepared to accept their dismissal without protest and approached the National Union of Railwaymen to take up their case. On 8th December John Marchbank, the General Secretary of the NUR, wrote to Austen warning him that the dismissals would be referred to a higher authority and that he reserved the right to claim full wages for both men during the whole period of their suspension. Before taking matters further he would be glad to be favoured with Austen's 'early observations' on the matter.

Austen replied on 11th December regretting that Marchbank had failed to obtain the 'true facts' before writing to him. He pointed out that the crew had acted contrary to all regulations in leaving the wagons as they had done, that two wagons had been demolished and that the line had been blocked for five to six hours as a result of the incident. He added that he had had to reprimand

Buttifint 'only a few months since' for allowing a train of 18 coal wagons to be propelled into the platform road at Shepherdswell while it was fully occupied with WD vehicles and personnel. As a result one of the WD vehicles had been pushed over the buffer stops for half a coach length and had been seriously damaged. Fortunately nobody had been injured. As to Griffin, Austen had cases 'too numerous to mention' of breaches of rules and regulations and consequent damage to the company's property.

Austen emphasised that it was not a case of suspension, the men had been dismissed and would not be reinstated, 'Indeed they were fortunate they were not facing a charge of manslaughter!' Austen's reply concluded with an apology for not dealing with the matter more promptly but he had been confined to bed with appendicitis for the last three weeks. As the incident had only occurred 10 days previously and Marchbank's letter had only been posted on the 8th it is hard to see how Austen could have acted more promptly. The problem seems to have been that Austen had acted too promptly.

Further correspondence passed between Marchbank and Austen during the final weeks of 1941. Marchbank asked for a full enquiry at which the dismissed men could be represented by the local NUR organiser. Austen refused. Marchbank then took the case up with 'higher authority' as he had promised.

1942

Cole Deacon, Railway Executive Committee, January 1942: 'This fellow Austen does seem to lack tact . . . in wartime, when other people's nerves, as well as his, are on edge, it is more than ever necessary to adopt a spirit of tolerance and that his 'Colonel Blimp' methods will, at the end of the day, lead to his defeat'.

1942 started with the continuing dispute over the dismissal of Griffin and Buttifint. Under the combined pressure of the Ministry of War Transport, the Railway Executive Committee and the Southern Railway Austen finally agreed to meet the dismissed men with their NUR representative on 4th February. Even this meeting was nearly cancelled when Austen refused to make an appointment until Buttifint handed in his uniform. The meeting cannot have entirely resolved the matter as Austen reported to the Directors on 26th March, 1942 that he was arranging to meet the NUR '. . . to settle on the best terms possible'. The Directors' next meeting did not take place until 23rd July, 1942 and there is no indication of the actual date of the final settlement which was reported at that meeting. Austen had agreed to pay the dismissed men four weeks wages in lieu of notice, £16 14s. 0d. for Griffin and £12 8s. 0d. for Buttifint. The Minutes continued: 'The General Manager stated that he had paid these out of his own pocket as he may have been to blame for this payment having to be made'. Moving a successful motion to reimburse Austen for the payment, Lord Courthope expressed the opinion that the Directors did not consider Austen to blame, '. . . but in the circumstances of today and in the national interest it was essential to maintain peaceful relations with the men's unions wherever possible'.

Austen really seems to have been out of his depth throughout this affair. His narrow experience of minor railways and the example set by Holman Stephens had hardly prepared him for national grievance procedures or the arts of negotiation. Whilst there was undoubtedly a serious breach of regulations at the heart of this matter, it never seems to have occurred to him that free and easy work practices are just as much the fault of inadequate supervision as of the employees concerned. Even in the days of Holman Stephens it cannot really be said that there was ever an effective day to day management presence on the East Kent.

Reuben Griffin went from the EKR to Tilmanstone where he was employed as a miner. He had been with the railway since the 1920s at least and was well liked by the other staff. Dick Cash, an East Kent guard at that time, said of him, 'He was a gentleman, he was too good to work on the East Kent'. Percy Buttifint also went to Tilmanstone but not as his first choice. He had first elected to join the Merchant Navy but was instead directed to go to work at Snowdown Colliery. He successfully appealed against this on the grounds that Snowdown was further away from his home than Tilmanstone and that three of his brothers were already working at Tilmanstone. His departure ended a long family association with the railway. Not only had his father died in 1912, while working as a brakesman on the construction of the line, but various brothers and cousins had also worked on the line and his widowed mother had worked as a cleaner at the house occupied by Kent Coal Concessions Ltd at Shepherdswell.

Meanwhile other events were taking place on the railway. In February 1942 the Directors had agreed to the breaking up of 'six useless wagons' and the relaying of a further mile of track. Tilmanstone Colliery had agreed not to put up the price of their coal to the railway and the traffic rates agreement had accordingly been extended for another year. However, the quality of Tilmanstone coal supplied to the railway was proving so poor that the Directors resolved to buy coal from Betteshanger instead for a trial period.

On 26th March, 1942 the Directors were pleased to learn that the problems arising from the military traffic over the line had been recognised by the authorities and resolved to charge the War Department 10s. a mile for their use of the line. The War Department must have felt that this was excessive as the question of military traffic came up again on 23rd July, 1942. The Directors had claimed an annual lump sum of £500 as compensation but the War Department had made a counter offer of £400. The Directors agreed to accept this but reserved the right to claim again should military use of the line increase or the damage prove greater than expected.

The same meeting also heard that all four of the Fairlight Cottages at Sholden had been damaged in an air raid and were now unoccupied. The Directors ordered that they should be repaired sufficiently to render them habitable. They also authorised the purchase of carriage wheels and axles from 'another light railway' but hoped that part of the cost might be recouped by selling the existing wheels. It is not clear which line these items came from but it seems likely to have been the Kent & East Sussex. The final business of the meeting was to allow Austen a short holiday. This was, of course, the meeting at which the dispute with the NUR had been resolved and it may well have been considered that Austen had been suffering from overwork.

When the Directors met again on 26th November, 1942 they found another crowded agenda. A bid of £156 to repair the cottages at Sholden was accepted. One mile 10½ chains of track relaying remained to be completed before Eythorne Junction would be reached. The Southern Railway had sold a brakevan to the East Kent for £100 but on inspection it had proved to be an old vehicle and it was hoped that the Southern would reduce its price. Missenden undertook to see what he could do. There had been a recent fall of chalk in the tunnel and the Directors authorised spending £162 12s. 0d. to carry out repairs. By way of contrast the railway had purchased £3,500 of Savings Bonds.

It was also reported that the Government had requisitioned Richborough wharf from the railway. Austen was instructed to obtain the best possible rent for this. Payment of £600 had now been received from the War Department for excess wear and tear of the permanent way from 30th October, 1940 to 6th April, 1942. A claim was also being lodged against the War Department for £126 11s. 4d. arising from a collision between a bren gun carrier and a coal wagon as a result of which a new signal had had to be obtained for £61 13s. 0d., £27 had been spent on engine repairs and £5 13s. 7d. on fence repairs. It is believed that this incident occurred at Eythorne.

The requisitioning of the wharf indicates that the military authorities were starting to take an interest in Richborough again. There is little evidence regarding the use of the wharf for military purposes at this time but, 1942 did see the establishment of a small Royal Navy depot at Richborough. This subsequently became a Commando Training School named HMS *Robertson*. Investigations carried out by local historian Robert Butler while preparing a history of Richborough Port suggest that there was no railway activity involved in the operation of this establishment. Although nothing had yet been done towards dismantling the bridge over the Stour it is unlikely that any EKR traffic was travelling through to Richborough Port at this date. At some point during the war the track on the bridge was lifted but we have not been able to find a date for this event.

1943

MINUTES OF A MEETING OF THE DIRECTORS 18th February, 1943: GOODS BRAKE VAN FOR COAL TRAINS - The General Manager reported that the price had now been reduced to £60, which he thought was a very reasonable figure and this was accepted.

1943 was to prove a busy year on the EKR, not least because the available figures appear to indicate a resurgence of traffic over the line. It is not entirely easy to reconcile the two sets of figures available for the wartime years. Austen gave the following figures for traffic in his *Railways in War Time*:

Year	Goods	Minerals	Coal & Coke	Total
	Tons	Tons	Tons	Tonnage
1940	7,950	4,390	330,684	343,024
1941	8,205	5,617	285,188	299,010
1942	11,733	5,955	263,925	281,613
1943	14,365	7,547	274,987	296,899
1944	18,336	6,248	278,033	302,167

However, when these are compared with a set of figures found amongst documents rescued from the Tonbridge Office a much more dramatic pattern emerges for 1943:

Year	Passenger receipts	Goods receipts	Total receipts
1939	£126	£12,245	£12,371
1940	£178	£5,663	£5,841
1941	£115	£2,550	£2,665
1942	£184	£2,052	£2,236
1943	£622	£7,895	£8,517

The figures for 1942 and 1943 tally with receipts inserted in an office copy of the 1943 Annual Report to Shareholders which were omitted from the published version as required by the regulations for Railway Control. The figures for receipts would therefore seem to be accurate and can only be explained by a significant change in accounting procedures in connection with the calculation of the fixed sum payable under the Railway Control procedures. Whatever the explanation, it is clear that during 1943 all classes of traffic were on the increase.

The Directors' Minutes also reveal a busy and varied pattern of activity on the railway. On 18th February Austen reported that despite delays due to bad weather the track relaying to Eythorne only required the relaying of two points to be completed. The Directors now authorised the purchase of 600 yards of bullhead rail to continue track relaying up to the boundary with the colliery. Austen also reported that repairs to the tunnel were proceeding and that the price of the brake van had been reduced.

The Government requisition of Richborough wharf also seems to have been satisfactorily resolved from the railway's point of view. The Government was prepared to pay £100 pa which would exactly cover the cost of the rent paid by the railway to PDL while retaining the right of access to the wharf when the Government moved out. Austen was asked to press for additional compensation in respect of wear and tear of the sidings on the wharf.

It would appear that the railway's own collection and delivery service had been discontinued. It may be that Carnell, the Staple agent, was operating this service on his own account by this date. Austen produced figures to show that £451 had been paid for cartage in 1942 although the figures subsequently given in the railway's own accounts show receipts of £425 against expenses of £422. It was Austen's view that the railway should resume its own service but that this would require a 2-3 ton lorry and the employment of a driver, indicating that the railway no longer had its own lorry. The Directors left the matter for further consideration.

The railway still had a number of surplus girders in hand. The Kent & East Sussex Railway wished to purchase two of these weighing approximately 10 cwt each. The Directors agreed a price of £10 and asked Austen to obtain offers for the remaining girders.

The question of renewing the Traffic Agreement with Tilmanstone Colliery then arose. It was pointed out that Tilmanstone's Accounts showed the colliery to have been in profit in 1941 to the tune of £9,950 and that the aggregate profit for the past four years amounted to £30,494. Additionally, '. . . the quality of the Tilmanstone coal had been growing steadily worse since the outbreak of the war, which rendered it necessary to clear out the large accumulation of clinkers from fire-boxes after only very short runs, which was a very serious handicap to the efficient and economical working of the traffic'. The Directors resolved that any renewal of the traffic agreement must be dependent on suspending the requirement that the railway purchase its coal supplies from Tilmanstone. The Accountant, E.F. Marsh, was asked to take this up with the colliery and to see whether the colliery would make cash payments in lieu of the free coal supplies to which the railway was entitled under the Agreement.

Little fresh business was conducted at the next meeting on 25th March but some outstanding issues were cleared up. The War Department had met the railway's claim for damage resulting from the bren gun carrier collision in full. Enquiries had shown Betteshanger coal to be too expensive for the railway and, since the quality of Tilmanstone coal had conveniently improved, it was decided to continue to obtain supplies from that colliery after all. The Traffic Agreement could therefore be renewed without amendment. Austen had not yet found any buyers for the surplus girders but was pursuing a new claim against the War Department in respect of Richborough wharf. This was based on a claim for compensation in respect of the railway's loss of use of the wharf. This claim dragged on for some time as the railway must have had some difficulty in proving that it had actually lost anything of value. Arguably the EKR was better off to the extent that the Government was paying enough to cover the rent on the wharf.

One claim that went unreported in the Directors' Minutes, but for which the invoice and a letter confirming payment survive, concerned two baulk timbers 'missing from Tank Bank, Richborough'. One was 30 feet long by 11 in. by 9 in. and the other was 26 feet long by 11 in. square, hardly the sort of property to be mislaid inadvertently. The culprits were 464 Battery of the Royal Artillery who paid up the £9 6s. 7d. value of the timbers without demur. Quite what 464 Battery were up to and quite what the 'Richborough Tank Bank' was remains unanswered.

When the Directors next met on 22nd July, 1943 they had to review the railway's locomotive position. Austen reported that the railway had seven locomotives of which two were unsuitable for its needs. These two were evidently Nos. 2 and 5 as he considered that these should be sold and one locomotive purchased to replace them. Surprisingly, Austen seems to have been mistaken as to the total of locomotives as by this date the railway only owned six locomotives, Nos. 1, 3 and 8 having already been broken up. The East Kent Locomotive Mileage Register shows that not only Nos. 2 and 5 but also No. 7 had only been working intermittently during 1942 and the early part of 1943. From April 1943 the railway had been hiring Southern Railway 'O1' 0-6-0 No. 1430. Possibly Austen included this locomotive in his figures. Another Southern 'O1', No. 1426, is shown as having been hired during September 1942 but this was just for that month, whereas No. 1430 remained on the East Kent until 17th December, 1943 to be replaced by sister locomotive No. 1066 on the 20th December.

The East Kent 'O1' No. 6 had been out of use since August 1942 but had returned to traffic in July 1943. Unfortunately Austen had to report that No. 6 had been damaged on 19th July as a result, in Austen's opinion, of its driver's carelessness. It would require a new cylinder to be fitted and would have to go to Ashford as the work was beyond the railway's own facilities.

Despite Austen's views as to the driver's fault it is significant that no mention is made of dismissal or disciplinary proceedings. The same Minutes also refer to a serious shortage of manpower on the line. Under such circumstances the EKR could hardly afford to lose a driver.

Moving on from locomotive matters Austen reported that a claim was to be submitted to South Eastern Command for damage caused by gunfire concussion. No details are given so that it is not possible to determine which of the howitzer batteries was to blame. The military presence on the line must have brought back memories of Longmoor to Colonel Gore Vesey when he made his annual Chairman's tour of inspection on 6th July.

Austen also reported that rails for relaying the colliery branch had now been received and there had been a request from Tilmanstone Colliery for the railway to reinstate the Colliery North Bank Junction and to lay in a connection with the Southern at Richborough. The colliery was advised to apply to the Ministry of War Transport as '. . . this company was not prepared to pay any of the cost of same'. It is tantalising that the EKR should have got so close to realising part at least of the original intention behind the Richborough branch and to have been unable to carry out the necessary work. Had this scheme been possible it would have generated far more income in mileage receipts than the short trip between Tilmanstone and Shepherdswell. The route would also have been easier to work as loaded trains would have travelled downhill for all but short sections, and none of these presented any of the difficulties faced in bringing coal up to Shepherdswell.

The Directors met for the last time in 1943 on 25th November. Austen was able to report that all but two rails of the colliery branch had been relaid and that the spur to the Southern at Shepherdswell had been realigned. The only regret on the permanent way situation was that the track through Golgotha tunnel was now in need of further attention.

The locomotive situation had been assisted by the return to service of locomotive No. 6 which had come back from repair at Ashford on 7th October. Locomotive No. 2 had been sold for £575 and it was hoped to get £450 for No. 5. Austen was authorised to approach the Southern Railway with a view to obtaining an additional locomotive.

In the absence of any further developments in 1943 it may be considered that the year ended on a much more positive note than was usual. The business section of the railway between Shepherdswell and the colliery was in better shape than it had been in a long time. Traffic was increasing. Damage was being paid for. There was hope of an additional locomotive. Even the coal supplied by Tilmanstone was improving!

The body of Cheshire Lines Committee carriage No. 6 at Staple is believed to have been used by the military authorities during the war together with the heavily sandbagged shelter to the left.

0-6-0ST No. 2 was sold in 1943. Here it is seen standing in Shepherdswell yard in 1939 in the new standard green livery. *Jim Jarvis*

1944

Railway Observer August 1944: EAST KENT RAILWAY - Nos. 4, 5, 7, 100 and SR No. 1371 were at Shepherdswell on 21/7/44. 1371 retains her SR number and as she was repainted with SR standard lettering and number on cab-sides just before her acquisition by the EKR she is likely to keep it for some time. The 5.0 Shepherdswell-Wingham, consisting of one ex-SER six-wheel coach and 22 wagons, left Shepherdswell headed by No. 6 running tender first.

The quest for an additional locomotive proved successful. The first stage in its acquisition was reported by Austen on 17th February. He had been offered a locomotive by the Southern Railway for £750 and sought the Directors' authorisation to inspect it and to accept the locomotive if it proved satisfactory. Meanwhile no offers had yet been received to purchase locomotive No. 5. The Directors also authorised the relaying of the track through the tunnel and 'the short spur at Shepherdswell'.

Further damage had been suffered since the Directors had last met. The reservoir at Shepherdswell had been damaged by concussion but the War Department was prepared to pay the £72 quoted to repair this. A number of fences had been broken by the military and there had been two collisions at level crossings but it was not expected that any liability would accrue to the railway.

The Royal Engineers had asked to dismantle the Richborough bridge over the Stour and undertook to leave the girders removed in this operation alongside the track pending reinstatement of the bridge in the future. The Directors do not appear to have felt that there was any option but to agree to this request. Similarly the Traffic Agreement with Tilmanstone Colliery was renewed without comment.

The Directors met again on 16th March. Austen had inspected locomotive No. 1371, another 'O1' 0-6-0, and considered that it would be fit for work for some time, though he was concerned that the tyres and cylinders would require repair in the future. The Directors authorised its purchase and it subsequently arrived on the EKR on 3rd April, 1944. It continued to carry its Southern Railway number and identity throughout its time on the railway.

Austen also reported that the Royal Engineers were about to commence dismantling the Richborough bridge. The fact that the railway disclaimed responsibility for any injuries that might be incurred in this work is probably as much a comment on the state of the bridge as on the prudence of the Directors.

The final issue discussed at this Meeting was the fact that Carnell, the station agent at Staple responsible for local collections and deliveries, was refusing to serve either Woodnesborough or Eastry stations. There would presumably have been little difficulty in arranging for all collections and deliveries to be made through Staple station, but the Directors authorised Austen to stop the 7s. weekly allowance paid to Carnell for serving the other stations.

Bad news outweighed the good at the Directors' next Meeting on 13th July, 1944. The good news was that Eustace Missenden had received a knighthood and that the Shepherdswell reservoir had been repaired. The bad news was that work had not yet started on dismantling the Richborough bridge and that the relaying in the tunnel had been delayed by overtime disputes. Locomotive No. 5 remained unsold and War Department locomotives had caused £102 worth of damage to pointwork. A claim had been made.

The Directors met again on 9th November. Dismantling had still not started on the bridge but it was hoped to complete the relaying through the tunnel in three weeks as the Railway Executive Committee had agreed to double time payment for Sunday working. Locomotive No. 100 had gone away to Ashford for firebox repairs. In fact this locomotive went away on 20th October and returned on 11th December. Unreported in the Minutes was the hire of 'T' class 0-6-0T No. 1604 from the Southern from 28th September; it was to remain on the EKR until 13th January, 1945.

No. 100 was not the only locomotive in need of attention. No. 6 needed new wheels. Austen had a spare set of locomotive wheels in stock, probably salvaged from No. 8, but would need to obtain new wheels for the tender. Less understandable is a report in the Minutes that 'locomotive No. 3' needed a new boiler which might possibly be obtained second-hand from the Southern. As locomotive No. 3 had been broken up in the 1930s it would have needed rather more than a boiler! The locomotive concerned is probably 0-6-0ST No. 7 for which the Southern did have a boiler available. Unfortunately this was fitted to locomotive No. 3334 which had been tried and rejected by the Kent & East Sussex in 1938 and had lain derelict at Eastleigh ever since. If locomotive No. 7 was the locomotive in question it is not surprising that there is no further mention of it getting a new boiler.

The November Meeting was also significant for the re-appearance of the Hammill Brickworks in the affairs of the railway. The brickworks had been in Receivership since December 1938 but had taken on a new role during the war. The rotary clay dryer had been pressed into service to salvage damaged grain at the rate of about 100 tons a week. This was delivered by rail from London and other towns and required about 10 to 15 tons of Tilmanstone coal to be delivered each week. The grain was later milled on site for use as livestock feed, the final weekly output being some 60 to 80 tons a week. In all some 12,000 tons were dealt with during the war. On 26th May, 1944 the brickworks company had been able to discharge the Receiver and was re-formed with a new Board of Directors. It is not clear whether the company's business at this date was grain milling or brick making but they had offered to pay off their debt to the EKR with 232 shares at 2s. 6d. each. The railway's response to this offer is unclear. The EKR could hardly object to a practice in which it had itself indulged for so many years, but must have known from its own experience that payment in cash would have been preferable.

Whilst on the subject of shares it should be added that since 1937 the railway had only sold 23 shares and was only ever going to sell 4 more. It seems unlikely that there was a real market for EKR shares by this date except amongst collectors of financial exotica or students of minor railways. There was no likelihood of a dividend ever being paid on the Ordinary Shares and even the 5 per cent Debentures only paid 1 per cent in 1944.

Before leaving 1944 we should mention that the year had seen a brief revival of rail-connected military activity at Richborough. The Pioneer Corps had established a depot for constructing the floating metal spans which were to form the Mulberry Harbours used in the Normandy Landings. A number of steam cranes were employed in this work, and the maintenance of these was entrusted to a detachment of Royal Engineers who worked from a railway mobile workshop train converted from Southern Railway luggage and goods vans.

A separate activity at Richborough was the marshalling of United States Army Transportation Corps wagons which had been brought to Britain in kit form and then put together at various points around the country. On arrival at Richborough it was found that many of these wagons were defective and considerable remedial work had to be carried out before they could travel onwards to France in late 1944. The Normandy landings took place in June and by the end of 1944 it appears that all the equipment assembled at Richborough had departed and the site resumed its ghost status. An important reason for carrying out all this work at Richborough was to give the appearance that the Allied Invasion would be launched from Kent and aimed at the Pas de Calais, thus diverting attention from the real invasion plans.

By December 1944 the howitzers based on the EKR had departed and the War Department had vacated the sites at Shepherdswell and Eythorne but continued to occupy their sidings at Staple and Poulton. Whilst the war was far from over it may be said that the railway's active role was finished at the end of 1944.

1945

Edwin Course *The Railways of Southern England: Independent and Light Railways*: I made my first pilgrimage to see what the East Kent looked like during a weekend leave in February 1945. Although I knew that it was unlikely that there would be any movement on the East Kent on a Sunday, in the days following the invasion of Europe anything might happen, and I did entertain some faint hopes of seeing an East Kent locomotive in steam. So on Sunday morning, I boarded a bus of the East Kent Road Car Co., and asked a slightly puzzled conductress for a single to Wingham station. She knew what I meant but hastened to assure me that she had never seen a train there.

Professor Course was unsuccessful in his hopes of finding any EKR locomotives in steam during his walk along the tracks from Wingham to Eastry and thence to Sandwich Road. Although he recalls the presence of vans at Poulton Farm siding he found no evidence, either there or at Staple, of the recent presence of the War Department. Had he continued towards Shepherdswell rather than taking the Richborough branch he might have been more successful in finding signs of life on the railway as a new programme of permanent way work was under way. At the Directors' Meeting on 22nd February Austen reported the purchase of 4,000 new sleepers as well as four tons of sole plates for flat-bottomed track to be used to preserve the track alignment on curves. However, he also had to report that he had had '. . . considerable difficulty owing to absenteeism and the men refusing to work on Sundays but there had recently been an improvement in conditions'.

The same Meeting reported a wide range of other activities in hand. Locomotive No. 6 had gone away to Ashford again for repair. The Mileage

Register shows No. 6 to have been out of service from 26th January to 6th June, 1945 but does not record the actual dates of departure and return. Locomotive No. 4 which had been out of use since April 1943 apart from one solitary turn in January 1945 was now receiving repairs at Shepherdswell. It returned to service in May. The Mileage Register shows that Southern Railway 'O1' No. 1373 was hired from January to May 1945 to cover the motive power shortage in the meantime.

Under an item headed 'Wagons for Internal Use' Austen asked for authority to dispose of 10 'very old' wagons and to replace them with 10 'disused' wagons from the Southern. The Draft Minutes are somewhat more blunt: 'Get 10 old wagons from S.Rly'. Obviously somebody considered it was better to replace 'very old' wagons with 'disused' ones rather than 'old' ones.

Another curiosity was Austen's report that three signals at Eastry had been blown down in a gale. He requested authority to replace them with three 'tubular cast iron signals'. As subsequent photographs show no apparent difference in the signals at Eastry it seems that Austen was able to re-erect the existing signals.

The Royal Engineers had still not dismantled the Richborough bridge by February 1945 and Austen was considering carrying out this work using the railway staff '. . . as otherwise the girders might fall into the River'.

The only other significant business of this Meeting was to appoint surveyors to deal with the disposal of lands on the Mongeham and Deal branch. There followed a steady trickle of sales which it is not intended to catalogue in detail. Although most of the land found buyers there were still isolated pockets here and there to be inherited by British Railways on Nationalisation.

As usual the Directors met again in March but had relatively little business to transact. Austen produced his draft of 'A Memorandum of a History of the company' for publication in *Railways in War Time* for the approval of the Directors and with a view to publication by the Association of Minor Railways. This organisation had been set up in 1938 to represent the interests of those railways which had not been included in the Grouping of 1922. Although the Directors were happy to approve publication, it does not seem that this was ever proceeded with and only the sections devoted to the EKR and the KESR appear to have survived.

Otherwise the Meeting was mainly concerned with a further renewal of the Traffic Agreement with Tilmanstone Colliery and the submission of a claim to the Government for compensation for 'abnormal wear and tear' on the same basis as a claim recently submitted by the main line companies. This claim was subsequently settled by the Ministry of War Transport in October 1945 but only amounted to £20. It seems that the Ministry had taken into account the many claims already submitted by the EKR, as the KESR was awarded £250 on its claim.

The end of the war in Europe was declared on the 8th May, 1945 and the EKR celebrated this fact by returning locomotives 4 and 6 to traffic in that month. From May the EKR began an unusually regular pattern of locomotive operations with locomotives 100 and 1371 running services one week and locomotives 4 and 6 running the next week. This pattern of running pairs of locomotives alternate weeks continued with only occasional interruptions until

Nationalisation. The actual locomotives paired changed from time to time but the general principle seems to have suited the railway well.

The Directors next met on 12th July. Lord Courthope was congratulated on his elevation to the peerage and the sale of further pockets of land was discussed. Amongst the properties concerned were the Fairlight Cottages at Sholden. A reserve price of £700 had been set on these before the war but it was now hoped to obtain £1,000. The subject of these cottages was to continue to occupy the Directors for some time but they appear to have been eventually sold for £500 in 1946. The difficulty with many of the land sales was that the property had originally been bought at inflated prices by the East Kent Contract and Financial Company. Any sale at a lower price reduced the capital value of the railway without any corresponding increase to its income.

The railway was luckier with its long-standing claim for compensation in respect of its loss of use of Richborough wharf, which was met by a retrospective lease of the wharf by the Admiralty at £125 pa from September 1942 to March 1945. Success breeds success and the Directors were encouraged to lodge a claim for £400 for the 'Staple Bungalow destroyed by gunfire'. It is not clear which of the various sheds and old carriage bodies at Staple this claim related to, but it should be remembered that the RAF had already paid for damage caused to a 'bungalow' at Staple during their occupancy of the site.

The Directors next turned their attention to rolling stock. Ten wagons had been purchased from the Southern at £25 apiece and it was agreed to break up 10 old wagons. It was also decided to break up four carriages and to replace them with two Southern bogie brake thirds. As to the locomotive fleet it was decided to seek offers from Geo. Cohen and from T.W. Ward for locomotives 5 and 7. In this the Directors may have been encouraged by the fact that the railway had recently sold a quantity of rails to T.W. Ward for £7 a ton whilst replacing it with heavier bullhead rail from the Southern at only £4 a ton! The Richborough bridge had still not been dismantled.

World War II ended with Japan's surrender on 2nd September, 1945 but the railway remained under Government Control. A Labour Government had been elected on 26th July and public ownership of both the coal industry and the railways was now clearly a distinct possibility.

The Directors had more mundane concerns when they met on the 8th November. Further lands had been sold but the War Department was only offering £75 for the destruction of the Staple bungalow. Austen was instructed to try for £100. Even more disappointing were the bids for locomotives 5 and 7. T.W. Ward were offering £61 for the pair and Geo. Cohen's offer of £80 was little better. Austen was directed to approach the Southern Railway '. . . with a view to the Chief Mechanical Engineer giving his opinion on such offers, and, if possible, put the company in touch with a Merchant who might make a better offer'.

Austen also reported that locomotive 100 had gone to Ashford for repairs and that the Southern was looking out two suitable carriages for the railway. No. 100 did not actually leave for Ashford until 21st November. During its absence 'O1' No. 1373 was hired from the Southern and paired with No. 4, while No. 1371 which had previously been paired with No. 100 was now paired with No. 6.

The EKR was one of the few railways in the United Kingdom to emerge from World War II in better condition than when the war had begun. Its locomotive stock was leaner but a great deal fitter than it had ever been. It had acquired 'new' wagons and a substantial part of its permanent way had been renewed. Traffic figures had improved and, even though it was unlikely that passenger or general goods traffic would continue at the same levels under peacetime conditions, it was to be hoped that coal tonnages could be maintained or even increased.

One of the last regular passengers on the line at Knowlton Halt.

P. Ransome-Wallis/National Railway Museum

Chapter Twelve

The Last Years of Independence - 1946-1948

Despite the prospect of Nationalisation the EKR did not rest on its laurels when peace returned and continued to make repairs as far as its modest means would allow. There was, admittedly, no attempt to restore the connection to Richborough but there was little traffic of any sort beyond Poison Cross anyway. It might be argued that it was in the railway's interest, for compensation purposes, to maintain its assets during this period. However, the picture that emerges is of a railway continuing to go about its business as it had always done.

1946

ANNUAL REPORT TO SHAREHOLDERS: The arbitrary fixation by Parliament itself of the value for Compensation purposes of the undertakings to be compulsorily acquired is unsatisfactory and without precedent.

1946 saw the first tangible steps taken towards railway nationalisation with the introduction of the Transport Bill. The EKR felt itself to be particularly vulnerable as the Bill proposed that undertakings would normally be acquired at their quoted price on the Stock Exchange. As there was no such quotation for the EKR it was feared that its assets might not be valued as highly as the Directors or shareholders might wish.

For all their protests it is unlikely that the Directors had any serious hope of avoiding Nationalisation. The Southern Railway's holding in the EKR inevitably meant that where the Southern went, there the EKR must also go. Moreover by 1946 it was becoming apparent that the wartime levels of traffic would not be sustained. We only have figures for traffic originating on the line but the following comparison between 1945 and 1947 shows a general pattern of declining traffic:

Traffic originating on the East Kent Railway

Year	Passengers	Merchandise	Coal	Other minerals
1945	985	12,202 tons	263,195 tons	1,538 tons
1946	766	7,411 tons	243,522 tons	2,248 tons
1947	556	3,296 tons	255,658 tons	2,791 tons

Whilst coal traffic remained comfortably above the levels of most pre-war years the only other comfort to be gleaned was from 'Other Minerals'. This may possibly have been gravel, clay traffic or sugar beet. However, the increase in this traffic was not going to make up in any way for the continuing haemorrhage of the railway's merchandise business. This was not only more lucrative by item and train mile than mineral or coal traffic, but was the only real reason for keeping the line open beyond Eythorne.

4-4-2T No. 5 at Shepherdswell in considerably better condition than when it was eventually sold to the Southern Railway in 1946.

0-6-0ST No. 7 awaiting scrapping at Ashford in 1946. Someone has thoughtfully restored its identity with a liberal application of chalk.

The Directors' first meeting in 1946 took place on 28th February and heard a number of welcome reports. Austen had succeeded in obtaining £100 compensation for the Staple bungalow instead of the £75 originally offered, and the Southern had offered to purchase locomotives Nos. 5 and 7 for £120 and £90 respectively. No. 7 appears to have been purchased for scrap but No. 5 was destined to be completely rebuilt for service on the Lyme Regis branch. Austen could also report the return of locomotive No. 100, now renumbered No. 2, from overhaul at Ashford and an offer by the Southern to sell two carriages to the railway for £75 each.

The Directors also had to consider the matter of 460 yards of track laid by the War Department during the war. It is not clear what arrangements were made elsewhere on the line but the 150 yard extension at Wingham Canterbury Road was being offered to the railway and Austen was instructed to purchase this for up to £75. The Directors were less inclined to consider an offer from Cementation Limited to remove defence works along the line for £6,026 11s. 9d. which seemed rather high! The traffic agreement with Tilmanstone Colliery was renewed without comment.

The Directors met again on 27th March to hear that locomotives Nos. 5 and 7 had been 'taken over' by the Southern on 14th March but the carriages had not yet been delivered. Austen had offered £50 for the track at Wingham Canterbury Road and was awaiting a reply. A quote of £1,600 had been received to dismantle the bridge over the Stour but this was considered too expensive. The railway's Accountant, Mr E.F. Marsh, was retiring from the Southern Railway but the Directors hoped that he would continue to serve the EKR in this capacity.

The Chairman's annual tour of inspection on the 17th May was but one of the items reported at the Directors' next meeting on 24th July. The bogie carriages had at last arrived from the Southern. The War Department had accepted the £50 offered by Austen for their track at Wingham Canterbury Road and the railway had undertaken the removal of defence works at Shepherdswell with its own staff at an estimated cost of £90, compared with the £500 asked by Cementation for this particular site.

One unprecedented item of business was a complaint by fitter Davis concerning his weekly pay of £5 8s. 6d. The Directors resolved to consult the Southern as to rates of pay. Finally, Austen reported that it had not been possible to dismantle the bridge over the Stour as the electricity company had failed to remove its cable. It seems strange that after so many years of consideration, nobody had previously identified this particular problem.

The bridge was still standing when the Directors held their final meeting of 1946 on 7th November. The Directors were possibly more concerned by the news that locomotive No. 2 and carriage No. 10 had been derailed at Woodnesborough on 13th September as a result of the gauge spreading. Although such incidents were not uncommon this seems to have been the only one formally reported to the Directors.

Even if funds had been available for refurbishing the track beyond Eythorne it is by no means certain that labour could have been found to carry out the work. The railway was finding it increasingly difficult to recruit staff. This may

0-6-0 No. 6 pauses at Staple on its way to Wingham with carriage No. 5 and assorted goods vehicles on 25th April, 1947.

H.C. Casserley

have prompted the Directors to increase fitter Davis's pay by 10s., but any beneficial effect this might have had on staff morale was undermined by the dismissal of a guard and a fireman following the disappearance of a small quantity of cherries and a sandbag. The Directors were also informed of the resignation of one of the other guards and of one of the clerks at Shepherdswell.

The same meeting reported the renewal of the traffic agreement with Tilmanstone Colliery for the last time before Nationalisation of the mines. Although the Directors were informed that Tilmanstone (Kent) Collieries Ltd had made profits of £182,974 since that company had been reconstituted in 1937, they do not seem to have felt that it was necessary to increase the traffic charges. With Nationalisation of the mines and railways in sight it seems that the time for local disputes was over. It may also have been feared that an increase in charges would turn the Tilmanstone management's thoughts to re-opening the ropeway to Dover. Although the ropeway had ceased operations in 1939 it had not been entirely forgotten and there was even talk of serving Guilford Colliery with a branch from the ropeway should it be decided to renew work there.

On 28th November, 1946 the Directors received formal notice of the Government's intention to include the EKR amongst the lines to be nationalised.

1947

ANNUAL REPORT TO SHAREHOLDERS: The proprietors may rest assured that the Directors will do their best to obtain an equitable settlement of their claim for compensation.

The Nationalisation of the coal industry from 1st January, 1947 had little immediate effect on the railway. The onset of the most severe winter conditions for many years was of much greater concern to everyone involved with fuel or transport and the Directors' Minutes make no reference to the changed status of the coal industry at all. By a curious anomaly the one surviving enterprise of Arthur Burr's coal empire, Kent Coal Concessions, escaped Nationalisation and continued to charge the National Coal Board for royalties on coal raised at Snowdown.

On 26th February the Directors heard from Austen that bad weather and staff shortages had prevented any work on the Richborough bridge. By this date the railway's main concern was to salvage the girders used to build the bridge. The only other significant business of the meeting was to consider the electricity supply to the locomotive shed at Shepherdswell. Hitherto this had been provided by accumulators but these were worn out and it was resolved to obtain a mains supply instead.

The Directors' next meeting on 26th March was mainly concerned with the problem of chalk falls in the cutting leading to Golgotha tunnel. It was estimated that more than a thousand tons of chalk had fallen but the railway had been able to continue operating. Austen hoped to be able to remove the chalk on Sundays without interfering with services on the line. On a more positive note it was recorded that the Government had set up a buffer depot for

No. 6 on the curve out of Eastry in 1947 with 'new' bogie carriage No. 5 and a Southern Railway brake van in tow.

P. Ransome-Wallis/National Railway Museum

emergency food supplies on the Hammill branch. This was briefly responsible for bringing additional traffic over the railway.

A serious problem had to be addressed when the Directors met on 23rd July:

> It was . . . reported that Carnell was running practically nightly with market produce with his own lorry to the London Markets, same having been confirmed by the Southern Railway, and for such action, which was against all the railway company's rules and detrimental to the railway, it was resolved and agreed that the services of Carnell should be dispensed with at the earliest possible moment.

Carnell was the station agent at Staple and in a unique position to corner the agricultural traffic that had previously travelled over the railway. It is likely that if Carnell had not taken up this opportunity then others would have done so, but there was certainly a dramatic reduction in the traffic dispatched from Staple in the post-war period.

On the 1st October Eustace Missenden retired as a Director of the EKR on his appointment as Chairman of the Railway Executive Committee. No attempt was made to fill his place on the Board.

The remaining Directors held their last recorded meeting on 6th November, 1947 and heard that Carnell had appealed against his dismissal. It is not clear what argument Carnell put forward but it fell on deaf ears as his 'termination' was confirmed.

The final item of business was to hear that the Government had de-requisitioned the 'Queenborough wharf' on 1st October. The draft minutes actually read 'Richborough' as they should have done but it is a significant commentary on all the efforts to reach the sea that had been made since 1910 that the last official reference to the railway's destination should have got the wrong name.

1948

A Postscript

The EKR should have become part of the Southern Region of British Railways on 1st January, 1948. In the event British Railways must have had its hands full absorbing the East Kent's larger neighbours and Austen continued to manage both the EKR and the KESR from the Salford Terrace office in Tonbridge until May 1948.

A tour of inspection of the EKR was eventually arranged on 1st April, 1948. The following memorandum records the findings of the inspection. We have added our own comments in square brackets.

Memorandum of visit of inspection to East Kent Railway, 1st April, 1948

Preamble

In company with Messrs W.H. Austen (Senior and Junior) and J.A.Iggulden, the Superintendent of Operation, Commercial Superintendent, Assistant Civil Engineer, Divisional Engineer, Divisional Superintendent and other Departmental Officers and Chiefs of Sections, visited the East Kent Railway, 1st April, 1948.

1. Track layout

The East Kent line commences with a junction with one of the down sidings at Shepherds Well and proceeds in a more or less north-easterly direction to Eythorne, with a junction leading to Tilmanstone Colliery and thence to Eastry, where the line divides north-westerly to Wingham (Canterbury Road) and north-easterly to Richborough, the approximate total mileage being 16½, single line.

There are short stretches of double line at Eythorne and Eastry.

There is one tunnel between Shepherds Well and Eythorne named 'Golgotha' - one third of a mile in length. The tunnel has been constructed for double-line working. [No reference is made to the chalk blocks on the spare line through the tunnel.]

2. Level crossings

There is one gated level crossing at the public highway known as Roman Road [confusingly the roads at both Sandwich Road and Roman Road were known as Roman Road - this refers to Sandwich Road] and several public road level crossings (without gates and equipped with cattle guards), also numerous accommodation crossings (equipped with ordinary field gates).

3. Fencing

Generally speaking, the railway boundary is defined by post and wire fencing.

4. Locomotive water facilities

Shepherds Well

One water crane in shed road; one on 'main' line near passenger station platform.

Woodnesborough

One water crane.

Staple

One water crane supplied by Windmill pump. Suggestion in hand to connect with main water supply laid in by Military during the war to a point near station platform.

Notes on Stations and Halts

5. Shepherds Well

One platform with station buildings. The platform line is a terminal almost at right angles to Southern Region main line.

Details of the siding accommodation at Shepherds Well were not taken but there is apparently sufficient capacity for several hundred wagons [something of an over-estimate!], including an old rarely used spur siding situate at high level with connection somewhat remote from the station.

These sidings are situate on the down or west side.

6. Eythorne

A connection on the up siding facing for up trains exists to Guildford [*sic*] Colliery. This colliery is not operating and the Tramway is not used. [Most of it had been lifted in 1937 but the War Department had relaid a short length of the surviving line for their locomotives.]

A connection facing for down trains exists on the up side forming a loop to Tilmanstone Colliery. Goods Yard on down side. Two sidings with connection facing for down trains.

Short platform with small brick built structure containing office and store.

Tilmanstone sidings

Situate on up side with single line approximately half a mile in length fanning out into several sidings serving the colliery which is on higher ground than the East Kent Railway proper. There are gravitation sidings in the colliery.

There is no line of demarcation between British Transport Commission property and colliery property and it was gathered that no agreement existed regarding the terms and conditions for maintenance of operation of the sidings.

7. Elvington

Short brick faced platform only on down side, in reasonably good condition.

8. Knowlton

Short platform with waiting shed up side. Both in poor condition.

9. Eastry South

Off loading siding on up side with facing connection to down trains.

Beyond the public road level crossing and on the down side is a short platform. The platform is in poor condition.

10. Eastry

Siding forming a loop on down side; short platform with waiting shed and office up side. Accommodation in fair condition.

Shortly after passing the junction at Eastry, a turn out facing for down trains exists on the Canterbury Road section leading to the Hammill Brick Works, at which point is also a Ministry of Food Buffer Store. There is some brick traffic and the Food Store is regularly served by rail.

It was gathered that no agreement exists for the maintenance of operation of the brick works siding, but that there is some reference thereto in the Light Railway Act. Certain expenditure is required here and Mr Austen will be handing over correspondence relating thereto. [This correspondence has not come to light.]

11. Woodnesborough

A siding on up side with connection facing for down trains, also side loading dock.

Short platform with structure containing shed and office on down side. Accommodation in fair condition.

Note - about a mile beyond Woodnesborough station there is a connection facing for down trains to Moat Farm siding situate on up side.

It was not made clear whether there was any agreement relative to this siding.

12. Ash Town

Short platform, with shelter, on up side.

Note - A short distance beyond Ash Town there is a connection facing for down trains to Poulton siding. It was not made clear whether there is any agreement as to this siding.

13. Staple

Sidings on down side consist of a loop with a short siding in the rear.

There are 3 sidings on the up side with connection facing for up trains.

The platform is on the up side with a brick built shelter and store, all in good condition. An old coach body is used as an office.

There are several lettings at Staple, particulars of which are in the hands of the Estate & Rating Surveyor.

14. Wingham Colliery

Short platform up side. The colliery is not being worked. There is an agricultural siding. [There is rumoured to have been a siding beyond the Halt at one time but it had long since gone. Plans drawn up by British Railways in April 1948 show no signs of a siding here.]

15. Wingham Town

Short platform up side.

Note - Immediately south of Wingham Town station there is a connection facing for down trains on the down side leading to the Wingham Engineering Company's Works. The siding runs through a large shed. It was not made clear whether there is any agreement relative to this siding.

16. Wingham (Canterbury Road)

One siding up side with connection facing for down trains.

An old van body with loading dock (foul of gauge) exists on up side. This van body is used as a Goods Shed.

Beyond the public road level crossing is a short platform on down side. Platform in fair condition.

Note - It was understood that the line extended beyond Wingham Canterbury Road for about 300 yards, this extension having been laid in by the Military (the extension was not visited).

17. Section Eastry to Richborough

Poison Cross Halt (Eastry Goods)

Sidings on down side consisting of a loop with outer siding connected thereto.

Short platform up side.

Note - It was understood that this is a sugar beet area and new coal borings are also under consideration. [One of many rumours of new collieries current at this date; another favourite was the re-opening of Guilford Colliery.]

There is at present no traffic of any description beyond Poison Cross Halt [interviews with staff suggest that seasonal workings still brought back market produce from beyond Poison Cross].

Roman Road Halt

Short platform up side, immediately south of gated crossing. [Further confusion between the two 'Roman Roads' - this crossing had no gates.]

Sandwich Road

Short platform up side, also loop siding down side. [No mention of the real gated level crossing.]

Beyond [some way beyond] Sandwich Road, the line bifurcates, the 'left hand' leading to several short sidings (Richborough Castle sidings) partly overgrown by bushes, the 'right hand' turn leading to a bridge over the River Stour with a loop between the junction and the river bridge. [No mention of bridge over road and Deal branch.]

Note - This bridge is unfit for use by rail traffic but it was understood that the extension over the river to Richborough Port was designed for the export of coal from the Kent Collieries.

Mention was made of a charge of £100 per annum payable by the East Kent Railway Company for the privilege of working to Richborough, which charge is a statutory one.

18. *Signalling*
Between Shepherds Well (SR) and Shepherds Well (East Kent)
No signalling exists and such movements as are made are conducted as shunting operations.

Shepherds Well (East Kent)
Electric train tablet.

Eythorne to Eastry
Electric train staff - out of order and 'one engine in steam' arrangements operating.

Eastry to Wingham
'One engine in steam' arrangements operating. Points released by key on train staff.

Eastry to Richborough
'One engine in steam' arrangements operating. Annetts key used for releasing points.
No fixed signals are in use throughout the line except at Eythorne. At other places semaphore signals existed but the posts apparently have been blown down or damaged sometime in the past and not replaced. [Most signals seem to have been in place still but simply not working.]

19. *Engines and rolling stock*

(a) Locomotives 4 - Depot at Shepherds Well
Notes - (i) These engines include No. 301 [presumably 1371] built in 1891 also an 0-6-0 side tank engine which is out of gauge for working over Southern Region.
(ii) Two engines are in steam on weekdays.
(iii) Heavy repairs are carried out at Ashford Works.

Locomotive coal supplies obtained from Tilmanstone Colliery.

It is to be decided whether the engines will be based on Shepherds Well or Dover. If it is decided to base the engines on Dover the Chief Mechanical Engineer will arrange the removal of the following machinery:-
6 in. Lathe, 2 in. Lathe, Vertical Drill, Gear cutting machine, Grindstone, Bench grindstone, Forge. An old vertical boiler and steam engine, originally used for power supply also to be removed together with an old circular saw and dynamo.
If it is decided to base the engines on Dover the cab of No. 4 will require alteration to meet gauge requirements.

(b) Passenger Stock
Of the 7 carriages taken over Nos 5 and 6 are old Western 8 ft 6 in. wide corridor coaches. They are still suitable to work and will meet the requirements of the traffic. They will be renumbered and marked 'To work on E.K. section only'. Nos 1, 4, 5, 10 and 11 will be broken up (No. 5 is an old 6-wheeled vehicle and is in addition to No. 5 Western type).

With nationalisation impending the EKR broke up some of its older stock on the embankment overlooking Shepherdswell yard. Here ex-LCDR carriages Nos. 8 and 9 await their fate whilst No. 7 has already bitten the dust.

0-6-0 No. 6 with 'new' bogie carriage No. 6 await departure on the embankment at Canterbury Road.

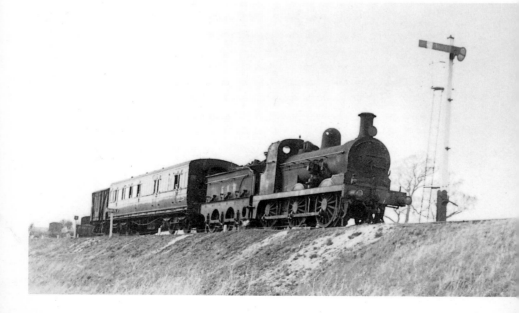

(c) Wagon Stock

Nos. 1 to 10 open goods are of Central Section wood frame type and are in fair condition to work on E.K. Section only. They will be marked accordingly.

Goods Brake No. 34 is also in fair condition for working on the Section. An additional goods brake will be selected by the Traffic Department and suitably marked. [A separate inventory carried out by the Finance Department recorded 3 brakevans at this time but probably included the NLR passenger brake No. 2 and a goods brake on loan from the Southern.]

LCDR Box Truck No. 33 used as a tool van will need replacement shortly if still required.

The following vehicles will be withdrawn from traffic:

Open Goods 12, 15, 20, 22, 26 and 28

Box wagon 17

Dumb buffered timber trucks 30, 31 and 32

(d) Cranes

Dumb buffered crane will be broken up.

20. Staff

A total of 19 Staff (excluding Head Office) is employed in the operating grades as follows:

Name	Grade	Station	Age	Date entered service	Rate of pay of pay	Qualifications etc.
Sampson	Clerk-in-Charge	Shepherds Well	27	1946	110/6	Compile accounts for Eastry
McAdie	Clerk	Shepherds Well	27	1947	102/6	Woodnesborough, Tilmanstone, Eythorne
Hudson	Shtr guard	'	33	1946	100/-	-
Coultham	Shtr guard	'	30	1947	100/-	-
Clements	Shtr guard	'	42	1947	100/-	-
Davis	Fitter	'	59	1923	126/-	-
Clements	Fitter's mate	'	26	1946	97/6	-
King	Driver	'	43	1923	119/-	-
Clements	Driver	'	60	1926	119/-	-
Rogers	Driver	'	44	1930	119/-	-
Abbott	Fireman	'	17	1944	99/6	-
Pope	Fireman	'	19	1945	99/6	-
Walker	Cleaner	'	21	1947	89/6	-
Smith	Carpenter	'	72	1916	100/-	Carriage & Wagon Dept.
Bell	Porter	Eastry	31	1947	89/-	-
Vacancy	Stn agent	Staple	-	-	-	-
Epps	Porter	Staple	59	1947	89/-	-
Burton	Porter	Eythorne	53	1928	89/6	-
Harffey	Stn agent	Wingham	51	1923	100/-	-

Engineer's Dept. staff comprises 1 Chargehand Ganger, 2 Gangers, 10 Lengthmen

Total Staff employed - 32

Total wage costs - £167 per week = £8,684 pa

Staff are not paid on National Agreement Rates and there is no Staff Pension Fund in existence.

Conditions of service, Rates of Pay, etc. have been examined.

21. Train Service

(a) PASSENGER - Total Daily Train Miles - 45

Weekdays only

Miles -		-	SX	SO	Miles -	-	-	SX	SO
-	-	am	pm	pm	-	-	am	pm	pm
-	Shepherds Well	7.30	5. 0	6. 3		Canterbury Road	8.40	6.20	6.50
1	Eythorne	7.37	5. 7	6.10	½	Wingham Town	8.42	6.22	6.52
2½	Elvington	7.40	5.10	6.13	1	Wingham Colliery	8.45	6.25	6.55
3½	Knowlton	7.43	5.14	6.17	2½	Staple	8.52	6.32	7. 0
5¼	Eastry South	-	M	M	3¼	Ash Town	8.55	6.36	7. 4
5	Eastry	7.51	5.22	6.23	4	Woodnes borough	8.59	6.40	7. 9
6½	Woodnesborough	7.55	5.26	6.27	5½	Eastry	9. 5	6.45	7.13
8	Ash Town	7.58	5.30	6.30	6	Eastry South	-	M	M
8	Staple	8. 2	5.33	6.34	7	Knowlton	9.15	M	M
10¼	Wingham Colliery	8. 8	5.38	6.39	8	Elvington	9.19	6.58	7.25
10	Wingham Town	8.10	5.40	6.42	9½	Eythorne	9.23	7. 2	7.28
11¼	Canterbury Road	8.12	5.42	6.44	11¼	Shepherds Well	9.30	7. 9	7.35

M = Stops by Signal to set down or pick up.

(b) Freight

The services shown in para (a) are run as mixed trains as required.

Five empty wagon trains run on weekdays serving Tilmanstone Colliery and five coal trains run from the colliery to Shepherds Well conveying the loaded wagons.

Maximum Train Load - 40 empty wagons or 18 loaded wagons.

22. Traffic Receipts

(a) Passenger Train Traffic - Year 1947

Station	No. of Passenger tickets issued	Receipts £	Number of parcels forwarded	Number of Parcels received	Receipts £
Shepherds Well	373	25	-	-	-
Eythorne	-	-	209	1,055	20
Woodnesborough	-	-	-	-	-
Eastry	-	-	-	703	-
Staple	-	-	220	997	52
Wingham	9	1	293	916	39
TOTALS	382	26	722	3,671	111

[Most tickets were issued on the train by this date and it would seem that these were all credited to Shepherdswell.]

(b) Freight Train Traffic - Year 1947

	Forwarded (tons)			Received (tons)			Receipts
Station	Goods	Minerals	Coal	Goods	Minerals	Coal	£
Tilmanstone	67	-	255,635	3,280	481	-	91
Eythorne	10	-	10	135	106	925	13
Woodnesborough	225	819	-	1,362	300	489	581
Eastry	127	420	94	502	371	1,687	239
Staple	1,903	1,199	-	1,374	1,547	2,121	3,390
Wingham	943	281	-	424	624	935	1,654
TOTALS	3,275	2,719	255,739	7,157	3,429	6,157	5,968

Livestock Traffic - NIL

[It is not clear whether Hammill traffic is included with Eastry or Woodnesborough. It is interesting to see the amount of goods traffic received by Tilmanstone; was this conveyed with the empty wagon traffic?]

(c) Summary of Receipts - Year 1947

Item	£
Passenger Traffic	26
Parcels Traffic	111
Freight Traffic	5,968
Coal from Tilmanstone Colliery 255,635 tons @ 6*d*. per ton	6,391 *
Rentals from eight bungalows and allotments	300
TOTAL	12,796

* Southern Railway revenue from coal in Year 1947 forwarded from Tilmanstone Colliery was £66,234, the traffic being conveyed chiefly to SR local stations.

23. General

The receipts on the East Kent Railway are very small, those accruing from passenger traffic being negligible and it is a matter for consideration by Commercial Superintendent and the Superintendent of Operation as to whether the line between Eythorne and Wingham Canterbury Road and Eastry and Richborough could not be closed.

The line between Eastry and Richborough is not worked beyond Poison Cross Halt.

The future of the East Kent Railway is being examined by Committee of Commercial, Operating and Engineering Assistants following a directive given by the Chief Regional Officer.

Estate Agent to be consulted as to the selling value of land of any line which may be abandoned (including the line from Eythorne to Guilford Colliery, now disused).

24. The appointed day for taking over

It was agreed that the 'appointed day' for taking over should be Monday, 3rd May, 1948.

The Memorandum was worded politely enough but it is clear that British Railways were less than impressed with their prospective acquisition. There was perhaps some reluctance to refrain from stronger criticism in the knowledge that the Southern Railway had held a majority of the seats on the railway's Board of Directors. It is, for example, strange that no mention is made of the state of the track on the line as this must certainly have influenced any decision on the future of the railway.

The early months of 1948 also saw negotiations taking place to fix a price for the railway's shares and debentures. The railway's case was prepared by its Accountant, Mr E.F. Marsh, and largely dwelt upon the prospects of developments at Tilmanstone Colliery to which, of course, the railway would prove essential. Marsh pointed out that Tilmanstone had so far only worked one of the many seams which it might exploit and that the present output of 220,000 tons pa could reach a million tons pa by 1956. With the ropeway out of use and derelict the railway had a monopoly of Tilmanstone traffic and even if only 75 per cent of the colliery's output were to go by rail the railway could look to an income of £36,800 pa. It was possible that the Guilford Colliery might yet re-open with potential coal reserves of 200 million tons.

Under these circumstances the shareholders could have looked forward to a return of 5 per cent to 6 per cent on their investments: 'The conclusion to be drawn . . . is that the East Kent Light Railways Company, in common with the Tilmanstone Colliery Company, has, so far, barely touched the fringe of its potential revenue earning resources, and is thus in a very like position to that of a new undertaking, which has only just begun to fructify; for this reason the past results are no fair measure by which the value of this undertaking can properly be assessed'. The shareholders and debenture holders should be entitled to compensation '. . . not on the basis of past results but on the basis of a just and fair return on the capital invested in an undertaking which events have proved to be of a perfectly sound commercial proposition, the fact that they have waited so many years without reward, only serving to strengthen their case for a just settlement of their claim'. One can imagine the figures of Arthur Burr and Holman Stephens beaming down with approval. Unfortunately the Valuation Tribunal was to prove less impressed but their award was not made until September and therefore properly belongs in the next chapter.

British Railways duly took control of the EKR on Monday 3rd May, 1948. The last Annual Report, for 1947, was published on 10th May, 1948 and the East Kent Light Railways Company officially ceased to exist on 3rd June, 1948 by a Board of Trade Certificate issued under Section 24 (1) of the Transport Act 1947. The offices at Salford Terrace closed shortly afterwards. An era had ended.

The end of the line at Wingham Canterbury Road.   *John Scott Morgan Collection*